Published under the auspices of
THE CENTER FOR JAPANESE AND KOREAN STUDIES
University of California, Berkeley

SUBURBAN TOKYO

Suburban Tokyo
A COMPARATIVE STUDY
IN POLITICS AND SOCIAL CHANGE

Gary D. Allinson

UNIVERSITY OF CALIFORNIA PRESS

BERKELEY · LOS ANGELES · LONDON

University of California Press
Berkeley and Los Angeles, California
University of California Press, Ltd.
London, England
©1979 by The Regents of the University of California
ISBN 0-520-03768-5
Library of Congress Catalog Card Number: 78-62852
Printed in the United States of America

1 2 3 4 5 6 7 8 9

FOR ROBIN

CONTENTS

MAPS AND TABLES

PREFACE

The book that follows analyzes political changes that have accompanied the growth of suburbs in western Tokyo since the late nineteenth century. Underlying the study is the methodological purpose of explaining political change contextually, by depicting the social environment in which it occurs. Drawing on work from several fields of study, I have tried to produce a more holistic image of the past than is common in many monographs, because I feel historians must be willing to unify the social sciences in order to create a comprehensive portrait of past behavior. I hope readers will find that the book contributes to this undertaking.

In striving to achieve this goal, I have selectively appropriated the concepts, techniques, and methods of several disciplines. The anthropologist's role as a participant observer and his use of the knowledgeable informant, as well as the sociologist's concern with demographic analysis and social structure, have shaped the first parts of chapters 2 through 5, where an attempt is made to illustrate the social, economic, and demographic processes through which suburban Tokyo has evolved. In the second parts of those chapters, I have employed concepts from political science, especially those current in the field of voting studies, in order to interpret the political consequences of suburban expansion. As an historian, I have tried to bring to life aspects of the past in language that is readily understood.

Employing selectively the concepts of several social science disciplines entails some risks. While many social scientists in the contemporary world are able to "create" their own data, the historian must rely on fortuitously surviving documentation. This makes it difficult for him to satisfy the exacting standards of proof demanded of contemporary social scientists, and especially difficult to meet current expectations for quantitative analysis. The study at hand has not escaped this dilemma. It would have been ideal if panel surveys had been available, for instance, that treated the mobility patterns and political preferences of selected urban sub-samples. Unfortunately, to my knowledge such data do not exist. In compensating for this hiatus in the historical record, I have relied primarily on aggregate data drawn from census reports and election returns printed by various government bodies since the 1880s.

Further risks arise in employing these materials. Although they enable one to make broad generalizations about social and political trends, aggregate data do not permit one to make uncontestable claims about the behavior of individuals. Nor do they offer assurance that one is always dealing with the same set of individuals or groups across time. Nonetheless, by combining analysis of aggregate data with personal observations, anecdotal materials, interviews, biographies, news accounts, and extant surveys, one can affirm some hypotheses and dismiss others.

Rather than devote the text to the lengthy, logical exercises that hypothesis-testing entails, I have chosen instead to present the most plausible explanation for what happened in a narrative analysis that sets forth my conclusions in standard English. This format does not satisfy the scientific requirement to follow procedures that may be replicated, but I think it results in a book that is easier to read. Those who wish to may consult the sources I have used by referring to the footnotes, where I have tried to cite my evidence as fully as possible.

To reach my conclusions, I have relied on a method that is comparative in two respects, one explicit and the other implicit. Explicit comparisons involve two suburbs that are the focus of the study, the cities of Musashino and Fuchū. I have systematically compared aspects of their history in order to illustrate the underlying complexity in patterns of social and political change in suburban Tokyo. Their comparison also serves as a kind of control over conventional socio-economic variables, and it facilitates analysis of other—often neglected and more subtle—social and economic phenomena that also shape political change. Implicit comparisons treat composite images of suburbs in western Tokyo with suburbs in the United States. Although these comparisons appear less systematically than those involving the two cities, I think they nonetheless illustrate how the development of Tokyo's suburbs has followed a different path from the one to which observers of the American scene have grown accustomed, and they suggest there is more than one alternative in our urban future.

I hope that such a comparative, cross-disciplinary study will have particular interest for three different audiences. The first includes students of comparative politics and urban history, for whom the book is intended as a contribution to the scant literature in English on Japanese cities and municipal politics. The second audience includes graduate and undergraduate students; they might use the book to achieve a novel perspective on aspects of Japan's modern history. And the third audience is the body of Japan specialists from several disciplines around the world who will, I hope, value the study for its analysis of change in an increasingly important type of community—the suburb—that has been scarcely studied to date.

It is a pleasure to acknowledge my appreciation to some of those specialists, without whose support and assistance this book could not have been completed, much less undertaken. I owe a heavy debt to Professor Sekijima Hisao of Seikei University, who graciously served as my sponsor, guide, and adviser during a year in Japan. He could not have been more helpful with his counsel, nor more generous with his time. I also wish to thank many others in Japan who willingly lent assistance. They include Professors Satō Atsushi, Satō Seizaburō, and Yanai Michio, Mr. Narita Tadayoshi, Mr. Mitarai Tateki, Mr. Katagiri Tatsuo, and members of the staffs of the Tokyo Institute for Municipal Research, of the Fuchū and Musashino city governments, and of the Tama Central Trust Fund. In the United States, Samuel P. Hays, Richard N. Hunt, Ellis Krauss, Thomas C. Smith, and Kurt Steiner all risked their credibility to support this undertaking. Mr. Wang Jen-yuan, formerly of the Hillman Library at the University of Pittsburgh, and Mr. Key Kobayashi of the Library of Congress both lent special help in gathering materials. For their stimulus and criticisms, I owe thanks to Ronald Aqua, Douglas Johnson, J. Victor Koschmann, Stephen Large, Evelyn Rawski, the members of the 1976 Fulbright Seminar in Tokyo, and the participants in the 1976 Social Science Research

Council Conference on Local Oppositions in Japan. Ellis Krauss deserves a special note of appreciation for reading parts of the book in draft form, and Chalmers Johnson deserves my thanks for keeping me honest and the book short.

The bulk of the research for this study was conducted with generous assistance from the United States Educational Commission in Japan (the Fulbright Commission), which sponsored a year's visit in Tokyo during 1975–76. The Faculty of Arts and Sciences of the University of Pittsburgh lent valued assistance during the summer of 1975, and the Joint Committee on Japanese Studies of the American Council of Learned Societies and the Social Science Research Council provided indispensable support during the summer of 1977. A grant from the Asian Studies Program at the University of Pittsburgh defrayed the expenses of typing, copying, and map-making.

As always, I owe an incalculable debt to my wife Pat. She has gracefully endured more than any author ever could, and she has helped in more ways than it is politic to enumerate. We have dedicated the book to our son Robin, who also participated, in the hope that his generation will develop an even deeper friendship with Japan and its people.

March 27, 1978

ABBREVIATIONS

CGP Clean Government Party (Kōmeitō)
DSP Democratic Socialist Party
JCP Japan Communist Party
JSP Japan Socialist Party
LDP Liberal Democratic Party
NLC New Liberal Club

Fss *Fuchū shi shi* [The History of Fuchū City]. Fuchū shi shi hensan iinkai, comp.
Ms *Musashino shi* [Musashino City]. Seikei daigaku, Seikei gakkai, ed.
Mss *Musashino shi shi* [The History of Musashino City]. Musashino shi shi hensan iinkai, comp.

one

INTRODUCTION

The growth of the modern Tokyo metropolis has occurred in three phases and three distinguishable areas. The first phase coincided with the period between 1868 and the 1920s and took place in what can be called the center (see map 1). Focused on the present downtown area near Tokyo Station, the center has a radius of about three miles and encompasses parts of eight of the twenty-three wards (*ku*) of Tokyo Metropolitan Prefecture.[1] Such famous sites as the Ginza, the Imperial Palace, and the Diet Building are in the center.

A second phase of growth occurred between the 1880s and the 1960s and took place in what will be called the periphery. We can envision the periphery as the part of contemporary Tokyo that essentially coincides with the fifteen outer wards of the twenty-three-ward area. It stretches to a radius of about ten miles from the center.

1. It is important to clarify what Tokyo Metropolitan Prefecture is. Although both a city (*shi*) and a prefecture (*fu*) of Tokyo existed between 1889 and 1943, since then Tokyo has been a metropolitan prefecture (*to*), the only one so designated in Japan. The prefecture has its own elected governor and assembly, and it covers an area on land of 667 square miles. (It also encompasses several islands to the south, with which this study is not concerned.) There are two major parts of the prefecture. Covering its eastern third are twenty-three wards (*ku*), each with its own executive head and elected assembly, also. These wards form the densely inhabited commercial and residential core of the metropolitan area and, were it not for peculiarities of administrative usage, would be the center city of Tokyo. Lying west of the ward area are twenty-six cities, five towns, and one village. They cover the westernmost two-thirds of the prefecture, about 447 square miles, or an area roughly comparable in size to the city of Los Angeles. At one time this area was divided into three counties (Nishi Tama, Kita Tama, and Minami Tama). It thus became known as the Santama (or Three Tama) region, a term this book employs interchangeably with the phrase "the western suburbs" to refer collectively to these thirty-two local entities, their predecessors, and the area they cover. Map 1 offers a visual perspective of the prefecture and its constituent parts.

I

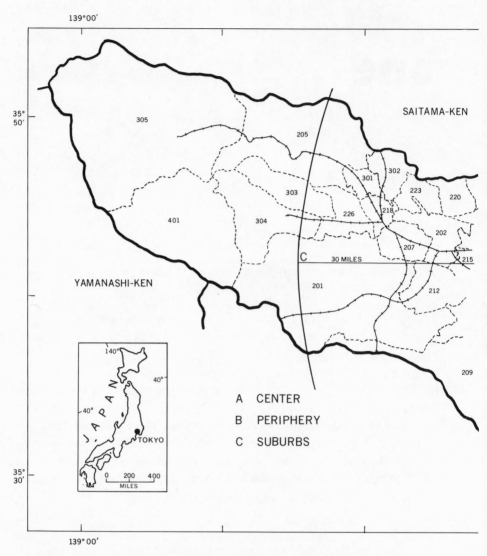

Map 1. Political Subdivisions of Tokyo Metropolitan Prefecture, 1975

WARDS (*ku*)

101 Chiyoda	109 Shinagawa	117 Kita
102 Chūō	110 Meguro	118 Arakawa
103 Minato	111 Ōta	119 Itabashi
104 Shinjuku	112 Setagaya	120 Nerima
105 Bunkyō	113 Shibuya	121 Adachi
106 Taitō	114 Nakano	122 Katsuchika
107 Sumida	115 Suginami	123 Edogawa
108 Kōtō	116 Tōshima	

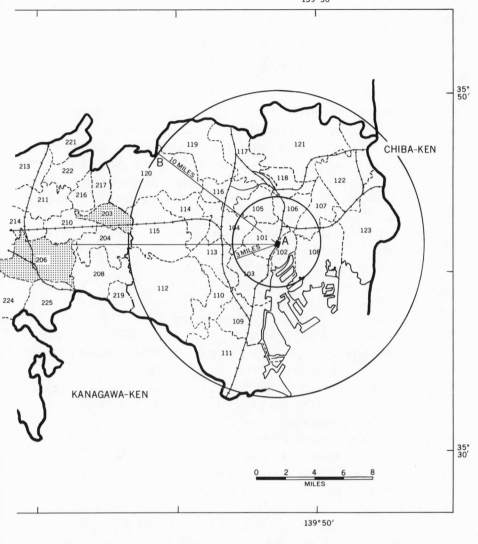

139°50'

35°50'

CHIBA-KEN

10 MILES

3 MILES

KANAGAWA-KEN

35°30'

0   2   4   6   8
MILES

139°50'

CITIES* (*shi*)

201 Hachiōji	210 Koganei	219 Komae	
202 Tachikawa	211 Kodaira	220 Higashi Yamato	
203 Musashino	212 Hino	221 Kiyose	
204 Mitaka	213 Higashi Murayama	222 Higashi Kurume	
205 Ōme	214 Kokubunji	223 Musashimurayama	
206 Fuchū	215 Kunitachi	224 Tama	
207 Akishima	216 Tanashi	225 Inagi	
208 Chōfu	217 Hōya	226 Akikawa	
209 Machida	218 Fussa	*Oldest first.	

TOWNS (*machi*)

301 Hamura
302 Mizuho
303 Hinode
304 Itsukaichi
305 Okutama

VILLAGES (*mura*)

401 Hinohara

Experiencing pervasive residential, commercial, and industrial development after the early twentieth century, the periphery forms what Herbert Gans has labeled the "outer city."[2] Some of its wards well known to Tokyo's foreign visitors are Setagaya, Nakano, and Suginami.

Beyond the twenty-three wards are the suburbs. They stretch not only into the western part of Tokyo known as the Santama region, but into the surrounding prefectures of Saitama, Chiba, and Kanagawa, in some cases to a distance of thirty miles or more. When they first emerged in the early 1920s, Tokyo's suburbs were an outgrowth of farm villages, market centers, or post towns. Even when the Pacific War ended two decades later, most were still small agricultural and commercial settlements of ten to twenty thousand residents. But since then, many have grown to become diversified cities of one, two, or three hundred thousand.

The suburbs which form the subject of this book are autonomous administrative entities, or municipalities, situated adjacent to or near a major city. In Japanese, they are referred to as *shi* (cities), and on some occasions as *machi* or *chō* (towns), especially during their early stages of development. For purposes of political analysis, this definition is appropriate. It enables us to deal with a persisting territorial unit, one possessing its own political structures and engaging in the political process at higher levels, in particular, the prefectural and national.

In addition to being autonomous politically, suburbs are distinguished in other ways from central cities and rural villages. They are always located near a larger city on which they are in many ways dependent. Most important perhaps is their economic dependence, for the majority of suburbs are residential communities for people who commute elsewhere (often to the larger, central city) to work. Employed suburbanites thus pursue nonfarm, and usually white-collar, occupations. As a last measure of suburban attributes, their population densities generally fall below those of the central city but well above those in the rural villages of the countryside beyond. For our purposes, therefore, the suburb is a rather densely inhabited, autonomous political entity where commuting, white-collar workers in the tertiary sector (and their families) are the largest social group.

2. Herbert J. Gans, "Urbanism and Suburbanism as Ways of Life: A Re-evaluation of Definitions," in Sandor Halebsky, ed., *The Sociology of the City* (New York, 1973), pp. 332–350.

The role of the suburb as an agent of political change is shaped by these attributes. Suburbs are territorial units in which have grown communities distinguishable from others, such as capital cities, resort towns, or farming villages. Having emerged in greatest number since the nineteenth century in industrializing societies, suburbs are a product of economic and social changes in an age of advanced technology. They have thus attracted people with special occupational, educational, psychological, and material attributes. Owing to this fact, suburbs have witnessed a range of political changes that have not been uniform across cultures. These changes were not always *caused* by suburbs. Rather, they *appeared* in suburbs as areas attracting certain social groups under special material and psychological circumstances. In sum, suburbs themselves do not in every respect cause political changes; they are a dynamic arena in which often unique political changes occur owing to a broad range of other factors. Some of these factors inhere in suburban developmental processes, but others are the product of larger, outside forces that may be national and even international in origin.

Japan's suburbs in general, and Tokyo's western suburbs in particular, provide a worthy topic of investigation for many reasons. They have, first of all, assumed considerable demographic importance, especially during the past quarter-century. Exactly how important they are is difficult to gauge, because Japanese census data do not treat them as a separate category. One can therefore only hazard rough guesses, for which the latest national census provides one approximation.[3] It indicates that 53 million people (nearly half the nation's population) resided in three major metropolitan regions, focused on Tokyo-Yokohama, Osaka-Kyoto-Kobe, and Nagoya. Of the 53 million, only 19 million (about 36 percent) lived in the six central districts; the remaining 34 million (or 64 percent) lived in contiguous metropolitan regions. These 34 million people, most—though not all—of whom were suburbanites, constituted over 30 percent of the nation's population. If one adds to this number people living in suburbs surrounding smaller cities throughout the country, it seems safe to assume that suburbs encompassed a third or more of Japan's total population in the late 1970s.

This already large share of the nation's populace has experienced

3. Sōrifu tōkei kyoku, *1975 Kokusei chōsa: Zenkoku todōfuken shichōson betsu jinkō gaisū* [1975 Population Census of Japan: Preliminary Count of Population] (Tokyo, 1975), pp. 7, 46–47. Hereafter, 1975 National Census.

rapid growth and will continue to do so. Tokyo is a case in point. Between 1950 and 1975, when the nation's population expanded by 35 percent, Tokyo Metropolitan Prefecture grew by 86 percent. This rate of growth paled by comparison with suburban increases, however, as table 1 illustrates. In the Santama region, the population rose from about 850,000 to nearly 3 million, an increase of 252 percent. Moreover, it seems likely that such suburban growth will continue, in Tokyo and elsewhere as well. Not all suburban cities grew at the same rate as those near Tokyo, nor will they in the future. But the rapidity of suburban growth, the already large size of suburbia, and the prospects for continued growth all attest to the demographic importance of suburban cities.

Japan's growing suburbs are also important socially, owing to the characteristics of their residents. During the past quarter-century, Japan has witnessed a major alteration in her occupational structure. In the face of rapid industrialization, the farm population declined while white-collar groups mushroomed. Having been a society where most workers were agricultural proprietors or unpaid family laborers, Japan became in a few decades a nation of company employees. The epitome of this new social type is the stereotypic middle-class, white-collar worker—the *sarariiman,* or salary man. Of equal importance is his counterpart, the middle-class, blue-collar worker employed on the production line of a large corporation. Symbolizing the changing character of Japanese society, men from such groups, and their families, are those who have settled in the largest numbers in the nation's suburbs during the postwar era. They represent the dominant social thrust in contemporary Japan, and they personify the future character of Japanese society as well.

Proceeding in pace with these social changes has been the modern economic development of such suburban areas as Tokyo's Santama region. In the early 1920s, when it was still primarily agrarian, the region's economy produced barely 6 percent of the prefecture's industrial output while employing a similar share of its industrial labor force. After abrupt growth in the 1930s and extensive development in the 1960s, its industrial stature rose. By the mid-1970s, Santama industrial workers, who made up a fifth of the prefecture's total, produced over a fifth of its industrial goods.[4]

4. Tōkyō fu, *Tōkyō fu tōkei sho* [Tokyo Prefecture Statistical Annual], 1922 (Tokyo, 1925), p. 281; Tōkyō to, *Tōkyō to tōkei nenkan* [Tokyo Metropolitan Prefecture Statistical Yearbook], 1973 (Tokyo, 1974), pp. 92–95.

TABLE 1. *Changes in Population of Tokyo Metropolitan Prefecture, 1920–1975*

Year	Absolute Numbers (in thousands)				Decennial Increase (%)				Distribution of Metro. Pop. (%)	
	23-wards (A)	Santama (B)	Tokyo-to (C)	Japan (D)	(A)	(B)	(C)	(D)	(A)	(B)
1920	3,356	316	3,699	55,391					91	9
1930	4,977	403	5,409	63,872	48	27	46	15	93	7
1940	6,786	537	7,355	71,400	36	33	36	12	93	7
1950	5,385	851	6,278	83,200	−21	59	−15	17	86	14
1960	8,310	1,335	9,684	93,419	54	57	54	12	86	14
1970	8,841	2,534	11,408	103,720	6	90	18	11	78	22
1975	8,643	2,992	11,669	111,934					74	26

SOURCES: *1950 Kokusei chōsa hōkoku* (Tokyo, 1953), vol. 7, part 13, pp. 28–39; *1960 Kokusei chōsa hōkoku* (Tokyo, 1964), vol. 4, part 13, pp. 54–55; *1970 Kokusei chōsa hōkoku* (Tokyo, 1972), vol. 3, part 13, pp. 3–5; *1975 Kokusei chōsa: Zenkoku todōfuken shichōson betsu jinkō gaisū* (Tokyo, 1975), pp. 46–47. Author, in all cases, is Sōrifu tōkei kyoku.

NOTE: Figures for Tokyo-to (C) include, in addition to the 23 wards and the Santama Region, the populations of several islands lying south of Honshū which are a part of the metropolitan prefecture.

Moreover, an influx of supermarket chains, discount houses, and major department stores after 1960 stimulated a sharp increase in commercial activity. Because of these developments, the Santama has assumed substantial economic importance, its population alone creating a market larger than thirty-seven of Japan's forty-seven prefectures.

The foregoing changes have sharply enhanced the political significance of suburbia. The 1975 Diet reapportionment is one indication. Of twenty seats added to the Lower House to adjust for population changes, sixteen were in suburban districts around Tokyo, Osaka, and Nagoya. In the late 1970s Japan still had relatively fewer suburban legislators than the United States, owing to a serious underrepresentation of urban constituencies, but, even so, about one in every eight Diet members was a suburban representative.

A perhaps more critical measure of suburbia's political importance stems from the partisan preferences of its residents, who have formed an expanding base of support for opposition and progressive parties.[5] Since the early 1950s, Japan's conservative parties have suffered a marked decline in their suburban strength, their share of the vote falling from nearly 60 percent in the mid-1950s to a historic low of 25 percent in 1976. This trend has been apparent in many suburbs around the nation's major metropolitan centers, but it has been especially conspicuous in Tokyo's western suburbs. In Diet elections, conservative candidates, who once took nearly two-thirds of the votes, captured less than one-third in the 1976 Lower House election, in a year when the Liberal Democratic Party (LDP) won 42 percent of the vote nationwide. At the municipal level; the conservatives, who once controlled all the mayoralty posts in the Santama, saw opponents capture control over more than a third of them by the late 1970s, a rate nearly double the national average. In the past two decades, therefore, voters in many of Japan's suburbs—and in Tokyo's western suburbs in particular—have been displaying their aversion to the ruling party by casting ever more ballots for the opposition.

5. Japanese commentators generally refer to the opposition parties as the *kakushin seitō*, or progressive parties, a usage that embodies explicitly subjective overtones which imply that these parties are more advanced, liberal, or progressive in their policies than the ruling conservatives. This book also employs the term "progressive," but merely as a convenient shorthand to refer primarily to the Japan Socialist Party (JSP), the Democratic Socialists (DSP), and the Japan Communist Party (JCP). It should be understood that the usage herein implies no empirical judgments about the real policies these parties pursue.

These partisan changes are important in their own right, but they assume even more importance when considered in view of the changing patterns of human settlement mentioned above. Since the 1930s, Japan has witnessed a marked shift of population that has carried millions of people out of rural towns and villages into large metropolitan regions. In the past three decades suburban communities on the fringes of major cities have grown at startling rates, producing in the course of one generation a body of suburbanites who constitute, as we have noted, a large and growing share of the nation's populace. By casting light on their behavior, we are illuminating patterns of political change in the type of community that may house a majority of the Japanese populace by the end of this century.

The primary purpose of this study is to analyze the growth of opposition party strength in the western suburbs of Tokyo by examining long-term political changes in two cities in the area. Historical changes in party preferences among the area's voters serve as the focus of analysis. Partisan change, however, is a complex phenomenon that itself has many facets. Those receiving fullest treatment in this study are the appearance of new political parties, their organizational features, their performance in election contests, the socio-economic attributes of their supporters, and the degree of identity between parties and those who vote for them. Underlying new partisan alignments are changes in other aspects of political behavior. These influence participation, the mobilization of voters, the recruitment of leaders, the policies that parties implement, and the political roles of voluntary organizations and pressure groups. By examining changes in these various aspects of political behavior in western Tokyo, this study may also be able to suggest why the Liberal Democratic Party is in danger of losing its controlling position in Japanese politics.

There is some urgency in attempting to understand the demise of the Liberal Democrats. As the party which has ruled Japan without interruption since 1955, it has faced relatively weak opposition while conducting one-party government at all levels of the political system. But its position began to deteriorate in the early 1970s, and a coalition government has become a realistic possibility. Whether the LDP aligns with another conservative party, or with a centrist or leftist party, its political freedom will be compromised, and a consensus on national policies may become more difficult to achieve.

The diminishing electoral support recently attracted by the LDP is a harbinger of another, perhaps even more crucial change in Japanese politics. The LDP's long period of uninterrupted rule was based, to a large extent, on voter apathy and public disinterest in issues of national significance. These attitudes persist among many voters in Japan, but they are less pervasive than before. Increasing numbers of persons are entering the electorate who have been educated in the postwar era, socialized in an environment of competitive party politics, and affected by problems for which they seek political solutions. They have lent a new tone to the Japanese political temper, and their behavior has heightened considerably the voter's importance in Japan's political system.

The inherent significance of these changes endorses the importance of understanding Japanese electoral behavior. In one respect, therefore, this book is an inquiry into the electoral history of modern Japan, focused sharply on two communities and a Diet district on the edge of the nation's capital. It seeks to understand the processes through which suburban political behavior has changed in Japan, and in a concluding chapter it offers an interpretation of the significance of those changes. The study begins with the creation in 1890 of a system of parliamentary government and continues through the late 1970s. At the outset of that period, Japan was an authoritarian state dominated by former samurai with a haughty disregard for popular opinion. By the end, it was a competitive polity governed by career politicians and bureaucrats obliged to acknowledge public demands. This sweeping evolution took place, moreover, against a background of pervasive social and economic change.

Although much has been written in English about Japanese politics during this period, most works have focused on the central government, political parties in the national arena, and national political figures, and more recently, on political attitudes and socialization.[6] Studies of electoral behavior are still relatively uncommon, and case studies of individual communities are rare.[7] Perhaps more unfortunate, few works provide sociological analyses

6. Major works published in the last two decades appear in the bibliography.

7. Scholars writing in English who have devoted greatest attention to electoral behavior in Japan are Scott Flanagan, Terry MacDougall, Bradley Richardson, Robert Scalapino, and Kurt Steiner, whose works are cited in the bibliography. For the two community studies now available, see Gary D. Allinson, *Japanese Urbanism: Industry and Politics in Kariya, 1872–1972* (Berkeley, 1975), and Yasumasa Kuroda, *Reed Town, Japan: A Study in Community Power Structure and Political Change* (Honolulu, 1974).

of change across this entire period. We therefore have an incomplete understanding of how the extensive social, economic, and demographic alterations Japan has experienced since the late nineteenth century have been reflected in patterns of political behavior, especially below the national level. Moreover, our image of Japan's modern politics is both fragmentary and discontinuous. Fine monographs exist dealing with aspects of political behavior in restricted periods, but virtually no study ventures to treat political behavior from 1890 to the present or to explore the continuities and discontinuities that span prewar and postwar Japan. A study like this one, which tries to analyze systematically the long-term changes in political behavior within a broad socio-economic context, may—by casting light in a dark corner—enhance our understanding of modern Japan's political history.[8]

Despite an obvious need for comprehensive studies, this book confines itself to one territorial setting. There is good reason for limiting a study of electoral behavior to a specific area, as one political sociologist has explained:

The facts on which the affluence has been based have in the main been gathered by means of poll-type social surveys, and it is a weakness of such investigations that they tend to concentrate on individual characteristics— such as age, sex, level of income and education—and fail to take into account the properties of the social structures in which the individuals in question are located; for example, those of work organizations and local communities.[9]

This critique of the synchronic, abstract nature of much research on electoral behavior contains an important corrective. Individuals responding to a survey questionnaire are neither unfailing prophets of future behavior nor infallible recorders of past actions. To understand their political behavior properly, it is essential to appreciate its social, economic, temporal, and territorial context. Historical case studies at the community level provide one means of achieving this end.

While this study is ultimately concerned with political history, it

8. "Systematic" is a vague term that can invite misunderstanding. I use it to mean comprehensive and methodical. This study of electoral behavior is systematic because it is based on all the data I could find that deals with all elections to the lower house of the national legislature since 1890, all Tokyo gubernatorial and prefectural assembly elections since 1947, and all municipal elections in Musashino and Fuchū for which materials survive.

9. John H. Goldthorpe, et al., *The Affluent Worker: Political Attitudes and Behaviour* (Cambridge, 1967), p. 73.

also treats social, economic, and demographic changes in the suburbs at some length. Neglect is one justification for such treatment. The only major volume on Japan's suburbs in English, Ezra Vogel's *Japan's New Middle Class,* is essentially a portrait of life among families of a "class" that has settled in large numbers in suburban cities.[10] Valuable for the light it sheds on social aspects of suburban Japan in the late 1950s, the Vogel book leaves untouched any discussion of the long-term development of suburbs as communities and any analysis of historical patterns of political behavior in suburban cities, two topics this study strives to illuminate.[11]

The need for a broader view is also underscored by the mechanisms of political change. While social, economic, and demographic changes have not been sufficient causes of new patterns of political behavior, many political changes have been inseparable from their socio-economic and demographic context. Cadences of economic development, patterns of migration and commuting, and social structures emerging from suburban expansion have all shaped the political environment. The book thus examines aspects of social change that have had a direct influence on political, and especially electoral, behavior. It is hoped the portrayal of these changes will lead to a realistic (though by no means comprehensive) account of the social history of suburban Tokyo since 1890, and to an understanding of the processes—social and economic as well as political—through which two suburban cities have evolved.

The two suburbs that provide the comparative subject matter for this study are the cities of Musashino and Fuchū. Musashino's 1975 population of 139,493 was fully twenty-eight times the size of that community in 1920, when the first national census enumerated fewer than 5,000 residents. Fuchū's growth was less dramatic, but it still increased from about 12,000 in 1920 to more than 180,000 in 1975. In both cities, the largest absolute increases came in the postwar era, during the 1950s in the former, and following the mid-1950s in the latter. Musashino's population stabilized at about

---

10. Ezra F. Vogel, *Japan's New Middle Class: The Salary Man and His Family in a Tokyo Suburb* (Berkeley, 1963). Subsequent references to this book are to the paperback edition of 1967.

11. Vogel's treatment of suburban politics is confined almost exclusively to one paragraph on page 98, where he essentially dismisses its importance by claiming, "Even in the local community salary men take little part in political activities." This study tries to demonstrate that suburban politics have been both more important and more complex than he implies.

140,000 in 1965, but Fuchū's continued to grow at rates that exceeded those of the nation and the perfecture.[12]

Musashino and Fuchū were both representative of Japan's suburbs in many key respects. As home for large numbers of salarymen, they were socially and occupationally similar to about 200 other suburbs that numbered almost a third of the nation's some 650 cities in the 1970s. They were also demographically similar to most suburbs, whose populations clustered in a range between 75,000 and 300,000. They differed from some suburbs in the timing of their initial development, Musashino being a prewar and Fuchū an early postwar suburb. In both cases, however, their rapid growth in absolute numbers after 1950 coincided with national trends. Like most suburbs, they were communities dominated by well-educated, white-collar workers (and their families) who commuted to central cities for work and enjoyed incomes in the middle range.

As cities that grew largely in the absence of rigorous planning, the two should, however, be distinguished from another type of Japanese suburb: the planned, mass community. While both Musashino and Fuchū had some large-scale housing developments, these were only a small portion of the housing stock in the two cities. They differed substantially, therefore, from sections of such cities as Machida, Hino, and Higashi Kurume, where huge housing developments for thousands of persons were built, creating virtually new communities overnight. Most observers agree that such communities have undergone a unique process of social evolution. We should note, therefore, that Musashino and Fuchū represent older suburbs that developed more haphazardly than the newer, large-scale suburbs.

As the older of the two suburbs, Musashino reached a level of maturity in the 1960s. Its most rapid rates of growth occurred in the 1920s and 1930s, when the city's population quadrupled. It continued to grow at a steady pace through the war years and into the 1960s. By then, however, its roughly four square miles of land, situated immediately adjacent to the western boundaries of the ward area, were almost entirely built up. With nearly 35,000 persons per square mile, Musashino was actually more densely populated than some of the downtown wards. In fact, it bore many social, demo-

12. 1975 National Census, pp. 46–47.

graphic, and physical features in common with the ward area, especially the suburban-like wards of the western periphery, such as Nakano, Shibuya, and Setagaya. It was actually so much like the ward area that many outsiders failed to recognize either the city or its location. Often, Musashino only came to mind when one mentioned Kichijōji, its major train stop, through which thousands of commuters passed daily on their thirty-minute ride to the center wards.

Musashino enjoyed a popular (and deserved) reputation as a cultural city (*bunka toshi*), a claim that many cities made but few deserved. It not only had an excellent public school system, several private academies, and five colleges and universities, it was also home for many writers, scholars, and intellectuals of national— indeed international—repute, including the novelist Niwa Fumio and the historian Maruyama Masao. Musashino was also alleged to be an expensive, upper-class suburb. This image oversimplified its social complexity, but many wealthy people did live in the city, almost as many per thousand as in the exclusive ward of Setagaya. Indeed, the 1974 per capita income of Musashino's residents placed it third among all cities in the country, at a figure of 182 (where 100 was the average).[13] Since white-collar workers constituted 80 percent of its resident employed (in 1970), two-thirds of whom commuted outside each day, Musashino was an almost classic white-collar, residential suburb.

Situated fifteen to thirty minutes farther by train from the city center than Musashino, and covering nearly three times more land with densities half as great, Fuchū was a new suburb in the throes of development. When the war ended in 1945, the old town of Fuchū and the two villages that subsequently joined it to form today's city had less than 40,000 residents. That number doubled by 1960, and doubled again by 1970. Later growth was less dramatic, since the city tried to control expansion, but it continued to attract several thousand new residents each year.

Like the residents of Musashino, most (about 67 percent) of Fuchū's were white-collar workers in the tertiary sector. Tending to be somewhat younger than those in Musashino, however, their incomes were lower. This placed Fuchū farther down the list of

13. Zenkoku shichō kai, ed., *1975 Nihon toshi nenkan* [1975 Japan Municipal Yearbook] (Tokyo, 1975), pp. 159–164.

wealthy communities at a ranking of 138, still above the national average but below Musashino and other nearby suburbs, such as Koganei (171), Mitaka (164), and Kokubunji (163).[14] In Fuchū, 30 percent of the resident employed were production workers, owing to the location in the city of several large electrical factories. These also drew substantial numbers of workers into the city each day, to replace many of the nearly 50 percent of the city's employed residents who commuted elsewhere to work. Fuchū thus bore features of both the residential and the industrial suburb, with the former gradually overshadowing the latter. While it still preserved the air of a rustic country town, Fuchū's movement toward a suburban future was pronounced and inexorable.

Despite fine distinctions, Musashino and Fuchū shared many social, demographic, occupational, and economic characteristics in common. The differences that did arise, such as the greater average age and income of Musashino residents and their greater concentration in nonmanufacturing activities, were conventionally associated with support for the conservative party in Japan. However, just the opposite was true. Musashino was a stronghold of progressive party support, while Fuchū was the more conservative.

The discrepancy appeared at all levels of the political system, but it was most pronounced below the national level. In Musashino, voters after the war always elected progressive candidates to the prefectural assembly; they elected as many progressives to city council as conservatives; and they returned a progressive mayor four times running after 1963. By contrast, citizens of Fuchū elected conservatives to the prefectural assembly in eight of ten cases; they nearly always elected conservative candidates to the city council; and they always elected mayors who were aligned with conservative parties. An important task of this study will be to explain why two suburbs with such similar social and economic characteristics differed so in their political preferences. This will contribute to the larger purpose of understanding the rise of the opposition in Tokyo's western suburbs, and, more generally, to understanding the nationwide decline of the Liberal Democratic Party.

The plan of this book is as follows: Chapter 2 presents a brief description of Musashino, Fuchū, and the Santama region in the

14. Ibid.

four decades before 1923, in order to convey an understanding of local society in the years before suburban growth began. The first phase of that growth occurred between 1923 and 1945. Chapter 3 analyzes the social, economic, and demographic processes that underlay it and evaluates the political consequences that ensued. The volatile early postwar period is examined in chapter 4, which explains the social and economic effects of recovery and examines the initial ascent of opposition political power. Chapter 5 depicts the social diversity found in contemporary suburbs and analyzes the causes and consequences of the segmented politics that characterized the two decades after 1960. A concluding chapter summarizes the findings of the study in light of several analytical themes and speculates on their significance for the future.

two

THE PROSPECTIVE SUBURBS

Few if any of Japan's suburbs developed on virgin soil. There was nearly always a rural hamlet of several hundred families nearby, or a small country town of several thousand. In some cases, there may have been several hamlets within the administrative boundaries of one suburb. By American standards, such communities were large settlements with long histories. They were, moreover, dominated by landlords and commercial proprietors who exercised firm control over local affairs. Power holders like these were well entrenched in the Santama region during the four decades before 1923, when they provided the local leadership for one of Japan's earliest political parties. The purpose of this chapter is to explain the social and political setting in which those men exerted their political influence, in order to describe the indigenous society that greeted the first suburban arrivals.

The Metropolis and Its Western Fringe

The years between 1890 and 1923 span one of the most eventful periods in Japan's modern history. That period witnessed its rise to power as a political and military force, and its ascent as an industrial nation. As Japan's capital and the focus of its economy, Tokyo was the center for many of the decisions and activities that shaped the era. Like London in the eighteenth century, Berlin in the nineteenth, and Seoul in the twentieth, Tokyo was a primary city leading the political and economic development of an emergent industrial society. It was always the largest city in Japan, and it discharged the widest range of urban functions.

Its political role was paramount. Following the Meiji Restoration of 1868, the samurai who formed the new government moved the nation's capital to the former shogunal headquarters of Edo, which they renamed Tokyo. They brought the emperor with them from the former capital of Kyoto to lend symbolic authority to the extensive powers they exercised. Relying primarily on fellow samurai in the early years, the new government eventually established a talented, loyal bureaucracy that quartered itself near the imperial household in what is now Chiyoda Ward. From the ministries there, and a variety of less formal sites nearby (such as the teahouses of Akasaka), several generations of leaders guided the political destiny of this energetic Asian nation.

Tokyo also created and fulfilled crucial economic functions. As early as the 1700s, one million persons or more had settled in the area; they created a huge market and a major center for handicraft production. In the decades following the Meiji Restoration, retailers, wholesalers, and small manufacturers in the old handicraft quarters remained active, some of them actually experiencing growth promoted by the new economic climate. During the late nineteenth century and after, other men of enterprise appeared who were more concerned with the opportunities accompanying Japan's role in an international economy. Among them were the first members of the white-collar ranks, the young men staffing banks, trading firms, and business houses in the Marunouchi and Ginza districts. Other newcomers to the economic scene were industrialists who settled away from the crowded downtown section in the counties of Katsushika and Ebara, where they found sites for their large factories. Responding to the opportunities offered by a growing, prosperous nation, these groups guaranteed Tokyo's continued primacy as the nation's economic center.

Tokyo enjoyed supremacy in other areas as well. While some in the elite performing arts preferred the sedate climate of Kyoto, many traditional artists and most of the new ones found the expansive atmosphere of Tokyo more conducive to their work. A new intelligentsia and the newspapers, magazines, and journals that printed their inexhaustible supply of writings clustered in the capital, where the beginnings of a new establishment in higher education also appeared. Resting at the pinnacle was a national university with a campus situated north of the imperial palace. Its status formalized

TABLE 2. *Population Changes in Tokyo Metropolitan Prefecture, 1880–1920*

	ca. 1880	1910	1920
City center[a]	885,445 (66%)	1,805,786 (68%)	2,173,201 (59%)
Periphery[b]	288,158 (21%)	574,940 (22%)	1,177,018 (32%)
Santama Region	178,812 (13%)	275,131 (10%)	316,103 (9%)
Totals	1,352,415	2,655,857	3,666,322

SOURCES: For Tokyo area, in 1882, Tōkyō fu, *Tōkyō fu tōkei sho: Meiji 15-nen* [Tokyo Prefecture Statistical Handbook: 1882] (Tokyo, 1884), p. 1; for Santama Region, in 1878, Fuchū shi shi hensan iinkai, comp., *Fuchū shi shi* [The History of Fuchū City] (Fuchū, 1974), II: 146; for 1910, Tōkyō fu, *Tōkyō fu tōkei sho* [Tokyo Prefecture Statistical Handbook] (Tokyo, 1912), I: 72–73; and for 1920, Naikaku tōkei kyoku, *Taishō 9-nen kokusei chōsa hōkoku: Tōkyō fu* [1920 National Census Report: Tokyo Prefecture] (Tokyo, 1929), pp. 2–5.
[a]The city center includes the 15-ward area of the City of Tokyo, as of 1920.
[b]The periphery includes what during this forty-year period were five counties: Ebara, Toyotama, Kita Tōshima, Minami Adachi, and Minami Katsushika.

in the 1880s, Tokyo Imperial University had become by the 1910s the gateway to success in Japanese society, through which virtually any aspiring and ambitious young man had to pass. Failing that chance, he could opt for one of the city's eminent private institutions, Keiō or Waseda, which became universities officially in 1920. Tokyo also expanded on other cultural and intellectual achievements of the Tokugawa Period during the late nineteenth century. By the twentieth, it was the undisputed center of the nation's cultural, intellectual, and scholarly life.

The extensive changes taking place in Tokyo exercised a powerful lure, drawing people to the capital in ever-increasing numbers, as table 2 indicates. Between the early 1880s and 1920, the population in the area of the metropolitan prefecture nearly tripled, from 1.4 million to 3.7 million. Data on the nativity of populations, which appeared for the first time in the 1920 census, reveal that nearly half the prefecture's residents in that year had been born elsewhere, the vast majority in surrounding prefectures of the Kantō Region.[1] While all parts of the Tokyo area—the center, the periphery, and the Santama region—grew discernibly during the four-decade period, each experienced different patterns of growth.

1. Naikaku tōkei kyoku, *Taishō 9-nen Kokusei chōsa hōkoku: Tōkyō fu* [1920 National Census Reports: Tokyo Metropolitan Prefecture] (Tokyo, 1929), pp. 34–37, 47. Hereafter cited as 1920 National Census.

During the forty years before 1920, the city center grew rapidly and attained a peak in the 1910s. Thereafter, its population stabilized at around 2.2 million. Covering an area of only thirty-one square miles, the center had population densities of more than 28,000 persons per square mile in 1880. When it reached the saturation point in the 1910s, densities exceeded 70,000 persons per square mile, a level almost three times that of New York City in the 1970s.

Tokyo's center was a swarm of human activity, encompassing all social ranks. Descendants of its old ruling class, and the members of its new, often lived in expansive residences of the Yamanote area. They sat in isolated splendor amidst lush gardens at the crest of breeze-swept bluffs. The sedate, leisurely mien of their occupants contrasted sharply with the otherwise frenetic pace of the city, where most families lived with their help in small apartments above tiny shops that buzzed with activity from dawn to dusk. One lived literally cheek-by-jowl with dozens of others, the noise of work and human chatter a constant presence, and privacy a vain ideal. Even by Japanese standards, the intensity of urban concentrations attained in Tokyo during the 1910s must have tested the limits of toleration.

Resistance to crowding, as well as more promising opportunities and possibly better housing, explains why many newcomers had already begun to settle in the periphery during the late nineteenth century. By the 1910s it was absorbing the largest share of the prefecture's population increase. Some 60 percent of the roughly one million new residents added between 1910 and 1920 settled there. While such areas drew heavily on in-migrants from surrounding prefectures, they also attracted many newcomers from within the prefecture itself. Young families moving out of the central city, unmarried men and women from the center and the Santama region, and younger workers and families from outside Tokyo were those who sped the periphery's rapid growth.

Most of them preferred to settle in the higher flatlands west of the city center, in what are now the wards of Shibuya, Shinjuku, and Toshima. Few settled in the river bottomlands to the east and north of the center: they were too steamy during hot summer months. The scene of most bustling growth during the 1910s was the town of Shibuya, situated advantageously at the junction of the Yamate Line with several suburban rail lines.[2] Indeed, until the consolidation of 1932, outlying communities such as Shibuya, Shinagawa, Ōji, and Ōkubo were the thriving suburbs of the expanding metropolis.

The newfound importance of the periphery was acquired at the expense of the Santama region, as figures in table 2 suggest. The Santama area did experience some growth in the four decades before 1920; in fact, its expansion rate of 77 percent exceeded the national rate of 60 percent. It did not, however, keep pace with the extraordinary growth taking place in the center and the periphery. The demographic importance of the Santama declined, and it served primarily to produce younger sons and daughters and other out-migrants who helped to populate the central and peripheral areas of the prefecture. One of its most important functions was to export labor to the metropolis.[3]

Where those workers went and how they were employed is suggested by table 3. Employment patterns in the center accord with what we would expect of the primary city in an industrializing society. Nearly four in ten workers were employed in manufacturing and construction. Another three in ten found work in retail and wholesale concerns, and the remaining three in ten were either unemployed or engaged in government and professional jobs or the service trades.

TABLE 3. *Distribution of Occupied Labor Force, Tokyo Metropolitan Prefecture, 1920 (in percentage)*

Category of Occupation	City Center	Periphery	Santama
Agriculture, fishing, mining	1	17	55
Manufacturing & construction	39	42	27
Commerce	31	17	9
All other occupations	22	18	9
Unemployed	7	6	0
Totals	100	100	100

SOURCE: Naikaku tōkei kyoku, *Taishō 9-nen kokusei chōsa hōkoku: Tōkyō fu* [1920 National Census Report: Tokyo Prefecture] (Tokyo, 1929), pp. 18–19.

2. Shibuya's development is analyzed in a study by Robert August, "Urbanization and Political Change in Tokyo, Japan: 1890–1932." Ph.D. diss., University of Pittsburgh, 1975.
3. 1920 National Census, pp. 2–5, 34–37, and 47.

In the transitional periphery, employment patterns were different. The 17 percent of the labor force engaged in primary industry were the descendants of an occupational group that had once dominated the area. They were being overshadowed, however, by newcomers arriving to work in its large modern factories or its small manufacturing shops. In addition, some workers employed in commerce, government, the professions, and the service trades had also begun to settle in the region, joining many small clusters of workers like them who had been there for generations. But this group did not compare in size with its counterpart in the central area, where government ministries, wholesale outlets, retail shops, and service establishments occupied most workers.

In addition to importing labor from the Santama, the center and periphery imported another essential commodity: food. Since the Tokugawa Period a popular saying in the region was that farmers from the Santama brought food baskets to the city and carried honey buckets home, a reference to their exchange of agricultural produce for human wastes used as fertilizer. They continued in this role after the Meiji Restoration, and by the twentieth century were actively engaged in feeding the metropolis. Given the data at hand, it is virtually impossible to examine how metropolitan demand for farm produce influenced the Santama. It seems certain that substantial changes took place in routes of trade, the sites of markets, the types of commodities produced, and the quantities of goods sold. But it seems equally certain that these changes did little if anything to alter the basic structure of the Santama's agricultural economy. Changes entailed extensive adjustments in the unit of production—the small-scale, family farm—but they did not lead to a radical redistribution of economic wealth and power among different segments of Santama society, a point to which we shall return later. We thus find the Santama region linked to the metropolis once again as an exporter, this time of agricultural produce.[4]

Assisting the Santama region in this role was an emerging network of railroads. The grandfather of them all was the Chūō Line, begun in the 1880s by private interests for the purpose of linking Yamanashi (a provincial city west of the Santama) with the me-

4. A discussion of the Santama's agrarian economy appears in Musashino shi shi hensan iinkai, comp., *Musashino shi shi (Mss)* [The History of Musashino City] (Musashino, 1970), pp. 487–503 and 587–596.

tropolis. Decades passed, however, before the line achieved that end. When it opened for service in 1889, it stopped at four stations in the Santama region (Hachiōji, Tachikawa, Kokubunji, and Sakai) on its way to Shinjuku. Not until 1919 was the line finally completed through the heart of the city to reach Tokyo Station. At that time, also, the line was adapted for the use of electric trains as far west as Kokubunji. For the first time people could realistically contemplate living in the Santama region and commuting into the city center for work.[5]

Several other lines also appeared in the region between 1889 and 1923. The Ōme Line, an extension of the Chūō from Tachikawa to the town of Ōme in the western mountains, was built in 1894 to bring that area's limestone into Tokyo. A second line built also for the purpose of hauling limestone (and silk) was constructed across the northeastern quarter of the Santama in 1915. It fell on bad times and only achieved some stability after 1940, by which time it had become a commuters' route, known today as the Seibu Ikebukuro Line. Yet another line was built in the mid-1910s across the southern tier of the Santama, linking Hachiōji, Fuchū, and Chōfu with Shinjuku. This line, the Keiō, remains today a major commuter route for those in the southern Santama.[6]

Indispensable as these railroads became, they played a negligible role as commuter lines before 1923. Stations were few in number, intervals between trains long, and the rides themselves time-consuming. A hint of just how isolated the Santama remained into the 1920s is contained in an anecdote reported by an elderly Santama resident, who recalled having taken a trip on the Chūō Line in the mid-1920s. He struck up a conversation with a wizened grandmother accompanied by her grandson and laden down with souvenirs. She informed him that she was returning from a visit to "Edo." Her somewhat embarrassed grandson had to explain that she had married before the Restoration of 1868, and even though the city had been known as Tokyo since then, she still called it Edo. The packages were filled with presents from relatives in the city, which she had just visited for the first time in her life. She lived in Tachikawa, a town in the center of the Santama that had been

5. Asahi shimbun sha, shakai bu, *Chūō sen: Tōkyō no dōmyaku imamukashi* [The Chūō Line: Now and Then on the Tokyo Main Line] (Tokyo, 1975), pp. 31–66.
6. Ibid, pp. 67–104.

connected with the metropolis by train since 1889.[7] One anecdote does not constitute a proof, but it suggests, along with the very low rates of ridership reported by these lines, that through the 1910s they were merely a path to the metropolis followed by only a few people on a regular daily basis.

This sketch of the metropolis suggests the outlines of its relationship with the Santama region in the four decades before 1923. Growth focused on the city center and on its proximate periphery, in what are now the wards of Shibuya, Shinjuku, Tōshima, and Shinagawa. This still left a vast expanse of undeveloped, agricultural land lying between these areas and the Santama region even farther west. Despite good lines of communication with the center and its periphery, the Santama functioned during this period primarily as it had for decades before, as an exporter of fresh foods, processed agricultural goods, and labor to the metropolis. It was, in short, still part of the capital's rural hinterland, as fuller comments in the following section affirm.

A Placid Agrarian Society

Travelers who visited the Santama at the turn of the century or two decades later all returned impressed by its natural tranquility. One moving description of the region appears in a series of essays written in 1898 by Kunikida Doppo, a popular author of the Meiji Period.[8] Kunikida was captivated by the silent grandeur, the freshness, and the expansiveness of the region. He could only compare it to the steppes of Russia, by relying on extensive quotations from Turgenev, undoubtedly a fanciful flight of the imagination.

Nonetheless, his enthusiasm may well have been justified by the view one had across the high, flat tablelands of the northern Santama, sighting to the right the rugged peaks of the Chichibu Range, and to the left the majestic and serene slopes of Mount Fuji. The vast spaces between were broken only by tall hedges, built as windbreaks to shield squat farm homes, and the scattered clumps of woodland that dotted the region. Kunikida delighted in following any small path he crossed. It might lead him to a quiet, forested glen where birds chirped above tree-sheltered gravestones; to a broad

7. Ibid, p. 183.
8. Kunikida Doppo, *Musashino* (Tokyo, 1975), orig. 1901, pp. 5–29.

plain broken by canals and radish fields; or alongside a levee protected by stands of soft green bamboo.

One site that especially attracted Kunikida, as well as many others, was the Tamagawa Canal at Koganei. Lined with cherry trees that burst into brilliant bloom during the spring, the canal drew thousands of tourists to the region in April. But at other times it was apparently desolate. Kunikida remarks that he and a friend once made a summer visit there in 1895. Disembarking from the Chūō Line at Sakai (now Musashi Sakai), they walked the fifteen minutes or so to Sakurabashi, where a small bridge crossed the canal. After a cup of tea taken at a small shop on the opposite side, they sauntered five or six miles along the canal toward Koganei, never seeing another person. The scene is noteworthy, not only because it describes the area's isolated simplicity at that time, but for what it also implies about change. Today, one risks life and limb to simply cross the road opposite Sakurabashi; it is plied throughout daylight hours by an unceasing stream of trucks, cars, and buses. Their gaseous fumes have destroyed virtually all the delicate cherry trees along the canal.

Comments by other observers also affirm the quiet, rural character of the Santama in the early twentieth century.[9] One elderly resident of Musashino recalled his memories of the Chūō Line about 1920 in the following way:

The area around Kichijōji was pure farmland. There were tea fields and mulberry trees along the line; from the windows of the train we would throw oranges at girls cutting tea leaves. . . .The trains that I rode to commute to school were virtually all single-car electric trams. Sometimes a double car would come along, to be greeted by cheerful clapping from the waiting riders. I remember that trains ran every thirty-six minutes. Those living west of Kichijōji would take a steam engine there and then have to change to an electric tram. Many did this, but the trains were still not very crowded. At that time things were not nearly as tense as they are now. We could avoid the ticket gate, cross over the tracks, and just jump on a train stopped at the platform. You really saved time that way.[10]

This commentary is highlighted by a comparison with the present.

9. Two other sources, more valuable for their photos than their commentary, that corroborate these assertions are Odauchi Michitoshi, *Teito to kinkō* [The Imperial Captial and Its Suburbs] (Tokyo, 1918), and Yokoyama Noboru, *Satsue Musashino meguri* [An Illustrated Tour of Musashino] (Tokyo, 1922).

10. Asahi shimbun sha, *Chūō sen*, p. 181.

In 1975 tracks ran on concrete piers forty feet above the street, reached after an arduous climb of several flights by the 250,000 commuters who passed through the station daily.[11]

Against the quiet serenity of this agrarian backdrop, slow but discernible changes were occurring in parts of the Santama. As was noted earlier, the region did experience gradual population growth. The slowest growing area was Nishi Tama, which covered the mountainous western half of the Santama. Its population rose from 55,066, in 1878, to 88,165, in 1920. Kita Tama, situated in the northeastern quarter of the region, grew from 62,643 to 109,399. But the fastest growth occurred in the southern quarter of the region, where the county of Minami Tama and its city of Hachiōji were located. The former grew from 61,103, in 1878, to 118,458, in 1920, while Hachiōji expanded from a small, rural market town of less than 10,000 to a bustling commercial-factory center of 40,000. Such growth was the product of the one notable economic change occurring in the Santama, the expansion of the textile trades in and around Hachiōji.[12]

Patterns of nativity and migration affirm how intensive the changes were in Hachiōji, especially by contrast with the rest of the Santama. Of the 38,955 persons enumerated in Hachiōji in the 1920 census, well under half were native-born. The high rates of in-migration that fed the city's growth accorded with similarly high rates that obtained in the rapidly growing periphery, but they contrasted with the markedly lower rates of in-migration in Kita and Nishi Tama. In those two counties, outsiders constituted only one-fourth of the population, while native-born residents constituted fully three-fourths. Moreover, the in-migrants to Hachiōji had traveled long distances in some cases, since more than half of them came from beyond Tokyo Metropolitan Prefecture. In the other villages and towns of the Santama, prefectural outsiders were rare. Most in-migrants were women, and they were likely to have come from nearby villages as wives for local men. Hachiōji, therefore, was veritably cosmopolitan beside the small, rural settlements populated so heavily by those who had lived there since birth.[13]

11. Musashino shi, *1975 Shisei tōkei* [1975 Municipal Statistics] (Musashino, 1976), p. 159.

12. Fuchū shi shi hensan iinkai, comp., *Fuchū shi shi (Fss)* [The History of Fuchū City] (Fuchū, 1974), II: 146; and 1920 National Census, pp. 2–5.

13. 1920 National Census, pp. 2–5, 34–37, and 47.

These comments should not imply that outside Hachiōji populations were immobile. It is apparent that many born in the area left when they grew older, to work at a variety of destinations, including other villages in the Santama, the periphery, the center, and even neighboring prefectures. Some of these out-migrants probably returned home later, thus exaggerating the image of permanence conveyed by nativity rates. In addition to these mobile natives, some outsiders also entered the Santama and its communities. But by comparison with the center and the periphery, outsiders were limited, constituting only 30 percent of the total population in the Santama but 60 percent in the center and 70 percent in the periphery in 1920. Moreover, outsiders were few in number. If one counts only immigrant males in the towns and villages, they averaged about 400 in the typical settlement of 5,000 in 1920. Therefore, amidst some movement in and out of local communities, what most stands out is the persistence of a large majority of the local populace. Such stability was the foundation of social continuity.

Continuity was the salient feature of occupational callings in the Santama as late as 1920. Table 3 provides an illustration of employment patterns in the region as a whole, indicating how demonstrably agrarian the Santama remained by comparison with the center and periphery. If one removes Hachiōji from the picture momentarily, this image is further reinforced. When only towns and villages are considered, fully 62 percent of the employed labor force was in agriculture. While there are no earlier figures on which to base a judgment of change, it is significant to note that in 1920 only 52 percent of the national labor force was employed in agriculture, making the Santama's labor force discernibly more agricultural than the national average.

Two patterns of landholding and land use obtained in the region. In the Kita Tama area north of the Tama River, land is relatively high and flat. Water was traditionally scarce in this area until the construction of canals in the seventeenth century. Owing to the scarcity of water, this part of the Santama was settled relatively late, in some cases not until the eighteenth century. In the absence of paddy land, and owing to the way in which farm plots were laid out by the *bakufu* (the Tokugawa government) when resettling former residents of Edo, many farms were of roughly comparable size. A large share of them were, moreover, owned by their cultivators, so that rates of tenancy in the northeastern quarter of the Santama were relatively low, by comparison with the southern and western regions. In the latter areas, living in the mountainous west and the river plain of the south, large landlords with substantial holdings either in forest land or paddy land were more numerous. As a consequence, tenancy rates were much higher in the south. There were no major changes in this basic pattern of ownership and cultivation during the period under consideration, but, as we shall see, these differences were reflected in varying partisan alliances during the late nineteenth century.[14]

The features of the region's industrial economy are explained by examining where its workers were employed, their sex, and the kinds of establishments in which they labored. Of the 38,007 manufacturing workers recorded for the region in 1920, 10,885 (or nearly 30 percent) were employed in Hachiōji alone, where 42 percent of them were females. In Nishi and Minami Tama Counties, women made up 62 percent of nearly 20,000 industrial workers, but they were less numerous in Kita Tama, where nearly two-thirds of the 7,543 manufacturing workers were men.[15]

The geographic and sexual division of labor reflected the structure of the region's industrial economy. There was one major industry, the textile trades. Dispersed throughout the entire region and neighboring prefectures as well, this industry was concentrated on Hachiōji. The city had many small factories employing twenty to thirty workers. It was also a center of marketing and distribution, the focal point of a putting-out system in cotton and silk spinning and weaving that persisted into the 1920s, despite some mechanization in parts of the industry during the 1910s. Even in the face of technological changes in the city, which had been going on sporadically since the 1880s under the leadership of new arrivals out to challenge old establishments, the putting-out system continued to employ large numbers of women and children in the farm villages of Minami and Nishi Tama during the first quarter of this century. Some other towns in the Santama also had small factories, where one or two dozen workers spun or wove cotton or silk. Outside the

14. This account relies on personal observation, discussions with local residents, and the work of a local geographer, Yajima Miyoshi, *Musashino no shūraku* [Rural Settlements of the Musashino Upland] (Tokyo, 1954).

15. 1920 National Census, pp. 18–29, 46–47.

weaving trades, where women were dominant, male manufacturing workers found jobs mainly in small shops and factories, where they produced a range of goods typical of a preindustrial, agrarian economy, such as milled rice, processed foods, lumber, and metal products.[16]

The Santama's industrial economy in 1920 was thus quite small, employing only a quarter of the labor force. A substantial share of the workers (30 percent) toiled in the spinning, weaving, and equipment establishments of Hachiōji. Women in small firms situated in the region's villages or working over looms in their own homes made up another segment of the manufacturing force (about 30 percent). And the remaining portion was composed of men employed in many small shops scattered throughout the region, with the largest group located in Kita Tama.

While it was not the largest community in Kita Tama during the period, the village of Musashino was one of the better known, owing to the location within its boundaries of two stops on the Chūō Line, Sakai on the west and Kichijōji on the east (see map 2). These were the names of two rural hamlets that combined with two others in 1889 to form the administrative village (*mura*) of Musashino. Kichijōji was the largest of the four. Situated on the eastern side of the village, it covered nearly half its area. Nishikubo was a thin slice of land abutting Kichijōji on the west, covering another 11 percent of the community. Adjoining it in turn was the hamlet of Sekimae, an additional 14 percent of the village area. The fourth hamlet was Sakai. It occupied the final one-fourth of the village area, lay on its westernmost edge, and enjoyed the mixed blessing of having one of the Santama's first four stations on the Chūō Line.

Musashino offers a good illustration of the somewhat limited impact the Chūō Line had on Santama communities, at least through the 1900s. Two local men were instrumental in getting a station for Sakai, both natives of that hamlet. One was a local political figure named Mitsui Kentarō, and the other was a landowner, pawnbroker, and entrepreneur named Akimoto Kihichi. Akimoto offered the line's developers a large plot of free land for the station, which apparently persuaded them of Sakai's superior location. Only four

16. Hachiōji shishi hensan iinkai, comp., *Hachiōji shi shi* [The History of Hachiōji City] (Hachiōji, 1963–1968), I: 529–572.

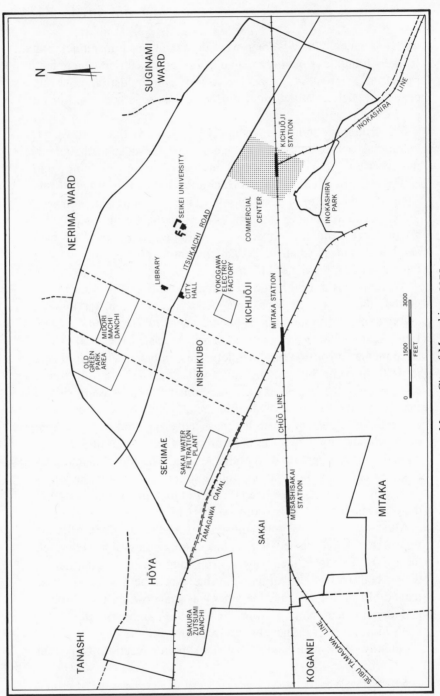

Map 2. City of Musashino, 1975

trains ran through that station daily during the 1890s, and they carried relatively little traffic. Nonetheless, the rail line eventually began to reorient the physical layout of the area as a cluster of small shops grew on a new street north of Sakai Station. After the station at Kichijōji opened in 1899, new shops began to crop up along its streets, too.[17]

Beyond these newly emerging commercial districts, most homes and shops in Musashino remained where they had always been, along the Itsukaichi Road. Cutting through the heart of Kichijōji, Nishikubo, and Sekimae, this was a major artery built during the seventeenth century to carry traffic from Edo to towns in the western part of the Santama. Kichijōji's first settlers were families from Edo who built their homes to front this road, while laying out their farms in long, narrow plots behind.[18] By the turn of the twentieth century, about half the homes in Musashino were situated along the Itsukaichi Road; another third were scattered in the natural farm settlement of Sakai; and the remainder were dispersed in the wooded areas of Nishikubo and Sekimae. There was little change in this residential pattern through the 1910s.[19]

Musashino was a small settlement. Barely 3,000 persons lived in the four hamlets when they amalgamated in 1889. In the next three decades, about 2,000 more residents joined them, to produce a total of 4,951 in 1920. The number of families had grown, probably owing in part to the in-migration of new family units and in some part to the division of long-resident families, a possibility suggested by the decline in average family size from 6.4 in 1889 to 5.8 in 1920.[20]

Arrival of new families led to changes that the city would experience far more extensively after 1923. Figures for the early 1910s indicate that nine in ten of the community's nearly five hundred households were engaged in agriculture. By 1920 the number of households had climbed beyond eight hundred, but the number of farm households had decreased slightly. Most of the additional households were engaged in retail trades, especially as shopkeepers

17. *Mss,* pp. 607–615.
18. *Mss,* pp. 202–232.
19. Seikei daigaku, Seikei gakkai, ed., *Musashino shi (Ms)* [Musashino City](Musashino, 1957), III: 650–677.
20. *Mss,* pp. 547 and 630.

in the new commercial districts around the train stations. Nonetheless, farm households continued to dominate village society, constituting nearly 60 percent of the total in 1920. They worked their dry, upland fields to raise cereals, vegetables, and some commercial crops, such as mulberry leaves, which became especially popular after 1910. Although it would soon experience unsettling changes, Musashino remained in 1920 a somnolent, agricultural village of the sort that typified the Santama.[21]

The town (machi) of Fuchū presented a different appearance because it had a long history as an urban settlement. Fuchū traces its origins to the seventh century, when the imperial government in Kyoto made it a provincial administrative center. Succeeding centuries were not always kind to Fuchū, but with the ascent of the Tokugawa bakufu and its construction of the Kōshū Road through the old town site, Fuchū's fortunes revived. By the nineteenth century, it was not only the residential quarter for some large landlords, it was also a rural market center and post town. In 1889, it resumed its historical function as an administrative center when it became the county seat for Kita Tama, a role it retained until the abolition of the county system in 1921.[22]

Today's suburb of Fuchū was actually three different communities in the period between 1889 and 1954.[23] The old post town of Fuchū sat in the middle of the three, flanked on the east by the village of Tama and on the west by the village of Nishifu (see map 3). The three had a combined population in the 1890s of some 10,000 persons, nearly half of whom resided in the town. In the next three decades, the village of Tama and the town of Fuchū experienced some population growth, giving the area a combined population of 12,864 in 1920, of whom 5,762 lived in Fuchū.[24]

The three communities together presented an image somewhat similar to Musashino's. In 1920 two-thirds of the workers were farmers. The others found employment in small commercial, man-

21.Mss, pp. 631–633.

22.For the early history of Fuchū, see the first volume of Fss.

23.The administrative history of Fuchū is far more complicated than Musashino's. In addition to the amalgamation of 1954, which brought together one town and two villages, amalgamations in 1889 joined five hamlets to form Fuchū Town, three to form Nishifu Village, and nine to form Tama Village. The difficulty of unifying so many formerly separate settlements may have exacerbated divisions in local politics, as the next section suggests.

24.Fss, II, frontispiece.

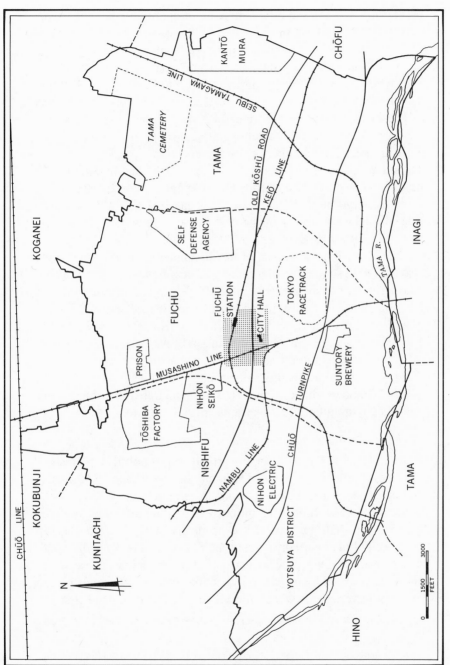

Map 3. City of Fuchū, 1975

ufacturing, and service establishments in approximately equal proportion. Most of these were located in the town, where only a third
of the workers were farmers and most were employed in retail shops
or small handicraft establishments. Several small spinning, weaving,
and dyeing shops in Fuchū during this period had mixed success.
The institutions that thrived, and provided what buoyancy there was
in the local economy, were the sake shops, the food stores, the
fertilizer dealers, and the hotel operators, whose maids were apparently a special attraction for sojourners along the Kōshū Road.
Their activities were a natural legacy that Fuchū had inherited from
its days as a post town during the Tokugawa Period, when there
were ten large brothels in its licensed gay quarters.[25] This seamy
side of Fuchū's history lent the community a somewhat tacky tone
that it has never really lost.

Like Musashino and much of the Santama region, the Fuchū area
also drifted in something of a social and economic backwater during
this period, to a large extent self-sufficient and isolated from the
bustling metropolis only fifteen miles away. If further proof for this
assertion were needed, we find it in a reply from the mayor of Tama
Village to a query from the county in 1918, whose officials worried
over the bad reputation rural laborers were acquiring. He remarked,
"The young people in this village are still rather simple and the
trends of modern thinking have not yet penetrated; we don't think
there is anything here that warrants special attention."[26]

The Political Process

To understand how this society articulated its political interests, a
brief description of its political structure between 1890 and the early
1920s is necessary, before turning to lengthier discussion of the
political process. Since our purpose is to illuminate electoral behavior, we shall be concerned primarily with the relationship
between political participants and their society, less concerned with
the decision-making process and policy formulation. These omis-
sions are justified by the sharp restrictions central authorities placed
on local government, whose formal structure is examined first.[27]

25. Fuchū shi, *Mukashi no Fuchū shashin shū* [A Photo Collection of Old Fuchū] (Fuchū,
1975).
26. *Fss*, II: 506.
27. This study will focus only on local and national politics in the period from 1890 to 1945.
It omits prefectural politics for three reasons: (1) the governor was an appointed official
during this period, so his selection was not part of the electoral process; (2) the powers of the

During the period between 1890 and 1923, towns and villages such as Musashino and Fuchū enjoyed limited rights of local autonomy. They could elect representatives to a local assembly, which in turn nominated candidates for mayor from among its members. The candidate finally selected had to be approved by the Home Ministry, an organ of the central government that kept close watch over local affairs. The suffrage in local elections was limited on the basis of age, residence, sex, and wealth; only males above twenty-five who were relatively permanent, wealthy members of the community could vote. The assembly and mayors had relatively little authority, because in Japan's prewar system of local government the central government retained any power not specifically delegated to localities. Thus, towns and villages were primarily responsible for staffing and financing the public schools (though not for their curriculum, which a central ministry controlled), for maintaining roads and bridges, for collecting taxes, and for maintaining vital records. They were allowed to raise their own revenues through a tax on households, which was usually progressive in practice. Other sources of revenue were closed to them, but in the absence of sweeping powers and responsibilities, this was not usually a problem for small communities.[28]

Restrictions on local autonomy merely reflected the autocratic outlook on politics held by leaders of the Meiji state. The product of their collective vision was the Meiji Constitution of 1890, which established a formal system of political authority that endured until 1945. The emperor rested at the apex of the system, theoretically exercising executive, legislative, and judicial authority alike. In practice, an increasingly powerful group of central ministries handled the daily operations of the government, under the supervision of imperially appointed ministers. While there was a "prime" minister, Meiji leaders sought successfully to restrict his authority, out of their anxiety over concentration of power. This anxiety was translated into a general conception of the state itself, which dispersed power through a wide variety of governing organs, most of them immune to manipulation by public demands.

Tokyo Prefectural Assembly in the prewar years were limited and of modest consequence to the communities studied; and (3) exclusion of prefectural politics will permit closer attention to local and national affairs.

28. The authoritative source on Japan's prewar government is Kurt Steiner, *Local Government in Japan* (Stanford, 1965).

The one exception was a national legislature, or Diet, the lower house of which provided a vehicle for limited expression of public demands. The Lower House was conceived as a body advisory to the emperor, but the constitution did vest it with authority to approve the government's annual budget. Seizing on this loophole, legislators soon made themselves an element in the equation of national power, albeit a small one with limited capacities. Such limits were in keeping with a body of this type, however, whose features as a representative organ were severely restricted. In the first election of 1890, only wealthy males over twenty-five and resident in their community for a year or more could vote; they numbered about 1 percent of the nation's population. Two reforms occurred in 1910 and 1919 that loosened restrictions somewhat, by reducing tax and residence requirements, but the suffrage was still limited to less than 6 percent of the national population as late as the mid-1920s.

A limited suffrage at both local and national levels kept politics the privileged preserve of a minority. Musashino offers an excellent illustration, for in that community the mayoralty and assembly seats were monopolized by men with substantial land holdings.[29] Four sat as mayor during the period. They were in their forties when they assumed office, and they remained on average about eight years. Since the first and third mayors of the village came from Sakai, and the second and fourth from Kichijōji, it appears there was an agreement within the community that the mayor's post would rotate between those two hamlets, as would the assistant mayor's position on an alternate basis. This not only reduced political competition, it kept conflict to a minimum—as long as the practice was followed.

The third mayor of Musashino, Akimoto Kihichi, illustrates the qualities of the village's political leaders. This is the same Akimoto whom we encountered earlier parting with some of his land to lure a Chūō Line station to Sakai. Only in his late twenties at that time, he was the adopted heir of one of Sakai's largest and oldest landlord families. Having attracted the station and its attendant developments to the site of the family's lands, Kihichi had also assured the family's fortunes for at least two generations to come. He then turned his

29. This overview is based on materials dealing with local politics that are dispersed throughout the two major sources on the city, *Musashino shi shi* and *Musashino shi,* both cited earlier.

attention to politics, where he had an active career as mayor (between 1900 and 1914), prefectural assemblyman (between 1899 and 1911), and Diet member (between 1915 and 1925). In politics, too, he established a lasting legacy. When he died in 1930, his younger, adopted brother Rokunosuke was already mayor of Musashino, where he served from 1922 to 1939, stepping down only to be succeeded by Kihichi's son, Toshio, who served until 1941. Kihichi's political status thus enabled members of his family to occupy the Musashino mayoralty for thirty-three years between 1900 and 1941.[30]

The Akimoto family is an exceptional case, but the men who sat as assembly members in the village during this period shared with it two attributes. They, too, were scions of long-resident families, and they held substantial land in their own right. That so many of them came from the Kichijōji area, where plots were on average larger than in the rest of the village, attests to this. Moreover, they were men born to rule, as the first group of twelve chosen in 1889 indicates. At least 75 percent were either themselves former officials during the late Tokugawa or early Meiji periods, or they were the sons or grandsons of men who had previously held local office. On average about forty-one years of age, the early council members of Musashino were clearly the socio-economic elite of the community. At the turn of the century, they were the political spokesmen for the one in twelve persons and two in three households in the village who enjoyed the right to participate in local affairs.[31]

They could carry those affairs lightly. They met perhaps twice annually for a session of a week or so, with additional meetings for special issues that arose. On other occasions, local affairs were handled by the mayor, an assistant mayor, and a handful of clerks. So leisurely was the pace of local administration that the routine clerical task of registering newcomers on the household lists was handled by the mayor himself through 1920. The main duty of the council members was to allocate the budget, the outlines of which were usually preordained with about 60 percent designated for education and the remainder divided almost equally between public works and administrative costs. Under the circumstances, it is little

---

30. Musashino machi, *Musashino chō shi* [The History of Musashino Town] (Musashino, 1932), pp. 225–226; *Ms*, III: 812; and *Mss*, p. 552.
31. *Mss*, pp. 525–535 and 549–556; *Ms*, III: 774–779.

wonder that an assembly election in the early twentieth century seldom attracted more than 30 to 40 percent of the voters from an already limited electorate.[32]

From the very sketchy materials that survive, it appears that local politics in Fuchū were similar to those in Musashino. The work load of the assembly was no heavier, nor were the administrative burdens of local officials; the town was getting by with only eight clerks as late as 1928. In Fuchū, as in Musashino, local funds were allocated for the same purposes, to support the public school system and to maintain major public roads and bridges.

On one count, however, Fuchū differed from Musashino. Dissension afflicted the local assembly. Divisions always arose when the assembly had to choose a mayor, and they nearly always split members into two camps. Owing to this instability, the local merchants and landlords who served as mayor in Fuchū enjoyed much shorter tenure than their counterparts in Musashino. Ten different men held the position of mayor between 1889 and 1923, for an average of 3.4 years per man. Since, however, one man served on three occasions for a total of fourteen years, tenure for most averaged only about two years.[33]

The origins and causes of this dissension are obscure, and will probably remain so. Although local histories contain substantial material on the split, they always stop short of providing decisive evidence. For example, council minutes are available that relate several disputes concerning selection of a mayor. However, it is impossible to learn who backed whom, what their affiliations were, and how they voted on the determining issues, because the decisive votes always took place during a council's recess. The minutes record only the final, formal vote, which was cast after the parties returned to their chamber to put the public stamp of unanimity on the behind-the-scenes compromise.[34]

In the face of such difficulties, one can only speculate about the sources of dissension in Fuchū. One conventional explanation can be dismissed. Simple economic cleavages between merchants and

32. Ibid.

33. *Fss*, II: 1265–1266.

34. See, for example, Fuchū shi shi hensan iinkai, comp., *Fuchū shi shi kindai hen shiryō shū: Fuchū shi no kindai gyōsei shiryō shū* [Materials Collection for the Fuchū City History: Fuchū City Modern Period Administrative Materials Collection] (Fuchū, 1970–1972), I: 198, 226–227; IV: 33–54; and V: 65. See also, *Fss*, II: 695–702.

landlords do not explain the split, because landlords and merchants worked together on both sides. Three other sources of division are more likely: (1) differences among the former hamlets that made up the town after 1889, (2) differences among kin groups, and (3) differences based on personal animosities. In the absence of direct evidence to affirm such cleavages, one can only note that these are intuitively logical points of division in Japanese society. One can also note that political divisions in contemporary Fuchū, which are the direct legacy of this earlier period, continue to align kin groups from certain districts against others from different areas, suggesting that a conjunction of the three causes might be the most plausible explanation.

Whatever the social basis of these political divisions in Fuchū may have been, one thing is clear: political parties crystallized the split. The parties around which Fuchū's political activists gathered traced their origins to a time of unusual activity in the Santama, the 1870s and the rise of the people's rights movement. Situated in an area where some of its important early supporters lived, Fuchū was inevitably drawn into the emotional and social fray of Japan's first party movement. Since that movement decisively shaped the outlines of Diet politics in this area through the 1920s, it must be sketched briefly before we can turn to an analysis of national-level politics in the Santama after 1890.

The people's rights movement was a spasmodic attempt by former samurai and landed interests to gain a share of power in a new government that appeared to be closing them out.[35] The movement originated in 1874 under the leadership of Itagaki Taisuke. A former samurai from the domain of Tōsa, he found himself and other samurai cohorts being shunted from center stage by the leaders of the Meiji government, who came primarily from Satsuma and Chōshū. Exploiting obvious sources of dissatisfaction among prospective adherents, leaders in its early days advocated three causes:

35. Major English-language sources on this subject are Robert A. Scalapino, *Democracy and the Party Movement in Prewar Japan* (Berkeley, 1962); George Akita, *Foundations of Constitutional Government in Modern Japan, 1868–1900* (Cambridge, Mass., 1967); and R. H. P. Mason, *Japan's First General Election, 1890* (Cambridge, 1969). A recent statement by the leading local student of the subject is Irokawa Daikichi, "Santama no hyakunen: Jiyū minken undō [A Century of Santama History: The People's Rights Movement]," *Asahi shimbun*, December 30, 1975, p. 13. Peter Duus presents a contrary interpretation in *Party Rivalry and Political Change in Taishō Japan* (Cambridge, Mass., 1968), pp. 6–8.

(1) reduction of land taxes, (2) revision of foreign treaties, and (3) creation of a representative national assembly. The movement fizzled quickly in the mid-1870s, but it revived again in late 1881, when Itagaki and his associates created a new political party, the Jiyūtō. After a short life of three years, this party disbanded in 1884, to reappear again in 1890 with the creation of the national legislature its adherents had been advocating. One decade later, most Jiyūtō adherents entered a new political party, the Seiyūkai, which finally achieved some power by becoming a pro-government organ.[36]

One region in which the people's rights movement found some of its most avid, early supporters was the Santama. The movement arose when the Santama was still part of Kanagawa Prefecture, and when a young former samurai from Tōsa named Nakajima Nobuyuki was governor. A close associate of Itagaki, Nakajima became vice-president of the Jiyūtō on its formation in 1881 and served later as the first Speaker of the Lower House. As governor between 1874 and 1876, he came into contact with many of the young mayors of the Santama, igniting in them a spark of political interest that some of them never lost.[37]

Nakajima's first major convert and the eventual patron of Santama political activists was Ishizaka Masataka (Shōkō).[38] Like many Santama activists, Ishizaka was the scion of a wealthy rural family with a history of political service, in his case in the village of Tsurukawa (now part of the city of Machida). Although he lost most of his land to political expenses, when Ishizaka began his political activities in the 1870s he managed 28 chō, or nearly 70 acres, an extremely large amount by Japanese standards, when most farms averaged about 1 chō, or 2.5 acres. Ishizaka soon recruited a number of protégés, including the son of a nearby local family that controlled over 15 chō of land, a young man eighteen years his junior named Murano Tsuneemon.[39] Others who became politically

36. A critical phase in the Seiyūkai's compromising path to power is examined in Tetsuo Najita, *Hara Kei in the Politics of Compromise, 1905–1915* (Cambridge, Mass., 1967).

37. For a judicious assessment of political events in another locale during this period, see James L. McClain, "Local Politics and National Integration: The Fukui Prefectural Assembly in the 1880s," *Monumenta Nipponica,* 31, no. 1 (Spring 1976): 51–75.

38. For Ishizaka, see Watanabe Shō, "Ishizaka Masataka no shōgai: Gōnō no seitai [The Life of Ishizaka Masataka: Conditions of a Wealthy Farmer]," *Tama bunka,* no. 21 (September 1969), pp. 21–45.

39. The authoritative source on Murano is a collaborative effort between a famous historian of the Santama area and Murano's son: Irokawa Daikichi and Murano Ren'ichi, comps., *Murano Tsuneemon den* [A Biography of Murano Tsuneemon] (Tokyo, 1969–1971), 2 vols.

active and gained reputations as the Santama *sōshi* were Morikubo Sakuzō, Aoki Shōtarō, Setooka Tameichirō, Nakamura Kokushō, Akimoto Kihichi, Hiruma Kuninosuke, and Uchiyama Yasubei, all of whom bore several traits in common.[40] With the exception of Ishizaka, all were born between 1850 and 1856; all were sons of major landlords; each served as mayor of his home village; and all went on during the 1880s and after to sit as prefectural assemblymen and Diet members. These are, in fact, the men who monopolized national-level politics in the Santama region on behalf of the Jiyūtō and the Seiyūkai for three decades between 1890 and 1920.

The extent of their political monopoly is measured by the votes they won and the seats they captured. In the fourteen national elections between 1890 and 1920, Seiyūkai candidates and other men coming directly out of the Santama *sōshi* tradition won exactly two-thirds of all votes cast in the Santama district, or the district of which it was a part.[41] This success is the more remarkable because it was maintained for seven elections between 1902 and 1917, when the Santama was part of a district including the periphery, where Seiyūkai strength was weak. Nonetheless, during that fifteen-year period, Seiyūkai candidates won 64 percent of the district's total vote. Even this support paled by comparison with the loyalty of Santama voters to their *sōshi*. In the first six elections, when the Santama was a separate district, local voters gave the Santama *sōshi* 86 percent of their ballots. These were converted to the type of power that counted: Diet seats. In the first six elections, *sōshi* won all the

40. *Sōshi* is a term that can be translated political activist, henchman, or political bully, and it bears all the connotations, negative and positive, implied thereby. The Santama *sōshi* frequently used staves and brute force to persuade voters, especially during the 1880s and 1890s. Disparaging connotations are not the only ones suggested by the term, however, which has come to be used with a certain amount of pride and approbation locally. I therefore use *sōshi*, rather than an English translation, when I refer to Ishizaka, Murano, Morikubo, and their cohorts collectively.

41. Changes in Diet districts affected the Santama as follows. During the first six elections between 1890 and 1898, the three counties of the Santama formed a single district, the Kanagawa Third District in the first two and the Tokyo Thirteenth District in the next four. Between 1902 and 1917 there were only two districts in all of Tokyo, one coterminous with the city of Tokyo, and a rural district including the rest of the prefecture. During this period it is impossible to determine exactly how many ballots Santama voters cast, because aggregate figures for the rural district as a whole are the only ones available. In 1920 a reorganization occurred which created sixteen different districts in Tokyo Metropolitan Prefecture. Two were in the Santama: the Twelfth, coterminous with the city of Hachiōji, and the Fourteenth, which included the rest of the Santama region. Between 1890 and 1898 the Santama sent two men to the Diet. When it was part of the Tokyo rural district, that district as a whole sent five members. After 1920, Hachiōji had one seat and the rest of the Santama two.

district's seats. In the next seven, twenty-six of thirty-five winners were Seiyūkai adherents, and in 1920, two of three seats in the Santama went to Seiyūkai members. Therefore, in the Santama District or the district of which it was a part between 1890 and 1920, Santama *sōshi* and their Seiyūkai cohorts won two-thirds of all the votes and captured forty-one of fifty Diet seats.[42]

It should be noted that the Santama *sōshi* were not part of one, trouble-free group. Within the Santama region there were several discernible factions, oriented toward leaders with strong personalities in several different areas. The major *sōshi* group, aligned with Ishizaka, Murano, and Morikubo, operated primarily in the southern county of Minami Tama and in the city of Hachiōji. Another faction that aligned with them on national issues but retained some autonomy regionally was based in the Nishi Tama area, where men with large holdings in forest land were the dominant figures. Nakamura Kokushō and Yoshino Taizō, two men who sometimes challenged the Ishizaka faction in electoral and ideological disputes, led what became a dissident faction in the Kita Tama area near Mitaka and Fuchū.

At a very early stage in the people's rights movement, some groups in Fuchū were drawn to the Mitaka faction under Yoshino while others aligned themselves with Ishizaka and his cohorts. Fuchū's geographic position, which placed it directly between both factions, reinforced differences among the community's politicians by providing dissidents with two political banners around which to rally. We may never know whether divided groups in Fuchū sought out various factions or whether factions gave rise to divided groups, but one thing is clear: political dissension in Fuchū found reinforcement in the people's rights movement during the 1870s.[43]

The men who dominated the list of *sōshi* Diet members bore familiar names. Ishizaka served eight years between 1890 and 1898. His protégé Murano established the local record for longevity by serving twenty-two years after 1898. Their cohort Morikubo sat for thirteen years, at the same time he was dominating the affairs of Tokyo through its city council. Musashino's Seiyūkai activist, Akimoto Kihichi, served nine years after 1915. And the less promi-

42. These figures are based on Kōmei senkyo renmei, ed., *Shūgiin giin senkyo no jisseki* [Results of General Elections for the Lower House] (Tokyo, 1968).
43. *Fss*, II: 210–232.

nent *sōshi* from the hinterlands of Nishi Tama, such as Uchiyama and Setooka, also served a term or two. Contacts with Ishizaka and his retinue, a reputation as a *sōshi*, and affiliation with the Seiyūkai were virtual guarantees of political success for any aspiring young man in the Santama during the early twentieth century—with two exceptions.

One was an unusual politician named Takagi Masatoshi (Seinen).[44] An anti-Seiyūkai candidate, Takagi was associated in later years with the Kenseikai and the Minseitō. His political career began at the age of thirty-four with the first Diet election of 1890 and ended in 1934, following seventeen campaigns, thirteen victories, and thirty-six years of Diet service. Throughout his political career, Takagi lived in an area called Shinagawa, situated near the shores of Tokyo Bay southwest of Tokyo Station and the imperial palace. During the early part of the century it was still dominated by farmers and fishermen, but it became a burgeoning industrial quarter following World War I. As a Shinto priest dedicated to the service of his parishioners and his locale, Takagi had close links to the fishermen, small farmers, and shopkeepers in his vicinity. They were the bedrock of his electoral base (*jiban*) in the Shinagawa area of Ebara County.

Takagi is an exception to the Seiyūkai monopoly in the Santama owing to his special relationship with Fuchū. When his father was the licensed sake brewer at the Oh Kunitama Shrine in downtown Fuchū between 1867 and 1877, Takagi lived there, studied with local scholars, and made friends among the residents. Therefore, when a reform of Diet constituencies took place in 1902 that put Ebara County and the Santama region in the same rural district, Takagi returned to Fuchū for support. He found it among relatives and friends who were willing to work for his candidacy. In the next fifteen years, while Ebara and the Santama remained a part of the same district, some Fuchū voters gave their support to Takagi Masatoshi, a prominent anti-Seiyūkai spokesman.

Once again, therefore, the leitmotiv of dissent running through Fuchū's local politics from the 1880s on recurred, this time in the form of a bond between local voters and a Kenseikai/Minseitō politician. Presumably, Takagi was able to exploit his position as a

44. The basic source on Takagi is Yokoyama Kendō, ed., *Takagi Seinen jijōden* [An Autobiography of Takagi Seinen] (Tokyo, 1932).

Diet member to benefit his backers in Fuchū. His ability to extract rewards from the center undoubtedly strengthened his supporters in contests for power at the local level and enabled them to stand against the Seiyūkai mainstream, despite their minority status.[45]

The second exception to the Seiyūkai monopoly arose in Hachiōji and stemmed from a markedly different set of causes. As the focal point of the Santama's only industrial district, Hachiōji underwent gradually increasing rates of social change from the 1880s onward, which found expression in political conflict, as a report from a local official to the prefectural government following a town assembly election in 1892 illustrates:

There was a battle in the town of Hachiōji between the landlord faction, in other words the wealthy group, and the newcomer faction. Although it was a rather dramatic struggle, it was less a battle between political parties and more a struggle between different political factions or cliques within the community itself. In the third rank [ed. that is, the one in which the least wealthy electors voted] the newcomers won, but the landlords won in the first and second ranks.[46]

These comments introduce a theme that will be repeated many times over in the evolution of the Santama's politics: divisions arising between newcomers and old-line groups.

Such divisions appeared first in Hachiōji because it was the only Santama community to experience major economic and social change before the 1920s. Its industrialization attracted, it appears, a group of entrepreneurs and technical innovators from outside whose needs and demands conflicted with those of established, old-line interests. Those conflicts simmered for nearly three decades, as more newcomers arrived to lend strength to the dissident faction. They finally exploded on the national political scene with the Diet election of 1920.

The election of 1920 took place on a new battleground.[47] Tokyo's two large districts had been divided to form sixteen, two of them in the Santama. The Fourteenth District encompassed the towns and villages of the Santama and had two seats. The city of Hachiōji, with a population of about forty thousand, was designated a separate

45. Ibid, pp. 22–27 and 66–68.
46. *Hachiōji shi shi*, II: 1277.
47. A general assessment of the 1920 election appears in Kimbara Samon, *Taishōki no seitō to kokumin* [Taishō Political Parties and the People] (Tokyo, 1973).

district and assigned one seat. Confident of its power, the Seiyūkai assigned their local warhorse, Murano Tsuneemon, to the Hachiōji district. He had been elected comfortably eight times running by relying on supporters from the Minami Tama area, and it seemed he would have no difficulty defeating the new candidate the Kenseikai was putting up against him. A forty-year-old lawyer from Oita Prefecture who had moved to Hachiōji following his graduation from Tokyo Imperial University, Yatsunami Takeji did not seem the kind of candidate to unseat someone of Murano's stature. Even though his party was conducting the election and he had ample money with which to offer gifts of appreciation to his supporters, Murano polled only 631 votes. Yatsunami won with 786.

Far more critical than Takagi's piecemeal support in Fuchū, Yatsunami's victory gave the Seiyūkai's opponents a foothold in the Santama region for the first time. They quickly moved to exploit it, for in the city council election of 1921 Kenseikai candidates took half the seats, an unprecedented share for any community in the region.[48] Yatsunami's ascent in Hachiōji was thus an exception to a general rule. His victory as an anti-Seiyūkai candidate occurred in a community experiencing rapid population growth, high rates of demographic mobility, occupational differentiation, and an expanding industrial economy. These changes undermined the solidarity of the old community and encouraged people outside the circle of power to lay claim to a share of it. They found social conditions ripe for their challenge by 1920, when outsiders finally surpassed native inhabitants in number. While their victory should come as no surprise, it is crucial to note that nearly four decades of social and economic change were required to assure it.

The placid, agrarian character of the Santama region and its political processes were intimately entwined in the three decades before suburbanization began. The political stability that the area witnessed was in large part, of course, the avowed aim of a political system that sharply restricted participation and local responsibilities. But political stability in the Santama was not only a product of formal structures. It resulted from a variety of factors—some general, some unique—that provided a salutary social foundation for the

48. *Hachiōji shi shi*, I: 80–100.

durable monopoly of political power achieved by the Santama *sōshi*.

The common socio-economic interests and backgrounds shared by the political activists of the Santama are striking. Virtually all were born during the decade of the 1850s into landholding families that had played a role in local affairs for many generations. They shared a common status in their home villages, therefore, as members of a hereditary ruling group whose claims to power were based on longevity of residence, demonstrated stature, and wealth. It is little wonder that men from such backgrounds found a good deal in common with their counterparts in other villages, especially during the 1880s. As landlords, they shared a common position on economic questions that affected their taxes. As creditors, they found a broader base of common interest among themselves than with a peasantry facing the dilemma of debt in a period of deflation. And as budding entrepreneurs with interests in banks, railroads, power companies, and warehouses, they shared a growing commitment to a competitive, capitalist economy. All these considerations resonated through their political activities after the 1880s.

Similar social and economic attributes were probably not sufficient to bring them together in a common political enterprise, but their desire for power compensated. The aspiration for high office must have flourished naturally among social groups whose forebears had for generations held political office as a hereditary right. With the Restoration and its new government, however, leaders established new patterns of ascent to office, not so much at local as at higher levels. As it became clearer during the 1880s that national institutions were going to be the repository of political power in the new state, men of local influence—like the *sōshi* of the Santama— grew anxious about their exclusion. The early program of the people's rights movement addressed their anxieties directly and gave them a rallying cry with which to campaign for influence at the national level.

This general aspiration for power was motivated in the Santama by peculiarly local impulses. During the Tokugawa Period, most of the Santama region was under the direct authority of the Tokugawa *bakufu* and administered by its lower-level officials. This did not give local men of influence any power in the Tokugawa shogunate, but it did comfort them in the thought that they were part of established authority. The overthrow of the Tokugawa house and the establishment of a new government led by former samurai from western domains ruptured these associations. Some have alleged that this left a legacy of pro-*bakufu* support among the villages of the Santama and their leaders.[49] If this was indeed the case, then the alacrity with which they challenged Meiji leaders in the 1870s and 1880s is more easily explained. The equal alacrity with which they conformed to government programs once they broke into the circle of power by joining the Diet might seem to require more complex explanation. But it will suffice to note that co-optation of dissidents in Japan's modern political history has usually mollified their discontent and elicited their conformity.

If common socio-economic interests and a desire for power brought these men together, the consensual nature of community affairs helped keep them in power. Few villages were without sources of conflict, but in most a low-keyed mood of consensus prevailed. Conflict usually arose on an intracommunity basis, as in Musashino, where sectional interests sought the rewards of office or the spoils of battle. But even dissenting interests within a community had a pragmatic appreciation of the proper dimensions of conflict. It was appropriate for landlords from Sakai and Kichijōji to quarrel over the allocation of road-repair funds within Musashino, but when the time came to elect a delegate to the national legislature, it was in everyone's interest to support a single candidate without discord. This general impulse operated in most communities and helps account for the longevity in office of so many *sōshi*.

It is also necessary to appreciate the ease of mobilizing voters during this period. In the first election of 1890, only ten persons enjoyed the suffrage in the village of Musashino.[50] This was a relatively low figure, but in most towns and villages of the region only a dozen or two persons were eligible to vote during the 1890s. This number increased about four times over by 1902, when, even so, a local electorate of one or two hundred persons remained common. Under such circumstances, large campaign organizations were not necessary. In their place, candidates relied on operatives em-

49. Irokawa Daikichi and Egawa Hideo, "Santama sōshi ni tsuite [On the Santama *sōshi*]," in Fuchū shiyakusho, *Tama shi shūi ki* [Gleanings from the History of the Tama Region] (Fuchū, 1972), pp. 1–24.

50. *Mss*, pp. 575–578.

bodying a range of roles, each of which was useful in persuading others to support him. For example, the operative who was a neighbor, fellow landlord, local assembly associate, and moneylender had access to other neighbors, landlords, assembly associates, business contacts, and even a debtor or two, all of whom might be willing to sign their ballot for his candidate. Moreover, a brother-in-law or a cousin in a nearby village might be persuaded to activate a similar network in his settlement. Candidates thus mobilized their supporters by relying on their own efforts and those of associates who were bound to a broad range of voters as a result of frequent, personal contact.

The task of reaching beyond one's own village or town was made easier by the langorous continuity of the rural economy. Many of the landlords who dominated the electorate in this period engaged with each other in banking and marketing activities, as directors of irrigation control boards, and as members of producers' associations. Although changes occurred in the Santama's agrarian economy, local interests promoted them through their entrepreneurial activities. While outsiders were numerous in the industrializing city of Hachiōji, few had penetrated the agrarian economy, where landed families dominant in the villages for generations held sway. Frequent intercourse arising from their economic activities fostered friendships that facilitated their political contact and very likely provided the basis for a common political outlook.

As the 1920s dawned, however, the somewhat languid air that hung over Santama society and politics was struck by new breezes blowing from the east. World War I had created large, noisome industrial quarters in many parts of Tokyo. The consequences of this growth were beginning to reverberate in other areas as well when the shock of a massive earthquake struck the city in 1923. This shattering force not only destroyed much of the metropolis, it also snapped the towns and villages of the Santama region out of their lethargy and confronted them with the first wave of suburban growth, whose pervasive effects the next chapter analyzes.

three

TOKYO STRETCHES WESTWARD

The initial phase of suburban development in the Santama region began with a disaster caused by the earthquake of 1923 and ended under a cloud of tragedy accompanying World War II. In the intervening years, the region witnessed many changes, promoted by housing needs, industrial development, and government policies. Out of the changes emerged a suburban society with features markedly different from those in the United States. This chapter offers an analysis of the processes which formed that society, and an interpretation of the political consequences that ensued.

FORMING THE SUBURBAN COMMUNITY

The first tremors of the Great Kantō Earthquake struck at 11:58 A.M., September 1, 1923, just as thousands of housewives were preparing meals over charcoal-fired hibachi in their small wooden dwellings. Houses caught fire like tinder, and within minutes Tokyo was a ball of flames. Nearly half the city was destroyed. Over 500,000 households were gutted by fire or badly damaged, and 100,000 people lost their lives. The fires smoldered for days as thousands fled the city for safer areas, taking advantage of free passes on the national railways.[1]

Coinciding with a period of already serious economic recession, the earthquake exacerbated the nation's economic problems. Japan's central government acted quickly to provide funds to speed reconstruction, and although costs were enormous, people accepted the

1. Tōkyō shiyakusho, *Tōkyō shiiki kakuchō shi* [A History of the Expansion of Tokyo City] (Tokyo, 1934), pp. 53–91.

task with dedicated energy. In the following decade, they rebuilt Tokyo and went on to expand it considerably. By 1932 nearly half a million structures had been added to the almost 600,000 that existed in 1924. They covered twice as much land and presented a markedly different appearance, because land built with two-storied structures had tripled and the space devoted to even taller structures had quintupled. It was during this period that many commercial districts in the center and the periphery began to assume the character of the modern, brick and concrete city.[2]

Despite the havoc caused by the earthquake and a prolonged slump in the national economy that continued until the early 1930s, Tokyo experienced greater absolute growth in the two decades after 1920 than ever before in her history. The population of the center and the periphery, combined after 1932 in an enlarged ward area, doubled from 3.4 million to 6.8 million. Virtually all the increase occurred in the periphery, especially in the wards on the western edge of the downtown districts. Their topography and their superior transportation facilities continued to attract thousands of new residents annually. By 1940, the periphery, which had been half the size of the center in 1920, was fully twice its size, with a population approaching 5 million.[3]

Its expansion attested in many ways to Tokyo's growing importance, especially in the economic arena. Owing to the government's reflationary policies after 1933, Tokyo assumed a commanding position at the center of a new, heavy industrial economy, dedicated to the production of machines, metals, and chemicals that would boost the nation's war potential. Expanding firms and new factories created a steady demand for workers. One hundred and fifty thousand joined commercial and service establishments in the center between 1920 and 1940, and 650,000 entered similar firms in the periphery. The largest single group of workers, however, included some 700,000 residents of the periphery who joined Tokyo's industrial labor force between 1920 and 1940.[4]

The geographic pattern of industrial development after 1923 followed its earlier course. Two areas on the periphery attracted the greatest numbers of industrial workers. One lay due east of the

2. Tōkyō fu, *Tōkyō fu tōkei sho: 1932* [Tokyo Prefecture Statistical Handbook] (Tokyo, 1934), pp. 1–40.

3. Sōrifu tōkei kyoku, *1940 Kokusei chōsa hōkoku* [1940 National Census Reports] (Tokyo, 1965), I: 101–103, hereafter 1940 National Census.

4. Ibid., II: 46–49.

downtown section and encompassed what are now the wards of
Sumida, Kōtō, and Edogawa. Textile and metal production were
dominant there by the late 1930s. The other was situated southwest
of downtown in the present wards of Shinagawa and Ōta. Small
shops in the metals and munitions industry as well as some larger
firms in electrical and vehicle manufacturing led that area's development. Tokyo's industrial expansion in the 1930s thus played
out historical tendencies that had always directed factories toward
the lowlands on the western shore of Tokyo Bay and toward the river
bottoms east of the downtown area. These two districts absorbed the
brunt of the bombing during the 1940s, suffering almost complete
destruction, and it was from them that some blue-collar, industrial
workers emigrated in the 1940s to find housing and jobs in the
western periphery and the Santama region.[5]

Industrial expansion, population growth, and the ensuing conges-
tion all placed acute pressure on a scarce resource—land. Construction materials and techniques used for residential purposes were
designed for lateral, not vertical, development. As more people
flowed into the metropolis, therefore, more land was needed to
house them, even in the small, modest dwellings characteristic of
the period. Industry had always had an appetite for land, but it grew
during the 1930s with the structural changes in manufacturing.
Heretofore, Japan's industrialization had taken place in many small
shops and some large textile mills. With the shift to heavy industry,
factories needed far larger sites than ever before. Public facilities,
too, such as hospitals, prisons, and sanitoriums, found themselves
in need of more space. Built during the late nineteenth century when
Tokyo was still a relatively small settlement, older facilities were ill
suited to the needs of the expanding metropolis. Exacerbated by the
rapid expansion of the center and the periphery, demand for land
increasingly turned the attention of homeowners, corporate managers, and government officials toward the Santama.

As development in the Santama region proceeded, it did not occur
spatially in the form of ever-widening concentric circles rippling
outward from the metropolitan center.[6] Rather, development conformed more closely to the visual image suggested by sets of lines

5. For an account of the nightmare Tokyo suffered in the early 1940s, see Gordon Daniels,
"The Great Tokyo Air Raid, 9–10 March 1945," in W. G. Beasley, ed., *Modern Japan*
(Berkeley and London, 1975), pp. 113–134.
6. A statement of this position in English is Yazaki Takeo, *The Japanese City: A Sociological
Analysis* (Rutland, Vt., 1963).

and points. Major public arteries, such as the Chūō route, and private commuter roads, such as the Keiō, formed the lines. They were paths for settlement radiating outward from the city center and periphery. The points were the stations along the lines, which often developed first as small commercial districts around whose edges residential areas then grew. The points began as small dots, but as houses increased, shops multiplied, factories appeared, and bus lines expanded, each dot grew larger and began to merge with the other dots or points along the line. Much of Tokyo's suburban expansion, both before and after the Pacific War, occurred therefore in three stages. First, small settlements arose at points along rail lines; the points then grew larger with commercial and residential expansion; and finally, land between points filled in and the points themselves merged into continuously built-up settlements.

It should be noted in passing that this pattern of development had crucial implications for social and political behavior. Until the gaps between points filled in, most land was retained for agricultural purposes by the landowners who operated it. This enabled families embracing agrarian mores to persist for many years amidst a population with markedly different values and occupations, creating a dual society whose characteristics will be examined later. Since many of the farmers were large landowners, they strived to preserve the control they had long exercised over local politics. Their efforts led to a perhaps surprising perpetuation of agrarian power in suburbanizing communities, as the second part of this chapter explains.

Implicit in the foregoing description of development by lines and points is the role of transportation technology and the physical constraints it imposed. The Tokyo suburbs whose evolution in the 1920s and 1930s is under discussion are to be compared with America's horsecar and electric streetcar suburbs of the nineteenth century, and most assuredly not with the automobile suburbs of the post-1920s. Not until the 1960s was auto ownership common enough in Japan to enable large numbers of workers to contemplate driving to work. For forty years, therefore, the Santama's suburban development depended on commuter services in the form of electrified railways. They shaped the patterns of development and they dictated its pace.

This explains why people came to Musashino after 1923 to find land on which to build their new homes, even though as late as 1939 over half the land in the periphery was undeveloped for urban purposes.[7] They were, among other things, measuring their commuting times closely. In the Kichijōji area, one could find open land in the 1920s only a three- to four-minute walk from the station, from which it might require forty more minutes to reach a destination near Tokyo Station. In Setagaya, however, available open land might be situated at a thirty-minute walk from the station, in the absence of well-developed bus routes. When added to the thirty minutes required to reach the same point downtown, economies of time favored settling in Musashino, even though it was farther, as the crow flies, from the downtown districts.

There was another reason for preferring a site in Musashino to one nearer the city: the cost of land. Although Japan has kept excellent statistics on many subjects, she is notorious for her data on land and housing values before 1945. They are narrow in coverage and poor in quality. Nonetheless, some data are available for Tokyo during the 1930s. One set of figures, for the periphery only in 1932, indicates that the most costly housing was found at such places as Shibuya, Shinagawa, and Ōkubo, towns near the center with their own train stations on the Yamate or Chūō Lines.[8] Traveling farther west on the Chūō Line to Suginami brought prices down about 30 percent, while moving southwest on private lines into Setagaya resulted in a reduction of nearly one-half. The lowest prices in the western part of the periphery were on the northwestern edge at Nerima, where housing was only a third the cost of that in Shibuya. A pattern common to metropolitan areas thus existed in western Tokyo during the early 1930s: increased distance from the center lowered land prices.

Another set of statistics, on rental rates in 1930, confirms this pattern.[9] Including all parts of the prefecture, these figures indicate that the most costly rental sites were in Nihonbashi, the center of the downtown commercial district, followed by the government quarter in Kōji *machi*. Land in the periphery near Shinjuku was valued at only 15 percent of the price of land in Nihonbashi. Moving westward on the Chūō Line to Suginami brought prices down to only

7. Tōkyō fu, sōmu bu, chōsa ka, *Tōkyō fu shichōsonzei yōran* [Outline of Conditions in Tokyo Metropolitan Prefecture's Cities, Towns, and Villages] (Tokyo, 1940), pp. 8–13.

8. Tōkyō fu, gakumu bu, shakai ka, *Tōkyō fu gogun ni okeru kaoku chintai jijō chōsa* [A Survey of Housing Rental Conditions in the Five Counties of Tokyo Metropolitan Prefecture] (Tokyo, 1932), pp. 129–130.

9. *Tōkyō fu shichōson zei yōran,* pp. 8–13.

5 percent of the Nihonbashi cost. And in the Kita Tama area as a whole, where both Fuchū and Musashino were located, average rentals were only 1.2 percent of those in Nihonbashi. The land near the station at Kichijōji would certainly have been more expensive than the Kita Tama average, but these figures highlight the basic pattern: land values dropped precipitously with distance from the center. In the periphery, one could acquire land for perhaps one-tenth its price in the center; if one traveled as far as Musashino or Fuchū, one might reduce that already low sum by another 90 percent. Such relatively low prices also help to explain why new residents began to arrive in the Santama in increasing numbers after the 1920s.

The absence of automobiles in large numbers and lack of extensive networks of connecting transportation imposed another constraint on the physical character of the Santama's early suburban development. Very little mass housing was built before the 1950s. There were some attempts at large-scale, planned communities, but they produced mixed results. One of the more successful was undertaken in 1925 at a site called Seijō in Setagaya Ward. Called in Japanese a *gakuen toshi,* a kind of "green town" focused on a private academy, this development was designed for wealthy families who would appreciate the benefits of an exclusive community of like-minded souls.

A less successful undertaking arose at nearly the same time in a small Santama village called Yabo. Conceived by the founder of the Seibu transportation and commercial empire, Tsusumi Yasujirō, this project was patterned after the model of Berne and sought to lay out a planned community with spacious, regular-sized lots. However, the lack of a nearby train station hampered development seriously. Even after 1929, when a new station was built and the village was renamed Kunitachi, commuters were reluctant to settle so far away from the downtown area. Several decades passed before Kunitachi matured as a kind of *gakuen toshi,* focused on Hitotsubashi University.[10]

People drawn to the Santama region to satisfy their housing demands did not, therefore, arrive in large groups to settle in newly built, large-scale units. Rather, they migrated as individuals or families and settled in small rental units or single-family dwellings built under private auspices wherever land was available. Ease of

10. Yamaga Seiji, *Tōkyō daitoshi ken no kenkyū* [Studies of the Tokyo Metropolitan Region] (Tokyo, 1967), pp. 212–220.

transportation and the relatively low price of land were two major attractions for all newcomers, but they came for a variety of reasons. Some were driven out of the center and the periphery by the disaster of 1923 or the bombing of the 1940s. Others were forced out by the rising value of real estate in the metropolis. Some came because they found the benefits of Santama living positively appealing. And others came because the region created a large number of new jobs during the period, especially in its expanding industrial sector.

The Santama region offered many appeals to companies in need of factory sites. By comparison with the periphery, where nearly half the land was developed for urban uses by 1940, the Santama was virtually pristine. Even its most populous Kita Tama area employed only 10 percent of its land for urban purposes. Transportation facilities were also good. The basic network of rail lines completed by the 1910s linked most major settlements with Tokyo, and when the Nambu Line opened in 1929 to connect Tachikawa with Yokohama through Fuchū, the Santama won easy access to the nation's major port and ingress to one of its most booming industrial areas. Abundant water supplies in the southern tier of the Santama were an added inducement to some types of industrial firms. The Santama's industrial appeal thus rested on its cheap open land, its sound transportation facilities, and its ample provision of water.

Owing to these inducements, a rash of major industrial firms put up large factories in the Santama. Hino, a small village in the southern quarter, attracted five factories that produced precision instruments, heavy machinery, photographic film, and electrical equipment. Two towns in the center of the region, Tachikawa and Fussa, drew a new industry that needed vast amounts of land, aircraft manufacturing. And towns in the north, such as Koganei and Mitaka, attracted firms producing electrical equipment.[11]

Musashino and Fuchū also drew electrical firms. The Musashino plant opened in 1930 when the Yokogawa Electric Works began production of precision instruments at a site in the Nishikubo area, five minutes north of the new Mitaka Station on the Chūo Line. Established in 1915 in the Shibuya area, this firm had hoped to build its new plant there. Finding prices too expensive, it bought land in Musashino instead, and by 1935 had moved its entire operation to

11. Ibid., pp. 203–211.

the site. During the war it built another larger factory in neighboring Koganei.[12] At almost the same time, one of the country's largest electrical firms, Tōkyō Shibaura Denki, or Tōshiba, was also building a giant factory in Fuchū. Covering three times the amount of land used by the Yokogawa factory in Musashino, the Fuchū plant was designed to produce electrically powered trains and electrical generators. Cheap land on the Nishifu-Fuchū boundary as well as convenient access to the home plant near Yokohama along the Nambu Line favored a location in Fuchū.[13]

Its distance from the center was an asset that lowered the price of land in the Santama, but it was an asset in another way, also. As the 1930s wore on, and the national economy assumed a war footing, military authorities grew concerned about the concentration of industry in Tokyo. When new factories producing war materiel were built during the late 1930s, the government required that they be situated away from the center of Tokyo but within a radius of twenty miles. These regulations also fostered industrial expansion in the Santama, which was an ideal site for firms subject to such rules.

As a result, Musashino and Fuchū were again singled out as sites for industrial expansion. The first establishment to arrive under these conditions was the Army Fuel Depot, which opened in 1937 on 150 acres of land east of the downtown area of Fuchū. It was followed in the next year by Nihon Seikō, a firm with factories in Hokkaido, Hiroshima, and Yokohama that would employ its Fuchū factory to manufacture tanks for the army. Construction on the tank factory started in November 1938; it began production in May 1940.[14]

At virtually the same time, Musashino was playing host to one of the region's largest manufacturers of military goods, the Nakajima Aircraft Corporation. Established in the 1910s by a retired officer named Nakajima Chikuhei, the firm originated in a small village in Saitama Prefecture where the founder had grown up. Parlaying the influence he won as a leading Seiyūkai politician, Nakajima eventually created a major industrial empire. He built a factory near Tokyo in 1925, another in his home village in 1931, and a third in Musashino in 1937. Located in the hamlet of Nishikubo, the

12. *Mss*, p. 702.
13. *Fss*, II: 733–746.
14. Ibid.

Musashino factory began production of engines for army aircraft in 1938. Three years later a second Nakajima factory in Musashino also began operations. Situated directly across the street in the Sekimae area, this one manufactured engines for navy aircraft. Operating for two years in virtually total secrecy, the two factories finally consolidated in 1943, by which time the Nakajima enterprise itself had expanded to more than one hundred factories around the country employing over 200,000 workers.[15]

In combination with industrial growth and residential expansion, the dispersion of public facilities was the third impulse behind Santama suburban development, one that wrought some unusual changes and bred lasting animosities as well. Although municipal governments resisted as many obligations as possible in prewar Japan, there were always some human needs that governments could not escape. These included the obligations to educate a citizenry, to provide sanitary facilities, to control deviance, to care for the diseased, and to bury the dead. Tokyo had built schools and colleges, waterworks and sewage plants, courts and prisons, hospitals, sanitoriums, and cemeteries to meet all these needs during the nineteenth century. In the early twentieth, however, when the population of the metropolis leaped from less than 2 million to nearly 7 million, most of these facilities were severely cramped and were no longer meeting the demands society placed on them.

As the national government and particularly the Tokyo prefectural government cast about for solutions to this dilemma, they discovered in the Santama region an answer to their problems. Its vast stretches of undeveloped land, its low prices, and its relative proximity to the metropolis all made the Santama a promising area for the expansion or relocation of public facilities. During the 1910s and after, therefore, the national and prefectural governments began locating more and more of their new, large facilities in the region.

These assumed a range of forms and promoted a variety of changes. The town of Kiyose offers one illustration. Anxious because outmoded facilities in the crowded downtown district were no longer adequate, government officials decided to build hospitals and sanitoriums in more distant areas, where patients could benefit from open spaces and clean air. In 1931 they established a new national

15. *Mss*, pp. 695–700.

hospital in Kiyose, then a small farm village about fifteen miles—
but more than seventy-five minutes—from downtown Tokyo.
In the next eight years, six additional hospitals went up in Kiyose. (By 1956 another seven had been added.) In one short
decade, therefore, this complacent farm settlement had become a
community of hospitals, presenting an appearance much like the
monzen-machi (or temple towns) of the Tokugawa Period. The main
street leading from the train station to the hospital district came to
be lined with flower shops, candy stores, book stalls, and inns,
frequented by the medical "pilgrims" arriving to tend and visit
patients.[16]

Other communities found themselves blessed—or saddled—
with different facilities. Tachikawa, for example, became a military
town. Following construction of the Tachikawa and Shōwa aircraft
plants in the late 1910s and early 1920s, the army built an ordnance
factory there and then a research institute for air technology, as well
as a major air base. Nearby Koganei also got a military facility, an
institute for research on army technology, as well as a large public
park. Kunitachi became the home of a major national university.
And Higashi Murayama, a small community in the northeastern
corner of the region, was designated the site of a major reservoir to
hold water supplies for the city.

Not surprisingly, both Musashino and Fuchū won their share of
public facilities. Musashino fared better than its counterpart, receiving a water filtration plant in Sakai and also one of the most beauti-
ful parks in Tokyo, the Inokashira. Situated a short walk south of
Kichijōji Station astride the boundary of Musashino and Mitaka, the
Inokashira Park was originally part of an imperial retreat. At the
instigation of Shibusawa Eiichi (a prominent entrepreneur), the emperor gave it to the people of Tokyo as a public park in 1914. The
dazzling beauty of Inokashira in springtime bloom struck a dramatic
contrast with the three public facilities imposed on Fuchū during this
period: a horse-racing track, a sprawling cemetery, and a prison.

Fuchū's fate suggests why dispersion of public facilities aroused
some animus in the Santama, especially as time passed. Officials
were initially successful in persuading communities to accept such
facilities by arguing that they would create jobs for local citizens. In

16. Yamaga, *Tōkyō daitoshi ken*, pp. 221–228.

some cases they did, but in many cases they created very few, certainly not enough to compensate for the hidden costs they entailed. These took two forms. One arose in the form of undesirable social consequences, probably best suggested by the petty gamblers attracted to the horse races in Fuchū. The other took the form of revenue losses; communities suffered income reductions when new public lands were removed from the tax rolls. Over the years, residents of the Santama, and especially its politicians and better-informed political activists, have nursed grievances about these costs. They provide a nagging presence in the collective consciousness that may contribute in some part to the mood of political dissidence evidenced in the area.

The special combination of circumstances under which the Santama developed during this period promoted the growth of communities that were, first of all, essentially unplanned, and second, socially heterogeneous. On both these counts, therefore, Santama's suburbs differed markedly from those that developed in the United States, especially after the 1920s. The absence of mass housing precluded the simultaneous arrival of large numbers of families with a monochrome social status. Instead, families migrated individually to the Santama region in large numbers owing to a range of private considerations that ultimately hinged on the availability of housing and jobs. It is important to note the rather laissez-faire quality of this development for one overriding reason: early suburban development in the Santama gave rise to a highly variegated society, the general features of which we should examine before looking more closely at changes in Musashino and Fuchū.

Population growth accelerated in the Santama after 1920.[17] The region grew as much in the two decades following that year as it had in the four decades preceding. The expansion of 70 percent perceptibly outpaced the rate of national growth, although it fell well behind rapid rates of growth in the periphery. In all, 220,736 people were added to the cities, towns, and villages of the area, most of whom (60 percent) came during the 1930s as the war boom gathered force.

17. Discussions of demographic and occupational change in the remaining pages of this part of the chapter are based on the following sources: 1920 National Census, cited earlier; Naikaku tōkei kyoku, *1930 Kokusei chōsa hōkoku: Tōkyō fu* [1930 National Census Reports: Tokyo Prefecture] (Tokyo, 1934), pp. 1–4 and 33–35; and 1940 National Census, I: 101–103, and II: 46–49.

Increases occurred in different parts of the region and fostered diverging patterns of development. In the mountains of Nishi Tama, population expansion reached barely 20 percent during this period, a rate that fell behind the national average of 28 percent. The Minami Tama area continued to grow, though not as rapidly as it had in the decades before 1920. Most of that area's 40 percent increase occurred in the bustling city of Hachiōji; the villages in the southern quarter grew hardly at all. As one might expect, given its proximity to the center and its superior rail connections, Kita Tama grew more rapidly than the other two counties. It experienced an increase of 142 percent over its 1920 population, and witnessed the arrival of more than 150,000 newcomers.

Owing to this exceptional growth, the demographic stature of Kita Tama rose significantly. Having absorbed nearly 70 percent of the region's increase, its share of the total expanded from only 34 percent in 1920 to almost 50 percent in 1940. In the earlier year most settlements in Kita Tama had been only small rural villages; in fact, not one had a population exceeding ten thousand. By 1940, however, nine settlements in Kita Tama had populations exceeding ten thousand, with two having more than twenty thousand and two others having over forty. While Nishi and Minami Tama remained beyond the edge of metropolitan influence, Kita Tama assumed the dynamic, urbanized character that had typified the periphery for several decades.

Some sense of the area's new demographic qualities is available from nativity data in the 1930 census. Although even more sweeping changes occurred in the following fifteen years, these data must suffice to illustrate the processes of demographic change, in the absence of such materials for later periods. The Santama as a whole had clearly begun to lose some of its parochial character by 1930, when nearly four in ten of its residents were newcomers to their place of residence. Indeed, two in ten residents in the region's settlements came from outside Tokyo Metropolitan Prefecture; they undoubtedly injected a new social tone into neighborhood and community relations. The Kita Tama area alone accounted for most newcomers, where they comprised 43 percent of the population. Among the outsiders, who were approaching half its population, one in ten had been born in Tokyo City, four in ten elsewhere in the prefecture, and five in ten outside the prefecture.

On the basis of such information, it is possible to infer two patterns of migration into the Santama during the 1920s. According to the first, newcomers born in the city, elsewhere in the prefecture, or outside the prefecture migrated directly to the region. It is likely that such newcomers included large numbers of adolescents migrating as individuals to find jobs for the first time, especially if they came from the latter two areas. Newcomers born in the city of Tokyo included mostly married couples with children, resettling after the earthquake of 1923, migrating to assume a new job, or moving to purchase their own housing. A second pattern involved second-stage migrants, people born elsewhere in the prefecture or outside it who had migrated first to the center or periphery and from there into the Santama. This group was more hetereogenous than the former, and included young adolescents changing jobs, middle-aged men with families, and older people moving after retirement.

It is impossible to define the magnitude of these flows, but it is possible to suggest two important observations based on these inferences. Increasing numbers of Santama residents after the 1920s were not socialized during their early years to the mores of the region. A large share of the region's growing populace came either from rustic villages well away from Tokyo or from downtown districts in the nation's largest, most dynamic metropolis. This suggests further that some share of the region's newcomers after the 1920s were people who had been exposed, before they settled in the Santama, to the values that emanated from the politically and intellectually most venturesome city in Japan.

Many newcomers also possessed, as well as different values, new occupational skills. A comparison of tables 3 and 4 suggests how the region's economic structure changed in the two decades between 1920 and 1940. Farming shrank to occupy only a third of the labor force, while the tertiary sector grew to occupy an almost equal portion. Despite their relative decline, farmers changed little in absolute number, experiencing a drop of less than two thousand in a group that numbered almost eighty thousand. Commercial institutions added 16,245 workers, and other occupations attracted 21,187, but the greatest leap in employment occurred in the industrial sector, where 55,948 new jobs were created for the region's residents.

The new industries that sprang up during the 1930s differed on

TABLE 4. *Distribution of Occupied Labor Force, Tokyo Metropolitan Prefecture, 1940 (in percentage)*

Category of Occupation	City Center	Periphery	Santama
Agriculture, fishing, mining	1	3	33
Manufacturing & construction	37	51	40
Commerce	37	23	12
All other occupations	25	23	15
Totals	100	100	100

SOURCE: Sōrifu tōkei kyoku, *1940 Kokusei chōsa hōkoku* [1940 National Census Reports] (Tokyo, 1965), II: 46–49.

virtually every count from their predecessors. Previously, a large factory employed thirty or forty workers; by 1939, twelve in the area employed between two and five hundred workers and another fifteen employed over five hundred. Early industrial development had taken place primarily in Minami Tama and its major city, Hachiōji, but between 1920 and 1940 the Kita Tama area created 77 percent of the region's new industrial jobs. As late as 1932 textiles had dominated the region's industrial economy, accounting for 75 percent of its output by value and employing 80 percent of its industrial work force. By 1939, however, textiles were completely overshadowed by the new, large, heavy industrial concerns in the Kita Tama area, whose machine-making establishments alone accounted for 62 percent of the region's industrial output. Female workers, who had once dominated the region's industrial work force, declined in relative importance in the face of a large influx of men who took jobs in the larger factories. In less than a decade, Kita Tama became the center of a large-scale, heavy industrial quarter where 86 percent of the workers were males.[18]

Since three of the largest firms settled in Musashino, that community witnessed a radical transformation. Many changes had already been set in motion during the 1920s, a decade of unprecedented growth that saw its population rise from 4,931 to 17,299. Exuberant and anxious at the same time about such growth, village elders petitioned the central government for the right to become a

18. *Tōkyō fu tōkei sho: 1932*, pp. 286–287 and 290–310, and Tōkyō fu, *Tōkyō fu tōkei sho: 1939* [Tokyo Metropolitan Prefecture Statistical Handbook: 1939] (Tokyo, 1941), III: 162–165.

town (*machi*), a status duly bestowed in 1928. In celebration of Musashino's new importance, the local council also planned and built what was, for the time, a monumental edifice to serve as the new town hall, situated northwest of Kichijōji Station beside the Itsukaichi Road. They little realized that their successors would still administer community affairs in that structure fifty years later, when Musashino had grown again almost eight times over.

Despite the rapidity with which it grew in the 1920s, Musashino retained its natural, verdant character. This was attributable in part to Inokashira Park. As an imperial gift, the park was made public on the condition that no bars, cabarets, or similar establishments be allowed in its immediate vicinity. Consequently, the area between Kichijōji Station and the park developed essentially as a residential district, especially after the early 1930s when a new commuter route (the Inokashira Line) that edged the park linked the Yamate Line at Shibuya with the Chūō at Kichijōji. The social tone set by the park and residential developments near it was further reinforced by a small, exclusive prep school for the emerging middle class, Seikei Gakuen. Originally located in the periphery, Seikei moved to Musashino in 1924, laying out its well-planned campus amidst a majestic stand of Zelkova trees near the future site of the town hall. Because leaders of the Mitsubishi industrial combine were financial supporters of the school, Seikei not only attracted sons of Mitsubishi executives to its doors, it also lured many of their families as well, who built new homes in the appealing setting near campus.

Many of the families attracted by the Seikei ethos enjoyed comfortable financial circumstances, if the quality of the homes they built is any guide. But not all the newcomers were so well off. After only three years of rapid growth, officials petitioned for consideration as a "special locality" in 1925, pleading that rapid growth was overtaxing their resources. They defended their position by claiming the house tax was no longer sufficient to keep the village solvent, "because over half the in-migrants are poorly paid salary workers."[19] This is not surprising, given the circumstances under which many of Musashino's first suburbanites arrived. The Mitsubishi executives could afford to move to Musashino to be near the academy their sons attended, but many of the white-collar workers

19. *Mss,* p. 648.

who arrived after 1923 were young men struggling to maintain a family and find housing at a time when it was scarce and expensive in the center. Musashino thus attracted a large number of persons drawn from the full range of a nascent class of salary men. By 1930 over half the employed residents worked in commerce, in the services, the professions, or for the government. In a loose sense, most of the newcomers during the 1920s were white-collar workers (and their families) who formed part of a "middle" class, situated between a large, economically stricken peasantry and a smaller class of wealthy landowners and entrepreneurs.

Exactly where Musashino's new residents came from remains unknown because the household registers that contain this information are by law closed to scrutiny. In compensation, inferences can be drawn from aggregate data on nativity, some of which date from 1910. Still a small farm village of only 3,595 residents, Musashino had attracted very few outsiders by that year. Records list only 154 persons for whom Musashino was not their settlement of official residence (honsekichi). There would have been other outsiders, especially among women who had married into Musashino families, but since they transferred their place of residence at the time of marriage, they would not have been listed as outsiders. There were also 203 official residents of Musashino who were temporarily absent from the community, most likely younger people working in the city, the periphery, or neighboring villages.[20] Mobility rose during the next decade, and by 1920 one-third of the community's population had been born outside. Since most of them were women, however, male newcomers heading their own families were still not a dominant force in the community.

Growth in the 1920s changed all this, however. By 1930 native-born inhabitants included only 30 percent of the population. Of the remaining 70 percent, 11 percent had been born in Tokyo City, 16 percent elsewhere in the prefecture, and an extraordinary 43 percent outside the prefecture. These outsiders constituted a greater share of the populace in Musashino than in any other Santama community, indicating that it was attracting by far the most diverse array of newcomers. While it is reasonable to suppose that some of them came directly to the town from other prefectures, it is also logical

20. Tōkyō fu, *Tōkyō fu tōkei sho* [Tokyo Prefecture Statistical Handbook] (Tokyo, 1912), pp. 52–69.

to assume that many of them were second-stage migrants who had spent some time in the center and periphery of Tokyo before settling in Musashino. Both the comfortable Mitsubishi executives and the poorly paid salary men fit this latter mold perfectly.

With the arrival of the Yokogawa Electric Works in 1930, Musashino entered a new phase of suburban development. Just as rapid as before, this one was propelled by a different force—industrialization. Within eleven years after Yokogawa's arrival, two giant factories of the Nakajima firm began production in Nishikubo and Sekimae, attracting many small subcontractors as well as a massive industrial labor force. Their need for workers stimulated a new spurt of growth that attracted over five hundred families a year during the 1930s. At the peak of its prewar development in 1944, Musashino's population numbered nearly sixty thousand, twelve times its size in 1920.[21]

Since most statistical efforts throughout Japan ceased by 1941, it is difficult to understand precisely the nature of Musashino's economy by the end of this period, but scattered materials enable one to produce a sketchy portrait. Prior to the outbreak of war in China, the Yokogawa factory employed about seven hundred workers at its new site in western Kichijōji. At the end of the war, the firm employed nearly sixteen thousand, most at a larger facility in Koganei, but many in Musashino.[22] At the Nakajima plants, employment shot up at rapid rates after 1938. The army plant employed about ten thousand workers in early 1941. Joined by the navy factory after 1941, the two employed nearly twenty thousand in 1943. This figure grew to a peak of forty-five thousand in 1944, when production began to decline. While many of these workers were commuters who lived outside Musashino, many also lived in the community, especially in a large housing project the Nakajima firm built in northern Sakai. A last piece of evidence, a sex ratio of 127 in 1942, suggests finally that Musashino attracted after 1930 an industrial labor force made up predominantly of men, who, given recruitment practices in Japanese firms, were mostly unmarried adolescents or young heads of households in their twenties and thirties.[23]

21. *Mss*, p. 722.
22. *Mss*, p. 702.
23. *Ms*, III: 782–783, and United States, Strategic Bombing Survey, Nakajima Aircraft Company Limited. Report no. 2, June 1947.

Considering its size, its proximity to the capital, and its importance to the war effort, one might think that Musashino was a
bustling, mature community by the early 1940s. A broader view
modifies that conclusion.[24] Despite its growth and accompanying
construction, residential, commercial, and industrial structures covered only one-fourth of the town's area in 1940. Another
65 percent was still employed as farmland, and the final 10 percent
was forest land. Since most of the newcomers had settled in the area
north and south of Kichijōji Station, Nishikubo and Sekimae were
still sparsely inhabited, even though three giant factories jutted up
on their horizon. Sakai had grown somewhat, but most of it was still
farmland.

Roads in town befitted the agricultural village Musashino had
been, not the industrial city it was becoming. Only 4 percent of
them had hard surfaces; the remainder were covered with an asphalt
compound or sand and gravel. Little wonder there were only
155 registered motor vehicles, only 34 of which were privately
owned. Most people got around by walking or riding a bicycle, of
which there were nearly four thousand, one for every second household. Goods were hauled in hand-drawn wagons. Four schools,
three in cramped quarters built at the turn of the century, educated
about five thousand stduents between grades one and eight, with
few amenities. Only every third house had a radio, every sixth a
phone, and none, of course, a television. Although 861 stores
served daily shopping needs, a single bank had to suffice for sixty
thousand residents. With its giant factories, large population, broad
farmlands, and tiny commercial districts, Musashino in the early
1940s was an awkward product of sporadic development under extreme conditions.

Fuchū was much the same. If anything, her appearance was even
more raw and unfinished. When the Tama Cemetery was created in
1923, it desolated a broad expanse of hilly land covered with scrub
forest. A year later construction began on a new prison north of
downtown. The massive structure of drab concrete that finally
opened in 1935 was a bland eyesore. And the racetrack, though built

24. *Mss*, pp. 722–723; Musashino machi, *Shōwa 14-nen Musashino chōsei yōran* [The
1939 Musashino Town Handbook] (Musashino, 1939); Musashino machi, *Chōsei gairan* [An
Outline of Town Conditions] (Musashino, 1942); and Sasai Taizō, *Tōkyō fu, Kita Tama gun,
Musashino chō zenzu* [A Complete Map of Musashino Town, Kita Tama County, Tokyo
Metropolitan Prefecture] (Tokyo, 1931).

in a fine natural setting at the foot of the bluff south of downtown, was a bleak misfit slashed out of bottomland beside the Tama River. Northwest of downtown in the new industrial quarter, the gigantic Tōshiba factory and its neighbor, Nihon Seikō, sprawled across the landscape. In the town of Fuchū itself, houses and shops covered less than 10 percent of the land area in 1939, most of which—62 percent—remained under tillage or in forest, a mute reminder of the community's agrarian past.[25]

Fuchū grew more slowly than Musashino did in this period. Growth in the 1920s, which resulted in a population of 16,558 by 1930, was confined largely to the town area. In the next fifteen years, the town and its neighboring villages shared almost equal rates of growth, bringing their combined population to 34,398 in 1945.

Slower growth obviously brought in fewer outsiders than in Musashino. Native-born inhabitants still constituted 60 percent of the populace as late as 1930, a rate double that in Musashino. Moreover, the outsiders who did arrive during the 1920s came from relatively close by. The city of Tokyo provided a few and other prefectures some, but fully half the outsiders came from other communities in the Santama. By contrast with Musashino, where seven of ten residents in 1930 were Santama aliens, eight in ten residents of Fuchū were natives of the region, socialized to its mores.

When the factories began recruiting workers after 1938, Fuchū had to find them at greater distances. But its industrial experience also differed from Musashino's and promoted less pervasive changes in the community. Its industrial labor force was significantly smaller. Again, reliable figures are difficult to find, but it appears that Fuchū never attracted more than twelve thousand industrial workers during the war, a figure that is only a fourth that of Musashino, or even less. Moreover, although many new workers were adolescent males recruited directly out of elementary school, or older, married males with experience at other factories, some had quite unconventional backgrounds. When labor shortages became acute near the end of the war, factory managers pressed for and won the right to employ inmates from the local prison. They also imported several hundred Korean and Taiwanese laborers from Japan's

25. *Tōkyō fu shichōsonzei yōran*, pp. 8–13.

colonies, not to mention thousands of local students, male and female alike, who were recruited for the war effort after 1943. Musashino's factories also employed students, but there is no evidence to indicate that they relied on prisoners or foreign nationals, who, under the circumstances, were closely guarded and isolated from the community.[26]

Therefore, if one counts only regular industrial workers, their numbers did not dominate all other occupational groups in Fuchū, even at the end of the war. They did constitute the largest occupational category, including perhaps four in every ten workers. Shopkeepers, professionals, service workers, and government personnel composed another 30 percent, and farmers, the remaining 30 percent. In Musashino farm families had been submerged by a wave of newcomers with heads of households employed in the secondary and tertiary sectors, but this was not the case in Fuchū. As a result, one of the largest groups in the community through the 1940s remained native-born inhabitants committed to an agrarian way of life.

Their persistence in Fuchū, and the persistence of a similar but proportionately smaller group in Musashino, fostered the evolution of a dual society in these two communities. Duality was identified by the social and economic attributes of community residents, and it had considerable importance for the way they engaged with each other. Before turning to a discussion of the political consequences of the changes examined above, it would be useful to comment briefly on this duality.

Native-born inhabitants formed one part of the dual society. Engaged primarily in the agricultural sector and, to a lesser extent, in the commercial, they were the descendants of families that had lived in a community for many generations. Many of them held land and were the pillars of such local institutions as shrine, neighborhood, veterans', women's, and youth associations. They also formed the pool on which the local citizenry had long drawn to provide its educational and political leaders. They harbored differences among themselves, of course, but to a large extent they shared a common perspective on what was right for them and their community.

Newcomers formed the other part of this dual society. They dif-

26. *Fss*, II: 733–746.

fered on many counts from long-time residents. They were often younger, either single people who came to work in factories or newlyweds rearing young children. They pursued an entirely different set of occupations, and they did so in organizations of a scale and complexity alien to the locals. In many cases, these were not even local firms, but large organizations with offices in the periphery or the center to which the newcomers commuted. Having come to the area from outside, probably after an education in high school, college, or university, many of the newcomers shared an educational background and a set of values that were also alien to old-time residents.

Differences separating these groups were not just sterile abstractions produced by census figures. They were social realities that people perceived and acted upon. In fact, their perception was enhanced by visible differences of dress and speech. A former schoolteacher in Musashino remembers that the first newcomers arrived in the 1920s wearing Western-style clothes—shoes, pants, shirts, and hats—at a time when the local children still attended school in native dress, with *geta* on their feet and a kimono-like garment draped around them. Moreover, while the hometown children still used terms from a local dialect, the outsiders spoke a more standard language taught in school texts.[27]

If dress and speech were not enough to set them off, local inhabitants assisted by referring to them as *kitarimono,* a term meaning newcomer but bearing a cold, pejorative connotation. Despite a rustic friendliness, natives in the Santama wore suspicion as a shield. Having been isolated for so long, they did not warm quickly to outsiders. They preferred to keep them at arm's length for awhile, letting them settle in and establish a measure of acceptability before inviting them to join local groups. So wary were Fuchū residents of outsiders that they did not let them stand fire watch in their neighborhoods.[28] The social distance implicit in this attitude was further exacerbated by the simple fact that many newcomers settled at a physical distance from the older urban neighborhoods and rural hamlets, in new residential districts around commuter stations or in

27. Interview on April 25, 1976, with Jitsukawa Hiroshi, who came to Musashino as an elementary school teacher in 1927.

28. I owe this observation to Takano Shōsei, a Fuchū *kitarimono* who arrived in the Tama Village area in 1938 to encounter such behavior, even though he was a police official. Interview, Fuchū, March 12, 1976.

company housing near factories. The social isolation that would have arisen from psychological causes was thus reinforced by their physical separateness, rendering interaction between the two groups even more difficult. It will be helpful to bear this in mind as we turn to examine how the political process altered under the impact of the extensive social changes described above.

DEFENDING POLITICAL PRIVILEGE

The early part of this period witnessed an "era of party politics." Beginning with the formation of the Hara Kei Cabinet in 1918, political parties assumed an unfamiliar position of power on the national scene, one they had sought ambitiously for more than three decades. The competence of their leaders assisted their cause, which also benefited by the retreat from power of the men who had guided national affairs since the 1880s. They passed from the scene in the 1910s and early 1920s, leaving behind them a pattern of oligarchic rule that never revived. The growing complexity of national affairs, the conflicting interests created by the constitution, and the divisive issues Japan faced all guaranteed a keen competition for power among elite groups in the capital. During the 1920s the parties succeeded as well as any other groups in this struggle, their leaders forming most governments, their members occupying most cabinet seats, and their supporters giving them equivocal, but helpful, pluralities.

The power they cultivated so successfully in the 1920s eluded the parties in the 1930s. Having managed to attract 93 percent of the vote in the election of 1932, the two major parties saw their share shrink to 78 percent in 1936 and to 71 percent a year later.[29] The emperor and his advisors stopped calling on party politicians to form cabinets, and prime ministers gave party members fewer portfolios. Their loss of power caused bickering that led to party splits and further weakened their already diminished position. Under pressures caused by impending war, the parties gave up their struggle in 1940, when they disbanded and nominally threw their support behind a

29. All statistics on Lower House elections and analyses of geographic bases of support for Diet members in this chapter are drawn from volumes treating the fourteenth (1924) through the twenty-first (1942) Lower House General Elections in the series: Shūgiin jimukyoku, *Shūgiin giin sōsenkyo ichiran* [Guide to Lower House General Elections], 8 vols., (Tokyo, 1924–1943).

new national organ of mass mobilization, the Imperial Rule Assistance Association (*Taisei yokusan kai*).[30]

Parties experienced a somewhat different fate at the local level during this period, one that can only be understood through a more careful definition of what political parties were. In their competition for power at the national level, political parties in prewar Japan were parliamentary bodies whose membership was drawn primarily from the Lower House of the national legislature. As one organ of the constitution, albeit one with limited powers, the Diet was a forum in which to compete for power with other elite groups, such as the surviving *genrō*, the military, the Privy Council, and the bureaucracy. Factional bickering within parties was common and splits frequent, but avowed adherents usually respected the need for party discipline on Diet matters.

This image of modest cohesion was utterly out of keeping with the nature of political parties in the prefectures, cities, towns, and villages of the country. If there was a link between political parties at the national level and those at the local levels, it was less organizational than personal, dependent on the voluntary activities of local men of influence, and not on the permanent staff of a local organization. Parties at the local level were basically a loose congeries of individuals drawn together to secure political rewards at the center but driven apart by their desire for office, because candidates commonly competed against their party brethren for votes that would send them to Tokyo. In seeking electoral support, local candidates relied on the national party for financial aid, campaign speakers, and a vague position on the issues, but the exhausting work of building a constituency and forming an organization usually fell on their own shoulders.

Promoting this competition among individuals within parties was the electoral system established in 1926, one without comparison. Based on the population distribution of the mid-1920s and ranging in number from one to seven per prefecture, the medium-sized districts created in 1926 sent three to five members to the Diet. The voters in these medium-sized, multi-member districts were allowed to cast one ballot for an individual candidate. Winners were determined in a simple rank order, those with the highest number of votes

---

30. The latest, and most thorough, treatment of the decline of the parties in the 1930s is Gordon M. Berger, *Parties out of Power in Japan, 1931–1941* (Princeton, N.J., 1977).

taking office. Since parties commonly ran more than one of their own candidates per district, party members competed against each other for votes. They usually sought to limit conflict by dividing their districts geographically, concentrating only in those areas where they—and not their party competitors—were strong. But it was difficult to guard against encroachments, and even under the best circumstances some conflict was unavoidable. Recognizing the dilemmas, the national party leadership stayed aloof from such battles in its role as a unifying force, leaving electoral politics in the charge of candidates with personal networks.[31]

Owing to these circumstances, it is necessary to draw an analytical distinction between political parties as national organizations based in the Diet, competing for power against other national elites, and parties as personal networks eliciting electoral support from voters at the local level. This study will not deal in any detail with the former topic, which others have already treated at some length.[32] It will attempt, however, to examine how the political parties articulated themselves with Japanese society at the grass roots level. These findings will be of value in complementing our understanding of political parties at the national level, by illuminating their relationships with and their functions in a rapidly changing society.

The so-called "established parties," or kisei seitō, that dominated national politics in this period were the Minseitō (and its predecessor before 1927, the Kenseikai) and the Seiyūkai. These major parties took over 70 percent of the vote in each of the six Lower House elections held between 1924 and 1937, the Minseitō winning a plurality on four occasions and the Seiyūkai on two. On a nationwide basis, the Minseitō, which enjoyed a popular reputation as an urban-based party advocating more "liberal" positions than the Seiyūkai, thus generally surpassed its opponent in electoral contests during this period, especially after the vote was extended in 1925 to virtually all men over twenty-five.

31. Although it draws no explicit distinction between political parties as national organs and local networks, an essay by R. L. Sims provides evidence from a prefecture in northern Japan in this period to support virtually every aspect of this discussion of politics in the Santama. See his "National Elections and Electioneering in Akita Ken, 1930–1942," in William Beasley, ed., *Modern Japan* (Berkeley, 1975), pp. 89–112 and 272–278.

32. The three major works on this subject in English are Berger, *Parties out of Power;* Robert A. Scalapino, *Democracy and the Party Movement in Prewar Japan* (Berkeley, 1962); and Peter Duus, *Party Rivalry and Political Change in Taishō Japan* (Cambridge, Mass., 1968).

In Tokyo Metropolitan Prefecture, the Minseitō enjoyed a pronounced edge over the Seiyūkai, especially in the periphery, where
the latter was relatively weak. Although Seiyūkai candidates always
attracted at least 35 percent of the vote nationwide in this period, on
four occasions Seiyūkai candidates in Tokyo slipped well below
30 percent. Their Minseitō opponents, by contrast, always captured
35 percent of the Tokyo vote and often more.

Partisan preferences in Tokyo differed from national trends in
other ways as well. The metropolis always gave a greater share of its
vote to candidates who were unaligned or who represented small
parties. It was an especially strong base for the Socialist parties that
arose after 1928. While they attracted on average only 5 percent of
the national vote in the five elections between 1928 and 1937,
Socialist parties captured an average of 15 percent in Tokyo, achieving a high of 22 percent in the 1937 election, which gave the
prefecture over a fifth of the Diet's Socialist contingent.

This relatively contentious political environment influenced developments in the Santama in several ways. Its proximity to the
center produced a spillover effect. Ideas, issues, and positions es-
poused by political activists in Tokyo found their way to the Santama in local newspapers, through the rumor mill, or in the persons
of commuters who worked in the city and returned to discuss them
at night. Proximity also facilitated party and campaign activity. It
was easy for a prominent politician to hop the Chūō Line at Yotsuya
and spend an hour or two campaigning for a party candidate in the
Santama region. Such ease of access proved especially useful during
the 1930s to the Socialist parties, whose leading figures often lived
in Tokyo. Tokyo's political environment also had important socializ-
ing effects. As was noted earlier, some of the newcomers to
Musashino and other Santama communities lived in Tokyo for a
time before settling in the suburbs. Exposed to patterns of political
activity markedly different from those in most rural towns and villages, they undoubtedly brought with them political dispositions
alien to the communities they entered.

This claim is affirmed by electoral trends in the Santama region
between 1924 and 1942, illustrated in table 5. As they had earlier,
candidates of the Seiyūkai managed to do very well, capturing
59 percent of the votes and winning thirteen of the twenty-one seats
contested. Their performance did not match that of the preceding
three decades, when they had captured 66 percent of the votes and

TABLE 5. *Partisan Vote in Lower House Elections, Santama Region, 1920–1942 (in number and percentage)*

Year	Total Vote	Seiyūkai	Minseitō	Socialist Parties	Others
1920	15,239 (100)	10,620 (70)	4,361 (29)		258 (1)
1924	16,809 (100)	10,096 (60)	5,486 (33)		1,227 (7)
1928	61,596 (100)	38,265 (62)	18,020 (29)	4,718 (8)	593 (1)
1930	66,173 (100)	39,591 (60)	23,793 (36)	2,789 (4)	
1932	66,191 (100)	48,458 (73)	17,733 (27)		
1936	74,229 (100)	43,053 (58)	21,219 (29)	5,810 (8)	4,147 (5)
1937	69,941 (100)	36,976 (53)	14,664 (21)	14,133 (20)	4,168 (6)
1942	92,310 (100)	48,665 (53)	20,611 (22)	23,034 (25)	

SOURCE: Shūgiin jimukyoku, *Shūgiin giin sōsenkyo ichiran*, nos. 15–21 (Tokyo, 1924–1943).

NOTE: In order to illustrate the continuity of personal attachments and partisan divisions, the table arranges the vote for 1942 according to the previous party affiliation of candidates, even though they did not run under such labels in 1942.

82 percent of the seats, but it nonetheless guaranteed a comfortable dominance.

Having secured a toehold in Hachiōji, the Minseitō struggled successfully to retain its supporters during this period. They were a volatile group, but they demonstrated enough loyalty to send one Minseitō representative to the Diet in every election except that of 1928. Part of the volatility was attributable to national trends. For example, when the Seiyūkai conducted the 1932 election during a political and military crisis and won a huge majority nationwide, the Minseitō suffered in the Santama. But part of the volatility was also due to the apparent ease with which candidates of the Socialist parties either nibbled away some of their supporters (as in 1937), or attracted new ones more successfully (as in 1942).

One of the most important elections in this period was held in 1928. The first to follow a grant of universal manhood suffrage that enfranchised virtually all males over twenty-five, the 1928 election witnessed a fourfold expansion in the electorate. In addition to the landowning elements that had always monopolized the franchise, the electorate now included the full spectrum of Japan's socio-economic classes. It is therefore important to determine whether the 1928 election produced dramatic changes in the district's partisan divisions, as one might expect in view of claims often made about "Taishō democracy."

Two adjustments are necessary if we are to draw a proper comparison between the 1924 and 1928 elections. We must add to the Seiyūkai column for 1924 the 570 votes that an unendorsed Seiyūkai candidate received. After this adjustment, we find that that party's adherents won 63 percent of the district total in 1924 and 62 percent in 1928. We might also subtract from the Socialist column and add to the Minseitō column the votes of Yabe Jingo in 1928, whose case will be discussed in a moment. Having done this, the Minseitō vote then amounts to 33 percent of the district total in 1924 and 34 percent in 1928. In both elections unaffiliated candidates took 4 percent of the vote. Voting returns thus indicate that a fourfold expansion of the Santama electorate in 1928 resulted in no change in the district's partisan divisions. To all outward appearances, universal suffrage merely enabled existing political networks to draw additional support from a broader spectrum of Japanese society.

TABLE 6. *Partisan Vote in Lower House Elections, Musashino, 1928–1942 (in number and percentage)*

Year	Total Vote	Seiyūkai	Minseitō	Socialist Parties	Others
1928	1,599 (100)	664 (42)	555 (34)	55 (3)	325 (21)
1930	1,890 (100)	996 (53)	810 (43)	84 (4)	
1932	2,121 (100)	1,324 (62)	797 (38)		
1936	3,182 (100)	1,299 (41)	1,167 (37)	363 (11)	353 (11)
1937	2,934 (100)	1,111 (39)	742 (25)	921 (31)	160 (5)
1942	6,356 (100)	2,770 (44)	1,351 (21)	2,235 (35)	

SOURCE: Same as table 5.

NOTE: 1928 is the first year for which election results are available at the town and village (*chōson*) level.

This finding offers a useful corrective to a misleading assertion. It is often alleged that the Seiyūkai drew heavily on landowning agrarian interests for its electoral strength. This was certainly true in the Santama District before 1924, as the preceding chapter illustrated. But its ability to attract nearly two in every three votes in the entire district even after 1928 strongly implies that it also drew support from middling farmers as well as some part of the tenantry. Returns from the rural portion of Minami Tama, the original stamping grounds of the Santama *sōshi*, offer compelling support for this observation. In 1928 fully 77 percent of the voters in that area cast their ballots for Seiyūkai candidates. Since tenant farmers constituted more than a third of that area's farm households, the Seiyūkai was obviously eliciting some support from every stratum of rural society.[33]

Voting trends evident at the district level were also reflected in local communities, though in different manner. In Musashino, for example, support for the Seiyūkai was always weaker than in the district as a whole, while that for the Socialist parties was stronger, as table 6 indicates. Consequently, the position of the Seiyūkai in Musashino deteriorated. The party experienced a similar fate in Fuchū, whose voters were more fickle than elsewhere. Much of the volatility stemmed from short-term considerations: the candidates,

33. Tōkyō fu, *Tōkyō fu tōkei sho: 1932* [Tokyo Metropolitan Prefecture Statistical Handbook: 1932] (Tokyo, 1934), p. 135.

TABLE 7. *Partisan Vote in Lower House Elections, Fuchū, 1928–1942 (in number and percentage)*

Year	Total Vote	Seiyūkai	Minseitō	Socialist Parties	Others
1928	2,634 (100)	1,077 (41)	289 (11)	1,268 (48)	
1930	2,696 (100)	1,047 (40)	1,473 (55)	176 (5)	
1932	2,623 (100)	1,823 (70)	800 (30)		
1936	3,200 (100)	1,466 (46)	1,266 (40)	326 (10)	142 (4)
1937	3,049 (100)	1,587 (52)	730 (24)	573 (19)	159 (5)
1942	4,261 (100)	1,635 (38)	1,507 (35)	1,119 (27)	

SOURCE: Same as table 5.
NOTE: These figures are the combined totals for Fuchū *machi* and Nishifu and Tama *mura.*

their parties, and the inducements—such as police harassment and bribery—that the parties could marshal for their cause. In Fuchū, as in Musashino and the district as a whole, however, perhaps the most significant trend to note is the steady rise in support for Socialist party candidates after the mid-1930s.

While an analysis of these partisan divisions is instructive, it discloses only part of the electoral process. To understand that process fully, it is necessary to set aside the images of the parties as national organs and to see them as networks of personal association active at the local level, where candidates created their electoral bases or *jiban*. Table 8 indicates the men whose *jiban* it is important to consider: the Seiyūkai candidates Tsugumo Kunitoshi and Sakamoto Ikkaku, the Minseitō candidate Yatsunami Takeji, and the Socialist candidate Nakamura Takaichi.

One reason the Seiyūkai had electoral difficulties in the 1920s is that it had reached a generational divide. Its leading figures— Ishizaka, Murano, and Morikubo—either had died or were too old to compete for office. After two elections in which the party ran several men who served only one term each, it finally found two candidates who were able to establish secure *jiban*. One was Tsugumo Kunitoshi. In 1928 a young man of thirty-five who came from a town in Nishi Tama, he had been a banker in Tokyo and neighboring prefectures before returning to the district to try his hand at politics, largely on his own initiative, it appears. The other

TABLE 8. *Victorious Candidates for the Lower House, Santama Region, 1924–1942*

Election Year	Victorious Candidates					
1924	Yatsunami	(M)	Setonuma	(S)	Kojima	(M)
1928	Nakamura	(S)	Tsugumo	(S)	Sakamoto	(S)
1930	Yatsunami	(M)	Tsugumo	(S)	Sakamoto	(S)
1932	Yatsunami	(M)	Tsugumo	(S)	Sakamoto	(S)
1936	Yatsunami	(M)	Tsugumo	(S)	Yamaguchi	(S)
1937	Yatsunami	(M)	Tsugumo	(S)	Nakamura	(Soc)
1942	Yatsunami	(M)	Tsugumo	(S)	Sakamoto	(S)

NOTE: (M) = Minseitō, or Kenseikai in 1924; (S) = Seiyūkai; and (Soc) = Social Masses Party. In order to illustrate the continuity of local political networks, the table indicates the previous party affiliations of candidates in 1942, even though successful candidates ran under the banner of the Imperial Rule Assistance Association.

was Sakamoto Ikkaku. Trained as a dentist and a lawyer, Sakamoto lived in Tokyo, where he pursued a varied career while occupying a seat on the Tokyo City Council. This brought him into contact with Morikubo Sakuzō, who recruited him to stand for the Diet from his old district.

The *jiban* of these two men provide evidence to support the claim that candidates tried to diminish intraparty conflict by cultivating sections of a district. Sakamoto inherited an electoral base that Morikubo Sakuzō had created during the early twentieth century. Living in the city, Sakamoto had to rely on the Morikubo legacy and a network of associates to win votes in Minami Tama, which provided 96 percent of his support in the 1928 election. In that same election, Tsugumo drew 97 percent of his support from Nishi Tama. A third Seiyūkai candidate named Nakamura, the son of the first people's rights dissident from Chōfu, drew 97 percent of his support from Kita Tama. In short, the three territorial subgroups of Santama *sōshi,* formed in the 1870s, still operated smoothly to divide the district's Seiyūkai supporters in 1928. As the region grew during the 1930s and a larger share of the electorate settled in Kita Tama, all candidates were forced to extract some votes from that area, but these two men always relied on their original bases in the south and west to provide the majority of their votes. Consequently, neither of them ever won many votes in either Musashino or Fuchū until 1942, when they were the only Seiyūkai candidates to stand in the district,

Seiyūkai candidates mobilized their supporters utilizing organizational techniques developed by the Santama *sōshi* at the turn of the century. Tsugumo's *jiban* is illustrative. A handful of local political activists, not always officeholders themselves, provided much of the manpower for an electoral effort. They contacted key political figures in each community where Tsugumo had support. These were often council members or mayors, sometimes prefectural assemblymen, and occasionally former Diet members. They marshalled networks of supporters by relying on the same ties political operatives had used during the 1910s: friendship, kinship, business, educational, and personal. Finally, a few families provided the funds needed to supplement those from the national party. The Uchiyama family of Itsukaichi, which had sent one man to the Diet and which controlled timberland, a power company, and a railroad, served this function for Tsugumo. Neatly meshed with the ongoing social activities of a stable, agrarian area, this method of cultivating support worked very effectively for Tsugumo in the western reaches of the Santama throughout the prewar period.[34]

Detailed scrutiny of election returns for Tsugumo's base in Nishi Tama indicates that the unit of electoral mobilization was not the administrative community (the *machi* or *mura*) but the hamlet (*buraku*). In 1928, for example, Tsugumo captured 58 percent of the vote in Nishi Tama. Two Minseitō candidates took an additional 36 percent, leaving only 6 percent of the vote to be shared by the remaining six candidates. A clear pattern appeared in each town or village. One candidate, in nearly every case Tsugumo, captured a clear majority of the vote, ranging from 50 percent to as high as 82 percent. One candidate, and on a few occasions two or three others, captured virtually all the rest of the votes. This implies, though it is impossible to prove, that individual hamlets backed particular candidates almost unanimously. Divisions within towns and villages are explained by differences produced among several hamlets each of which was voting en bloc for its candidate.

These findings suggest two important observations. First, it appears that in Nishi Tama as in Minami Tama, electoral support for particular candidates embraced all social strata. Partisan divisions were therefore underlain, not by class or economic interests, but by

34. Fuchū shiyakusho, *Tama shi shūi ki* [Gleanings from the History of the Tama Region] (Fuchū, 1972), pp. 26–59.

territorial interests contained in the hamlet and aggregated at the town or village level. Second, by implication, the unit of voter mobilization was a territorial entity rather than a voluntary or functional organization. Since virtually all the inhabitants of such entities were farmers, they were occupationally homogeneous. This facilitated mobilization, as did the familiarity that grew from long residence with the same families and individuals. In eliciting their electoral support, Seiyūkai candidates relied upon cross-stratal patterns of social intercourse indigenous to the hamlets that were the building blocks of their *jiban*.

Yatsunami Takeji, who had won office in 1920 with a surprise victory over the Seiyūkai's Murano in Hachiōji, won handily in that district in the following election also. The reform of 1926 hampered him in 1928, however, when the core of his support in Hachiōji and Minami Tama failed to return him to office. He solved this problem in 1930 and thereafter by cultivating voters in Kita Tama. Henceforth, they provided the majority of his supporters, the rest coming mainly from Minami Tama and Hachiōji, with only a small share from Nishi Tama. As one would expect, Yatsunami had a loyal core of supporters in both Fuchū and Musashino, where he attracted an average 33 percent of the ballots in each election after 1928.

Socialist party candidates faced widespread difficulties in building support during this period, but they enjoyed modest success in the face of them. Outright suppression led by police and government authorities, incapacitating factional splits created by themselves, and suspicious voters wary of their goals all complicated their task. Sometimes, however, a candidate could successfully cast these problems aside, if he combined the right personality, approach, and associates, as did an intriguing figure from Fuchū in 1928.[35]

The first candidate ever to stand in the district under the banner of a Socialist party was Yabe Jingo, a middle-aged charcoal dealer who had been active in organizing tenants from nearby villages since 1920. Son of an old-line family in town, Yabe's dealings with his wealthy landlord customers carried him through a countryside where he witnessed the economic difficulties faced by poor farmers in the precarious 1920s. Having built some political credit among them, he ran for office in 1928 as a candidate of the Japan Farmers'

35. The following account of Yabe Jingo is based on *Fss*, II: 478–492 and 514–517, and on an interview with his son, Yabe Takaji, in Fuchū, February 13, 1976.

Party (*Nihon nōmin tō*). He captured only 5 percent of the district's vote, but 48 percent of the ballots in Fuchū, Nishifu, and Tama, where he probably won support less as a Socialist candidate and more as the idealistic hometown boy he was. His only other support came from villages near Fuchū, where he was personally known and had been politically active.

Had Yabe lived beyond 1929, there is no telling how he might have influenced politics in Fuchū and the district. Returns for the 1930 election and later indicate that his supporters returned to the Minseitō, in which he had been quite active previously. One of the men who composed a eulogy for his memorial in 1930 was a familiar Minseitō politician whom Yabe had assisted in election campaigns, Takagi Masatoshi (Seinen). Other leading figures from the Minseitō attended his funeral service, as well as the district's own Yatsunami Takeji. In addition to these Minseitō figures, also present were Tsugumo Kunitoshi, Sakamoto Ikkaku, and other Seiyūkai officeholders. Whether they were associates paying homage or shrewd politicians exploiting the man's reputation, we cannot know, but one thing is certain: Yabe Jingo's short political career produced a potent symbolic legacy for his son Takaji, who became mayor of Fuchū in 1962.

After Yabe, several other candidates representing various factions of the Socialist and proletarian party movements ran for office in the Santama. One succeeded in establishing a constituency that returned him to office once in this period and seven times after the Pacific War. He was Nakamura Takaichi. Born in a village in Nishi Tama, educated at Tachikawa Middle School, and trained in law at Waseda University, Nakamura was a landowner's son who came under the influence of Socialist ideas and organizations during his days at Waseda, where leading Socialists like Abe Isō and Ōyama Ikuo were faculty members. Following his graduation in the early 1920s, he was a subaltern in the Socialist movement, concentrating his energies on tenants and their legal problems. Building credit among Socialist leaders, he won their approval to stand for election to the Tokyo City Council (where he won a seat), the Tokyo Prefectural Assembly (where he did not), and the Lower House of the Diet (where he captured a seat in 1937 as a candidate of the Social Masses Party, or *Shadaitō*). After serving five years in the Diet, Nakamura ran for reelection in 1942. Although he increased his support in the district, he lost his seat as the Santama's voters returned their three veteran members to the Lower House in the only wartime election.[36]

Unlike candidates from the major parties, Nakamura did not build a *jiban* with a discernible geographic concentration. Instead, he drew his support in snippets throughout the district, relying in almost equal proportion on Kita, Minami, and Nishi Tama. In the latter he drew in previous supporters of both the Seiyūkai and the Minseitō by winning votes from people in his home village and in others nearby where he, his family, and his relatives were known. In Minami Tama, he drew support from the city of Hachiōji, where Socialist parties had been sporadically active in tenant and labor affairs since the early 1920s. And in Kita Tama, he possessed small pockets of strength in the blossoming suburban and satellite cities of Musashino, Tachikawa, Mitaka, Koganei, and Fuchū, in all of which he captured about one in every five votes in 1942. Nakamura was not, therefore, drawing support from entire classes or groups, such as tenants or industrial workers, because if he had been, his base would have been far larger than it was in 1942. Rather, he was attracting support in small numbers throughout the district, both from people with whom he had social ties and from people who were not socially integrated into their communities of residence or into local political networks, owing to their status as newcomers or even to a personal contrariness demonstrated in political nonconformity.

Nor did Nakamura ever build a strong electoral organization before the war. He himself offered the most illuminating proof for this claim in an interview conducted in 1976. Unlike conservative party candidates, who were able to identify almost to the voter their bases of support, Nakamura revealed only a weak understanding of his *jiban*. He alleged that most of his supporters came from his hometown in Nishi Tama. In fact, they constituted less than 3 percent of his base in 1942. He also assumed that tenants whom he had helped with legal problems supported him, a claim that electoral returns do corroborate. And he suggested that the "labor and tenant

36. The following discussion of Nakamura is based on material gathered in an interview at his home in Musashino on April 16, 1976, and on his political biography, Nakamura Takaichi, *Santama shakai undō shi* [A History of the Santama Social Movement] (Tokyo, 1966), as well as on an analysis of the relevant volumes of the Guide to Lower House General Elections.

movement" organized votes for him. There was no "movement," in the sense of an ongoing organization with permanent staff or activists, in the Santama before the war. There *were* some intermittent political activists in Hachiōji and Tachikawa, and a few others in Musashino. They may have helped to collect votes for Nakamura, depending on factional relations at election time, but they did so as people committed to a vague set of shared ideals, not as the subordinates of a well-organized campaign machine. These observations are indicative of the mechanisms that the political left employed before the war to mobilize electoral support, and they have serious implications for the postwar performance of such parties, as the next chapter reveals.[37]

The electoral bases described above bear a direct relationship to the socio-economic structure of the Santama region. Seiyūkai candidates, such as Tsugumo, Sakamoto, and Nakamura, cultivated their support among old-line residents in the agricultural and commercial sectors, primarily in Nishi and Minami Tama, where Seiyūkai candidates received 68 and 65 percent of the vote, respectively, as late as 1942. Yatsunami of the Minseitō drew his support from Kita Tama and the region's first and largest city, Hachiōji, where, as the preceding chapter illustrated, forty years of social and economic change had already produced a complex society by 1920. And the Socialists, such as Nakamura Takaichi, although they relied to some extent on support from the peasantry in Nishi and Minami Tama, depended primarily on industrial workers and lower-level salarymen in Hachiōji and Kita Tama for their support. Thus, in the 1942 election, 54 percent of the district vote for candidates of Socialist extraction came from Kita Tama, 30 percent from Minami Tama (primarily Hachiōji), and only 16 percent from Nishi Tama. The relationships are by no means perfect, but they do illustrate that candidates from the three major partisan networks mobilized voters from different areas within the Santama and, by implication, from different social groups.

These findings suggest an explanation for the development of party support in the Santama during this period that is intimately

---

37. As Scalapino has noted, the moderate left, of which Nakamura was a member, "by the very nature of their philosophy, were dedicated to political procedures placing a premium upon popular enlightenment and rationality." Scalapino, *Democracy,* p. 344. One consequence of this philosophical bent was a concomitant inattention to the details and hard work of creating campaign organizations. Most Socialists preferred to make idealistic appeals instead.

related to the social and economic changes taking place. Natives of the region who had been introduced to political participation between the 1880s and 1920s had developed strong attachments to the political networks associated with the Seiyūkai from 1900 onward. They and their descendants appear to have maintained those loyalties through the early 1940s. In areas of the Santama where intracommunity conflict was evident before 1920, such as Hachiōji and Fuchū, dissidents seized on opposing parties and used them to challenge established powerholders with whom they had differences—often stemming, incidentally, from social causes. As more newcomers arrived in the district after 1923, many of them also adopted the techniques of their dissident predecessors. Outside the networks of political influence formed by the Santama *sōshi* and somewhat alienated from the new communities in which they were settling, they threw their weight behind parties readily distinguished from the entrenched Seiyūkai. For some, the Minseitō served this purpose; for others, the Socialist parties.

Underlying these electoral bases were discernibly different techniques of voter mobilization. In pure form, as ideal types, one was employed predominantly by the Seiyūkai; the other, by the Minseitō and Socialists. The former relied on territorial units as the foundation of its support, mobilizing voters from all social strata on the basis of diffuse obligations arising out of the intimate, reciprocal mores of farming hamlets. This mode relied on a relatively strong organizational effort. Manned by political activists and men of influence, such an organization aggregated support from individual hamlets at the village and town level to produce a strong base for a given candidate within a subsection of the district. By contrast, parties employing the alternative techniques appear to have relied less on territorial units and more on idealistic or symbolic appeals to newcomers from specific social strata, especially white-collar and industrial workers resettling in the area after living for a time in Tokyo. In contrast also, this mode of mobilization was organizationally weak; it did not enjoy the voluntary support of activists in every hamlet, village, and town, but relied more on public appeals. That these are only ideal types should be reiterated, since the Seiyūkai sometimes drew supporters by relying on the second mode, and the Socialists by relying on the first. But generally speaking, distinguishable modes of voter mobilization coincided with partisan differences in the Santama as this period wore on.

Newcomers lending their support to the Minseitō or Socialist candidates in the 1920s and 1930s were actually reifying the social divisions arising in Santama's rapidly changing communities. Isolated physically and psychologically from the native inhabitants of its former farm villages and market towns, the young bankers, salesmen, teachers, clerks, industrial workers, and company executives moving in drifted toward those parties whose supporters were like themselves. Content with its secure base in the agrarian sector, the Seiyūkai appears to have developed no new organizational mechanisms to deal with the different social structures that suburbanization was producing. The Minseitō and Socialists did no better organizationally. But they reaped the benefits of demographic growth and social change in greater measure than the Seiyūkai, in large part because of the previous political dispositions of newcomers socialized to partisan identities in Tokyo, and also because of the social distance between newcomers and old-line farming and commercial families.

Just as partisan labels defined lines of social cleavage in the district as a whole, so also did they serve that function in Fuchū. But as in the district, divisions based on the two major parties obscured more complex differences below the surface, which were really rooted in kinship, territorial, and personal considerations. A sketch of mayoralty contests in the community between 1928 and 1944 illustrates these claims concretely.

Six men held the office of mayor in Fuchū *machi* between 1923 and 1945. The first, Kuwada Hidenosuke, served from 1916 to 1928. A prominent local businessman, he was an adherent of the mainstream Seiyūkai faction and enjoyed widespread support from the eighteen council members who elected him. When he resigned in 1928, Seiyūkai adherents were still unified enough to return Ogawa Jun'ichi, who served the next four years. On Ogawa's death in 1932, however, the council faced an unusual dilemma. The racetrack would be opening in just one year, creating a new set of problems for the community. Some members of the council felt that greater attention to long-range planning was necessary to meet the challenges posed. Most of them were Minseitō adherents, but three were Seiyūkai members who differed with their fellow party supporters.[38] Numbering nine in all, the Minseitō supporters and the Seiyūkai dissidents controlled half the votes in council. As a result, after several inconclusive ballots, a Minseitō politician named Ogawa Yoshitarō (a distant relative of Ogawa Jun'ichi) took office in 1932, after winning a tie vote with his Seiyūkai competitor because he was the older of the two. This seems to mark the first time in Fuchū's history that the council chose as mayor a man outside the Seiyūkai mainstream.[39]

When Ogawa Yoshitarō died in 1936, the council chose as his successor a local landlord and banker named Kuwada Yūei, a relative of Kuwada Hidenosuke and the scion of a local family active in politics since the turn of the century. Kuwada had been everyone's favorite candidate for a decade, but he had always managed to plead the importance of his business obligations. In 1936 he succumbed to popular pressure. When a seven-man nominating committee representing each of the former hamlets in town recommended his choice unanimously after five minutes of deliberation, the council immediately voted approval. It appears, therefore, that Kuwada was able to serve temporarily as a candidate who stood above party divisions and elicited support from mainstream and dissident Seiyūkai members and from Minseitō adherents as well.[40]

When Kuwada stepped down in 1940, however, the coalition that had put Ogawa in office eight years before reappeared. On this occasion, again following a close vote, the council elected as mayor Yajima Kenkichi, the town's largest landlord and a leader of the dissident Seiyūkai faction. Yajima was probably redeeming the support he and his cohorts had given the Minseitō's Ogawa in 1932. The Seiyūkai dissidents called in further credit in 1944, when Yajima's cohort Ōtsu Shōji, son of a former Seiyūkai mayor who had served from 1912 to 1916, won office for the duration of the war.

38. It is conceivable that this breakdown in Seiyūkai unanimity in Fuchū reflected intraparty divisions at the national level, although it is virtually impossible to prove this. National election returns do indicate that the party found difficulty in choosing one viable candidate to elicit their natural electoral support in Kita Tama after 1930, and this problem may very well have split Seiyūkai activists in Fuchū.

39. Fuchū shi shi hensan iinkai, comp., *Fuchū shi shi kindai hen shiryō shū: Fuchū shi no kindai gyōsei shiryō shū* [Materials Collection for the Fuchū City History: Fuchū City Modern Period Administrative Materials Collection] (Fuchū, 1970–1972), IV: 33–58; interview with Yabe Takaji, February 13, 1976.

40. *Fss*, II: 695–702.

Two aspects of the foregoing discussion warrant special attention: (1) the continued ability of Seiyūkai adherents to dominate local office and (2) an apparent rise in Minseitō influence on the council. The explanation for both these phenomena rests on an understanding of the relationship between demographic change in the community and political participation. When Ogawa won election in 1932, there were about eighteen hundred households in Fuchū, and a like number of eligible council voters. Eight years later the number of households had risen 94 percent, the number of eligible voters by only 42 percent; thus, only 73 percent of the households were eligible to cast a ballot in the 1940 council election.[41] A requirement that voters be registered on the lists for two years prior to a council election accounts for the inability of one in four of the town's households to participate in the 1940 contest. A large share of the newcomers who arrived in Fuchū during the late 1930s were therefore prevented by registration requirements from participating in local elections. This gave undue advantage to the entrenched Seiyūkai and facilitated its continued domination.

Even this advantage may not have been necessary, if the observations of a local historian are correct:

Most newcomers to town took a very limited interest in elections for the town council. Votes assembled in the context of the old village society, according to ties between main houses and branches and on the basis of kinship and marital relations, largely determined the way an election turned out. In other words, bringing together the hamlet units of a localistic, communal society was the decisive act in shaping local developments.[42]

This analysis coincides with the explanation in chapter 2 for the political divisions in Fuchū; they may well have been based on kinship and hamlet differences. These comments also suggest that apathy among newcomers facilitated continued political dominance in Fuchū by the Seiyūkai.

The apparent rise in Minseitō influence may well be spurious. In the absence of returns that report the vote by party and the party affiliation of council members, we must rely on proxy evidence to determine partisan divisions in town. The outcome of mayoralty votes strongly suggests that there were three or four Seiyūkai dissi-

---

41. Fuchū shi shi hensan iinkai, comp., *Fuchū shi shi kindai hen shiryō shū*, V: 65.
42. *Fss*, II: 699.

dents who aligned with a Minseitō minority to build the coalition that brought Ogawa, Yajima, and Ōtsu to office. If this is correct, then Minseitō adherents held six or seven seats on the eighteen-man council of 1932 and perhaps as many as eight on the twenty-four-man council of 1940. These figures accord well with the roughly one-third of the vote that Minseitō candidates attracted in Lower House elections at the time, and they suggest that the Minseitō was still a minority. This conclusion is further reinforced by noting that only four first-time candidates won election to the council in 1940. One was a local Minseitō adherent; it is impossible to determine the background and party affiliation of the other three. Since, however, nearly 80 percent of the council members were incumbents, six of whom had served since 1928, it does not seem likely that many newcomers penetrated the council in Fuchū before the war. Their minority position in the community, their indifference to local politics, and the registration requirements working against them diminished the political role of newcomers and left Seiyūkai activists in continuing command.

In the face of even more sweeping changes than in Fuchū, the Seiyūkai establishment in Musashino also retained its firm grip on local power before and during the war years. Control over the mayoralty is one index of their continuity. Between 1923 and 1945, only three men held the mayor's post. Two were members of the Akimoto family of Sakai and the other was a landlord, real estate developer, and contractor named Ino, from the fast-growing Nishikubo section. Akimoto Rokunosuke, the adopted, younger brother of Kihichi and the operator of a small inn near Sakai Station, retained the position of mayor from his first election in 1922 until his death in 1939. The council sanctioned his choice of a successor, Kihichi's son Toshio, in 1939, and gave him a term in his own right at the next election in 1940. Toshio was apparently more eager to tend his patrimony, by developing the new bank his family had founded, and resigned after only two years in office.[43] Ino succeeded him through the end of the war. Landlords and entrepreneurs, these three Seiyūkai adherents were cut from the classic mold of the Santama *sōshi*.

43. The patrimony that Kihichi left to the Akimoto house developed briskly. When Toshio, at eighty-five still the chairman of the board of the family bank, sold a small parcel of the holdings near Musashi Sakai Station in 1975, he rose to the top of the Santama's list of taxpayers as a result of the $5.8 million (U.S.) proceeds.

There was never much question that a Seiyūkai politician would be chosen mayor in Musashino. In the 1929 council election, the first held after the grant of universal manhood suffrage, Seiyūkai candidates captured eighteen seats, Minseitō candidates five, and the head of the local tenants' union running on a Socialist ticket the last one. For the first time, three men born outside Musashino were elected to local office. In 1933, partisan divisions were virtually the same, with the Seiyūkai losing one seat to an unaffiliated conservative and eight outsiders being returned. Four years later the number of council seats rose to thirty, of which the Seiyūkai captured nineteen, the Minseitō nine, and unaffiliated candidates two. Because of the war, the next election was postponed a year until 1942. Although it was conducted under the banner of the Imperial Rule Assistance Association, twenty-one of the victors had ties to the Seiyūkai, six to the Minseitō, and three to no parties. Sixteen of the thirty were born outside Musashino. Seiyūkai control of the local executive thus rested on a comfortable majority in the council, and on the unity of that majority.[44]

The council itself, however, was a body divided by a number of splits, between farmers and non-farmers, oldtimers and newcomers, and Seiyūkai and Minseitō supporters. The composition of the 1942 council highlights these divisions. Farmers were unanimously Seiyūkai, eight local landlords all supporting the party of their interests. By contrast, the Minseitō had no farmers in its council delegation, all of whom were white-collar workers or professionals. Among the council's fourteen native-born members, twelve were Seiyūkai supporters and only two were Minseitō representatives. Therefore, while locals constituted nearly 60 percent of the Seiyūkai delegation (in a community where native-born residents constituted far less than 30 percent of the populace), they made up only a third of the Minseitō's six-man contingent. Council politics in Musashino thus reflected a general trend noted before. Opposition parties like the Minseitō were likely to attract heavy support from newcomers to the area, while long-time residents dominated the Seiyūkai.[45]

In the 1942 election, outsiders and insiders alike utilized another organization to mobilize their support, the *chōnaikai* or neighbor-

44. *Mss*, pp. 662–663, 713, and 742–744; *Ms*, III: 720–759.
45. *Ms*, III: 753–759; interview with Arai Genkichi, former mayor of Musashino, March 17, 1976.

hood associations established by national and prefectural decrees in 1940. Responsible for collecting taxes, for fire and police protection, for "social education," and for distributing rationed goods, the ninety-odd *chōnaikai* with some seventy families each were a natural vehicle with which to bring a candidate to the voters' attention. At one time that task had been easy. The residential clusters within the town simply designated a candidate, and everyone from that area was expected to support him. Since a candidate needed only 100 votes to win a seat, his campaign did not require much beyond word-of-mouth efforts. By 1942, however, a winning candidate required perhaps 200 to 250 votes, and such efforts in a single hamlet did not suffice. But a neighborhood chief *(chōnaikaichō)* with the support of his association and two or three others could be returned easily. It is no surprise that nineteen of the thirty victors in 1942 were *chōnaikaichō,* including eleven newcomers and eight natives. Many of this group were elected for the first time in 1942, and thus gave a new cast to the personal make-up, though not the party divisions, of the town council.[46]

The presence of many Seiyūkai supporters among newcomers to Musashino is a tendency that deserves emphasis. Preceding arguments that stressed how newcomers engaged in the political process by utilizing anti-Seiyūkai parties could be distracting. While many did, some did not, and their allegiance to political networks of the Seiyūkai breathed life into a body that relied primarily on native inhabitants in agriculture and commerce for its support. In the process, the Seiyūkai became a more socially diverse organ, of course, but most important from its point of view, the recruitment of some share of the newcomers enabled it to retain a firm grip on power— especially at the local level—in the face of intensive social changes militating against that achievement.

The fate of conservative political parties in the Santama between 1923 and 1945 was intimately bound up with the processes of social change and continuity occurring there. Persisting habits of social intercourse and economic activity that endured in the southern and western reaches of the Santama, as well as in some parts of the dynamic suburban towns of the north and east, were the foundation

46. *Mss,* pp. 742–744.

of conservative power. Social changes taking place in the suburbanizing area of the northeastern Santama advantaged the opposition parties.

We might expect, given the large number of newcomers entering the district after 1923, that Socialist parties would have fared even better than they did, but three critical factors operated against them: political apathy, registration requirements, and high rates of mobility. The earlier observation by a historian of Fuchū, who noted that newcomers showed little interest in council elections, is affirmed with material of a different type. Returns for prewar elections illustrate that, with the exception of the 1942 election (which witnessed a massive mobilization effort in the district), voting rates declined in every election. They fell from 85.5 percent district wide in 1930 to 78.3 percent in 1937. Moreover, they declined most rapidly in communities experiencing the greatest growth, such as Musashino, where turnout rates began at the relatively low level of 77.6 percent in 1930 and reached 62.1 percent in 1937. With the exception of the unusual 1942 election, declining rates of political participation accompanied the growth of suburban communities.

Voting regulations may have fostered such behavior. The requirement of extended residence before eligibility to vote probably encouraged newcomers to postpone their entry into the political process beyond the period imposed by law. Restrictions were most severe in local elections, where one had to be registered for two years before casting a ballot for a council member. Consequently, during the periods of rapid growth in Musashino after the early 1920s and in Fuchū after the late 1930s, often as many as three in ten households were disfranchised in local elections. Residence requirements in national elections were less stringent—one year on the name lists before 1934, and six months thereafter. But even these regulations kept men in about 20 percent of the households from voting. Since the majority of newcomers opted for Socialist parties, residence requirements postponing entry into the political system obviously advantaged the Seiyūkai's defense of political privilege, a cause also assisted by age restrictions that prevented many of the area's young industrial workers from casting ballots, since they were under twenty-five.

These advantages were reinforced by the district's high rates of mobility after the mid-1930s. Statistical materials are so poor we shall never be able to specify the rates and direction of migration patterns in that period. We can only note that the rapid growth in Musashino, Fuchū, and other Kita Tama towns is direct evidence that large numbers of people were resettling in the area. Given housing shortages, transportation problems, job reassignments, and other uncertainties that accompanied the war effort, we can safely assume that a large share of the populace was moving frequently. In the face of the residence requirements cited above, many of the area's inhabitants thus found political participation practically difficult or legally impossible.

It will perhaps seem odd that the war itself has not been mentioned as a factor behind Seiyūkai dominance. After all, it was alleged to be the more conservative and militaristic of the two established parties, and one might expect that it benefited from the chauvinistic atmosphere that prevailed in the 1930s. But such was not the case in the Santama, if one limits an analysis to changes in political parties as local networks. While the war effort did foster economic changes that greatly modified the structure of local society, it did not significantly alter the methods that local politicians had always used to build electoral support through their personal networks. The continuing victories of Yatsunami, Tsugumo, and Sakamoto attest to the remarkable persistence of voting patterns that continued through 1942, despite the dislocations of war.

Nor did the war and the nationalistic mood that accompanied it seriously dilute support for Socialist candidates, who were able to carve out a small electoral base for themselves during the decade before 1945. It could be argued that Socialists attracted support because they adopted a pro-government position on the salient issues of the day. If this ploy did not attract votes, it at least freed Socialists from government repression. But it seems more likely that Socialist electoral fortunes blossomed independently of their policies. Men like Nakamura appealed to some voters on the basis of personal ties, in the same way conservative party candidates did. In other cases Socialists won ballots because voters were simply returning favors done for them. And in still other cases, Nakamura Takaichi and his fellow Socialist candidates offered a political outlet for the grievances nurtured by newcomers and dissidents, who saw their own dilemmas of status and isolation reflected in the political weakness of the Socialist parties, which professed to be their political spokesmen.

During this period, the changing social structure of the Santama district magnified partisan political differences. Socialist parties benefited—almost passively—from the expanding suburban society. Owing to this process of partisan change, the relative strength of parties changed considerably, although the absolute power of the Seiyūkai diminished little. However, by their failure to penetrate the ranks of newcomers to the suburbs, conservative parties were undercutting their own prospects for the future, as the next chapter indicates.

four

FACING THE CHALLENGES OF RECOVERY

Forces set in motion during the 1920s continued to shape developments in the Santama region between 1945 and 1960. Despite problems caused by destruction, depression, and reconstruction, new
arrivals flowed into suburban communities at accelerated rates,
dramatically altering the social environment in some and paradoxically reinforcing social continuity in others. Musashino experienced
the former fate, and Fuchū the latter. As a consequence, both
cities—like the Santama region itself—witnessed pervasive but
subtle political changes that would set the stage for the emergence of
a new political drama in the 1960s.

REBUILDING THE METROPOLIS

Wartime damage in Tokyo devastated primarily the industrial
quarters lying east of Tokyo Station. Densely inhabited wards
packed with shops and factories, homes and apartments, they became infernos in the wake of incendiary bombing. Although they
had been targets before, the destruction rained down on them in
early 1945 effectively destroyed the capacity of their residents to
deal with the tragedies they faced. Despite prodigious efforts,
corpses piled up unburied as people fled their homes and shops, and
thousands disappeared without a trace.[1]

1. The following account of destruction in Tokyo during the war is based on the following:
Tōkyō to, *Tōkyō to senzai shi* [A History of War Damage in Tokyo] (Tokyo, 1953); United
States Strategic Bombing Survey, The Effects of Air Attack on Japanese Urban Economy,
March, 1947; *Asahi shimbun,* August 1, 1975, p. 20; and Gordon Daniels, "The Great Tokyo
Air Raid, 9–10 March 1945," in W. G. Beasley, ed., *Modern Japan* (Berkeley, 1975), pp.
113–134.

Early postwar estimates place the number of homes destroyed in the center at 280,000, in the periphery, at 392,000. It is estimated that over 90,000 persons lost their lives and that another 130,000 or more were injured. The population of the ward area, which had surpassed 7 million by the early 1940s, had begun to shrink by 1942, when people began deserting the city to take up residence either in safer communities on the suburban fringe or in their home villages. With the heavy devastation of 1945, millions fled the smoldering rubble that was Tokyo. At war's end a hasty census enumerated only 2.4 million residents in the capital city, a third of its number just a few years earlier.

While the Santama region experienced some destruction, it did not compare with the devastation in the ward area. About 15,000 structures were destroyed, only 2 percent of all those damaged in the prefecture. Well over 1,500 Santama residents were killed by the bombings, and an unknown number were injured. Virtually all the damage struck Hachiōji, since it was the largest city and sites were chosen on the basis of their size. American planes dropped 1,600 tons of bombs on the city's 1.4 square miles, destroying 80 percent of its built-up area and 82 percent of its 16,000 homes, and killing several hundred persons and wounding many others. Elsewhere in the Santama region damage was very light, most of it concentrated on the airplane factories in Tachikawa and Musashino.

Owing to its relative neglect by bombers, the Santama region became a sanctuary for refugees from the ward area who wished to remain at their jobs in the central district but feared the consequences of housing families there. By contrast with the ward area, therefore, the Santama witnessed a large influx of persons during the war. Its 1940 population of 536,839 rose to surpass 800,000 by late 1945, when it began to decline slightly as persons returned to their former housing sites in downtown areas.

Returnees eager to begin reconstruction only added to the difficulties Tokyo faced. Almost the moment the war ended, they poured back in huge numbers, 200,000 monthly between September and December, 1945, and another 400,000 in January 1946. Concerned about acute housing and food shortages, Occupation authorities pressed the Japanese Diet to pass legislation that prevented everyone except government officials, teachers, and their families from returning to the ward area between March 9, 1946, and March 31,

1947. This relieved the pressure on existing facilities, but it did nothing to solve the plight of several hundred thousand persons living in tin huts, cardboard boxes, or train stations where they sought shelter as they tried to regain a livelihood.

The pace of recovery was slow at first, but it quickened after the early 1950s. With so much of the city destroyed and over 80 percent of its industrial plant inoperative, Tokyo simply could not provide jobs for those who wanted them. Its labor force shrank from 3.1 million in 1940 to only 1.6 million in 1947; jobs in manufacturing fell from 1.2 million to less than 500,000. Following a period of acute inflation in the late 1940s and a painful period of deflation in 1949 and 1950, the national and local economies began to revive in 1951 as American military forces fueled the Japanese economy with dollars to purchase materiel for the Korean War. By 1955, the metropolitan labor force attained the level it had reached in 1940, although manufacturing employment still lagged behind. Five years rectified that disparity. Under the impetus of Japan's "postwar economic miracle," employment in Tokyo Metropolitan Prefecture rose to 4.6 million by 1960, including 1.6 million workers in manufacturing. Following a decade of reconstruction, Japan and its capital were already well launched in 1960 on an era of unprecedented economic growth.[2]

During the period of reconstruction and the first phase of growth, the ward area of Tokyo won more rewards than its suburban hinterland. Nearly 2.4 million new jobs were created in the ward area between 1947 and 1960, an increase of 151 percent. The Santama created barely 100,000 jobs in the same period, an increase of 61 percent that left it in a weaker position fifteen years after the war than it had enjoyed five years before the war. Having risen at one time to more than 10 percent of the prefectural total, industrial employment in the Santama fell to only 7 percent in 1960. While its industrial status diminished, however, the area doubled its share of the prefectural labor force in service trades. The industrial expansion that had given impetus to suburban growth in the 1930s and early 1940s thus receded in the 1950s, and residential expansion

2. Tōkyō hyakunen shi henshū iinkai, *Tōkei kara mita sengo Tōkyō no ayumi* [A Statistical Perspective on Postwar Tokyo] (Tokyo, 1971), pp. 22–23.

fostered a complementary increase in commercial and service employment in the Santama.[3]

As the prefecture rebuilt its economy and created new jobs, the ward area experienced a surge of population growth. Over 1 million people flowed back into the downtown sections within five months of war's end, before authorities proscribed reentry. After the lifting of these restraints, newcomers again returned en masse, causing rapid growth in the ward area, where populations rose to 5.4 million in 1950, 7.0 million in 1955, and 8.3 million in 1960. Ten years were thus required to restore the ward area's population to its prewar level.

The millions of residents swarming into Tokyo after 1947 first reclaimed old areas of settlement, then began pressing urban boundaries farther away from downtown. Less than half the ward area had been devoted to residential, commercial, and industrial use before the war ended, but 56 percent was so employed by 1950. Ten years later the figure stood at 68 percent. The open farmland that had once divided the Santama from the urban center disappeared quickly in this period, as the artifacts of an urban society pressed inward upon the region.[4]

While the wards grew at rates faster than the Santama during the late 1940s, this pattern reversed itself during the 1950s. As a result, the population of the Santama rose by 1960 to include 14 percent of the prefectural total. This was a sure sign of the maturation of the ward area and an impending surge of suburban growth. Indeed, the 1950s witnessed the initial large-scale impulse toward suburbanization, as more people resigned themselves to longer commutes in order to find less-expensive housing. Home buyers and apartment dwellers were joined in this quest by the central and prefectural governments, which sought less-expensive land in the Santama on which to build large public housing projects. These gave a new cast to local society, as later comments illustrate, at the same time they reinforced the residential impulse that lay behind suburban expansion in the 1950s.

Its proximity to the center and its superior transportation lines again advantaged the Kita Tama area in attracting new residents. In

3. Ibid, pp. 38–41.
4. Ibid, pp. 4–5.

the two decades between 1940 and 1960, while Nishi Tama added barely 50,000 residents and Minami Tama 134,000, communities in Kita Tama were deluged with more than 600,000 additional residents. Having commanded 50 percent of the Santama's population in 1940, its share rose to 66 percent in 1960, while that of Minami and Nishi Tama shrank to 23 percent and 11 percent, respectively. Such demographic change had profound political implications, as the second portion of the chapter explains, and it also had widespread social implications.

New arrivals continued to reshape the occupational structure of Santama society. The farm population declined in the face of more incoming blue- and white-collar workers, with farmers falling from 26 percent of the Santama labor force in 1950 to 12 percent in 1960. This period also witnessed the first absolute drop in the farm population, which fell from 82,326 to 66,311 as landowners in Kita Tama sold their holdings to home builders, apartment contractors, and public housing authorities. While farmers disappeared from the scene, the number of service workers doubled and the numbers of commercial and industrial workers more than doubled. Commerce continued to occupy a relatively small share of the resident employed (18 percent), while manufacturing occupied 35 percent and the services and professions the remaining 35 percent.[5]

The continuing changes in a society whose new arrivals had traits, skills, and backgrounds different from those of local inhabitants were enhanced by another development: a marked rise in commuting. Commuters before the war were limited in number and resided mainly in the periphery. Even in an older suburb close to the periphery, such as Musashino, perhaps no more than 20 percent of the employed labor force commuted outside to work in the late 1930s. In the postwar era that percentage rose dramatically, and by 1955 almost 60 percent of Musashino's resident employed were commuters. In six neighboring cities more than half were commuters, and in Kita Tama as a whole commuters constituted 45 percent of resident workers. With the exception of Tachikawa and Fuchū, virtually every settlement in Kita Tama had become a residential suburb, vacated during the day by the numerous *geshuku-papa*

5. Sōrifu tōkei kyoku, *1960 Kokusei chōsa hōkoku: Tōkyō to* [1960 National Census Reports: Tokyo Metropolitan Prefecture] (Tokyo, 1964), pp. 254–257. Hereafter, 1960 National Census.

(lodging-house fathers) for whom the suburban home was merely a nightly resting place between long stints of work outside the community.[6]

The absentee residents who were forming such a large share of the population in Santama's suburbs faced not just long stints at work but also long commutes. In older suburbs such as Musashino and Mitaka, where access to the Chūō Line put them relatively close to the center of Tokyo, about six in ten workers in 1955 traveled to the inner wards to work, a commute that would have required at least forty minutes and probably many minutes more. In cities farther west, commuters with jobs in the periphery became more numerous, and those making the trek into the center, less. Nonetheless, in the Kita Tama area, 44 percent of all commuters traveled to central district jobs in 1955. If one adds two hours of commuting time to their eight to ten hours of daily work in the office, then perhaps as many as one in four adult males spent less than a dozen waking hours during the work week in his community of residence. Such a phenomenon was causing inevitable changes in patterns of social intercourse and political behavior in the suburbs of the Santama, as a closer look at Musashino and Fuchū during this period attests.[7]

In the immediate postwar years, Musashino's development as an industrial city was arrested, and it reverted to a pattern of growth that characterized its expansion in the 1920s. It became essentially a residential suburb. Fuchū, by contrast, continued to experience industrial expansion after the mid-1950s, as well as rapid residential growth. Combined in a city with a still large and flourishing agricultural sector, these changes promoted the evolution of a diverse suburb whose economic base, occupational structure, migration and commuting patterns, housing, and social tone all differed in subtle but meaningful ways from those in Musashino.

The residential, commercial, and agricultural sections of Musashino emerged from the war unscathed, but the community's industrial quarter was badly damaged. Between November 24,

---

6. Tōkyō fu, sōmu bu, chōsa ka, *Tōkyō fu shichōsonzei yōran* [An Outline of Conditions in Cities, Towns, and Villages of Tokyo Metropolitan Prefecture] (Tokyo, 1936), pp. 48–55; and Sōrifu tōkei kyoku, 1955 *Kokusei chōsa hōkoku: Tōkyō to* [1955 National Census Reports: Tokyo Metropolitan Prefecture] (Tokyo, 1959), pp. 172–183.

7. Readers are referred to Ezra F. Vogel, *Japan's New Middle Class* (Berkeley, 1963), for a discussion of how these changes affected family life in the suburbs.

1944, and August 8, 1945, American bombers launched thirteen raids on the two Nakajima aircraft plants in Sekimae and Nishikubo, killing 220 and injuring 266. A one-story structure built of wood, the army plant in Nishikubo was soon destroyed. It stopped all work by April 1945. The navy plant across the street was better constructed of steel frames covered with ferroconcrete, but it, too, suffered damage that forced it to close before the war ended. While most of Musashino was spared destruction or even slight damage, the industrial quarter on the northern edge of the city was left a wasteland, dominated by the ghostly hulk of the half-destroyed navy factory.[8]

The fate of the Nakajima factory sites is of more than passing interest because their disposition had a considerable influence on the developmental path Musashino followed after the Pacific War.[9] Governments were too unstable and the economy too precarious to do anything about them for several years, but by 1950 several agencies were able to take action. The Japan Telephone and Telegraph Corporation, a public concern, assumed control over part of the army factory site and began construction of a research institute that still stands on the northern edge of Nishikubo. The Japan National Railway took control of another part of the site. It refurbished the old rail spur that once connected the Chūō Line with the army plant, built an expensive rail station, and put up a new stadium for a professional baseball team it managed called the Swallows. Unfortunately, the flat, dryland fields of the Musashino plain were swept with such strong winds in early spring that the dust blown up made it impossible for players to compete and spectators to watch. In the mid-1950s, the railway abandoned its investment, tore down the stadium and station, and built on the site a dormitory to house company employees, thus encouraging residential development in the area.

Following its lead, a government agency formed in 1955 and called the Japan Housing Corporation bought the old stadium site and began construction of the first mass housing unit in Musashino,

8. United States Strategic Bombing Survey, Nakajima Aircraft Company Limited, Report No. 2, June, 1947.

9. The disposition of the Nakajima sites is treated in Ms, III: 29–35; Musashino shi, Musashino shigikai hō [Reports of the Musashino City Council], September 10, 1952, p. 41; Interview with Arai Genkichi, April 17, 1976, Musashino; Asahi shimbun, October 3, 1975, p. 20, and April 2, 1976, p. 20.

the Midori Machi Danchi. Opened for occupancy in November 1958 and February 1959, the *danchi* contained 1,019 units in twenty-odd structures, each standing four or five stories high. As the government's answer to Japan's pressing housing problem, *danchi* were built with economy in mind. Apartments were small: the majority of them contained two multi-purpose rooms, a dining area and kitchen, and a bathing and toilet area all within the space of 360 square feet. By American standards such housing was embarrassingly insufficient, but for Japanese families who found it difficult to obtain shelter of any kind it seemed the answer to their prayers, the more so since monthly rents were the equivalent of only ten to twenty American dollars.[10]

So necessary and desirable did such public housing become that several other developments were put up in the city soon after. The largest arose on a site in Sakai that a government agency had bought in the early 1940s but left idle during the war. Called Sakura Zutsumi Danchi, it opened in 1959 to house another several thousand residents. Soon after, the prefectural government added several hundred units in a large development neighboring the Midori Machi Danchi and in several smaller compounds throughout the city. By the late 1950s, Musashino had over four thousand public housing units within its boundaries.

Like most *danchi* developments, these brought into Musashino large numbers of people with common characteristics. The size and price of *danchi* dwellings usually attracts young families, with one or two children in their early years and parents between their late twenties and mid-forties. Fathers in such households are, with few exceptions, college educated, and they hold high-status jobs as white-collar workers in commercial firms, industrial corporations, government offices, the professions, and the service trades. With commuting fathers absent most of the waking day, mothers assume the entire obligation of child-rearing, as well as the duty of representing the household in such local affairs as the parent-teacher association, the *danchi* council, and local voluntary organizations. Characterized at first by their tense, anomic character, social relations in such housing units can become more intimate—at least among the housewives—as uniform complaints about roads, traffic

10. *Asahi shimbun*, July 25, 1975, p. 15.

safety, and schools create a bond of common interest. The timing of their appearance, the age and background of their occupants, and the nature of the problems they create mean that *danchi* often witness similar patterns of political evolution, too, but this point should be reserved for later discussion.[11]

While several large-scale residential developments were rising where the old army factory had been, the navy site experienced a similar fate—of different quality. In 1950 a group impressively titled the Japan Cultural Housing Society *(Nihon bunka jūtaku kyōkai)* purchased the navy site from the Ministry of Finance, to which Nakajima had ceded it in payment of debts, and announced plans to restore the structure for use as dormitories by Diet members, some of whom were among the Society's directors. Unfortunately, the aspirations of the Society outstripped its resources, and when it failed to make payments in 1952, the Ministry of Finance repossessed the site. Soon after, government officials notified the mayor of Musashino that they intended to rehabilitate the old factory, to convert it to housing for American officers, and to call it Green Park. This offended the mayor and created an outpouring of protest led by both Socialist and conservative leaders that never abated completely until the final resolution of the Green Park problem in 1976. Protests were of no avail, however, and by 1953 American military personnel were living in a converted factory that their countrymen had almost destroyed a decade earlier.[12]

With two of its three largest industrial sites now devoted to residential uses, Musashino entered a new phase of suburban development. Its growth as an industrial community was almost completely arrested. Only the Yokogawa company remained as a major industrial employer. It had spawned a number of small, subcontracting firms which still survived, but while they and the parent firm

11. For a brief description of *danchi* in English, see Christie W. Kiefer, "Leadership, Sociability, and Social Change in a White-collar *danchi*," in James W. White and Frank Munger, eds., *Social Change and Community Politics in Urban Japan* (Chapel Hill, 1976), pp. 15–30. A fascinating account in Japanese is Suzuki Hitoshi, *Kinkō toshi: Aru chihō toshi no sengo shakai shi* [Suburban City: The Postwar Social History of a Regional City] (Tokyo, 1973). A helpful descriptive study is Ōshio Shunsuke, "Chiiki shakai to shite no danchi no seikaku [The Character of *danchi* as Communities], *Toshi mondai kenkyū*, 12, no. 9 (September 1960): 17–31.

12. Musashino shi, *Musashino shigikai hō* [Report of the Musashino City Council], September 10, 1952, p. 41; Musashino shi, *Musashino shihō* [The Musashino City Report], January 1, 1976, p. 1; and *Asahi shimbun*, April 2, 1976, p. 20.

employed about three-fourths of the community's factory workers in the early 1950s, the total factory labor force numbered barely three thousand. Some growth occurred during the 1950s, but the industrial sector in Musashino never again achieved the importance it had attained during the years when the Nakajima factories were operating at peak production.

The residential option had not risen in a completely fortuitous manner, it should be noted. To some extent it was a design imposed on the community by the national government. When they drew up long-range plans for urban development after the war, the concerned ministries of the central government designated Musashino and its neighbor to the south, Mitaka, as residential zones, to be treated in the same way as the wards on the periphery. Government directives thus sharply restricted the alternatives that local residents were able to adopt. This obliged the community to satisfy itself with one industrial quarter, where the Yokogawa factory was already situated, while it promoted residential and commercial development on the rest of its land.

Although national planners restrained Musashino's ability to raise revenues by taxing industry, they enhanced its developmental prospects in other ways. Most important, newcomers entering the city knew they would be settling in a community where they did not face the problems created by noisome factories, against which proscriptions had been leveled. Rather, fathers could move with some assurance that their families would be able to enjoy the city's prized advantages—its good schools, the serenity of Inokashira Park, the stately Zelkova around Seikei, and the radiant cherry blossoms along the Tamagawa Canal—at the same time they themselves retained easy access to downtown Tokyo.

These advantages, along with relatively low land prices, superior transportation facilities, and the availability of housing, all promoted a steep rise in the city's population during the first fifteen postwar years. When it finally won official approval as a city (*shi*) in 1947, Musashino had already regained the 10,000 people it had lost during the last years of the war and added another 7,000, producing a total of 65,799. Ten thousand more arrived by 1950. In the ensuing decade a constant rush of newcomers descended on the city. Although more than 15,000 persons departed each year during the 1950s, at least 16,000 and often 19,000 or 20,000 arrived to replace them. By 1960, Musashino had a population exceeding 120,000, among whom the equivalent of a third or more were moving in or out annually.[13]

The Kichijōji section of Musashino, which covered the city's eastern half, attracted most of the incoming residents. By the late 1950s it had nearly two-thirds of the city's population and three-fourths of its commercial establishments, most of them clustered in a warren north of Kichijōji Station. Vacated in the last years of war out of fears for the safety of businesses located there, that area attracted many former merchants and refugees from the ward area, who squatted on the vacant land after the war and developed the jumble of small, crowded stalls that was Musashino's major commercial center. Pushing steadily westward, newcomers had begun by the late 1950s to fill in the area of Nishikubo that lay north of Mitaka Station. In Sekimae and Sakai, however, farmers still worked farmland that constituted a fourth of the city's area, and salary men returning to the *danchi* in Sakura Zutsumi after an hour's commute from the center of Tokyo walked home along fields lined with tea bushes and choked with melon patches.

Newcomers entering the city after the war had diverse origins. Native-born inhabitants in the city made up only 24 percent of the total by 1955. Another 27 percent had been born in the ward area, and the remaining 49 percent were born in other prefectures of Japan, in its former colonies, or in foreign countries. Although materials are not available for Musashino to indicate where its people lived before coming to the city, there are data from Mitaka, its southern neighbor, which was attracting many of the same kinds of residents Musashino attracted. A sample survey of newcomers to Mitaka between 1958 and 1961 found that nearly half of them (48 percent) had moved to the city from the ward area. Another 18 percent had moved from other settlements in the Santama, and the final 34 percent had moved directly from outside the prefecture. The third group may well have included young persons moving in from farm villages and rural towns, but it would also have included many adults resettling from other urban prefectures, such as salary men being transferred to the capital from offices in Fukuoka, Hiroshima, or Osaka. It is impossible to say exactly what share of Musashino's population they were in the 1950s, but it seems that newcomers who

13. Musashino shi, *Musashino shisei yōran: 1962* [1962 Guide to Conditions in Musashino City] (Musashino, 1962), p. 8.

had lived in the ward area of Tokyo or in other large cities of the country before settling in this suburb may have constituted half or more of its population.[14]

As public officials and corporate employees, many of the entering heads of households brought with them an attachment to a new organization alien to the community: a labor union. Musashino was not entirely virgin ground for union enthusiasts. In the late 1920s construction workers had formed friendly societies to provide credit and funeral benefits for their members. A newcomer from Tokyo named Eguchi had formed a tenants' union in the late 1920s that provided a platform for his successful council candidacies in 1929 and 1933. But the great burst of industrial activity during the period after 1937 had not witnessed any union activity, owing to government repression, wartime conditions, and the social traits and political attitudes of factory recruits.

When Occupation authorities legalized collective bargaining and the right to strike in 1945, however, workers in many industrial, commercial, and public organizations in the city began to organize. In the absence of numerous, large-scale firms, where Japanese unionists are most commonly found, Musashino never became the base of a coherent, active union movement. Although many of the city's residents belonged to unions at their place of work (which was usually outside Musashino), these were too atomized and local unions were too small or indifferent to provide the foundation for an organized political effort in the city.

Another organization that had flourished previously in the city was emasculated after the war. Written accounts and observations by long-time residents both affirm that Musashino's *chōnaikai,* or neighborhood associations, had been powerful, effective organizations during the years between 1940 and 1945. They discharged a wide range of functions and, as the preceding chapter illustrated, provided a solid electoral foundation for numerous council candidates in 1942. Two of the first acts undertaken by Occupation authorities were to abolish *chōnaikai,* which they viewed as odious bodies indispensable to the war effort, and to purge their leaders,

14. Ibid.; *Ms,* I: 31; and Yasuda Saburō, "Mitaka shi no jinkō bunseki [A Population Analysis of Mitaka City]," in Kokusai kirisuto kyō daigaku, shakai kagaku kenkyūjo, ed., *Kinkō toshi no hen'bō katei: Mitaka shi sōgō chōsa hōkoku* [The Process of Change in a Suburban City: Report on the Comprehensive Survey of Mitaka City], *Kokusai kirisuto kyō daigaku gakuhō* II-A (June 1964), pp. 21–29.

which effectively ended their political careers. But with the signing of the peace treaty in 1952 and the revival of conservative forces in Japan, officials began to offer encouragement to restore *chōnaikai*, both as lower-level administrative bodies and as voluntary organizations to foster social harmony.[15]

Officials in Musashino's city hall were responsive to these directives, but they faced opposition from some residents. Intellectuals associated with local schools, as well as a coalition of novelists, critics, and reviewers, fought with determination to dissuade city hall from reestablishing the *chōnaikai* on a prewar model. Agreeing with Occupation officials, they found them archaic, nettlesome reminders of the war period. Deterred from reestablishing the organizations in their entirety, city hall was content to create several new organizations each of which fulfilled one of the functions the *chōnaikai* had previously undertaken, such as police and fire protection, collection of charity contributions, and transmittal of information concerning health and safety hazards. These never became subordinate organs of municipal administration in Musashino, as they did in many communities, and therefore the city never witnessed the return in force of officially sanctioned neighborhood associations.[16]

Nonetheless, voluntary organizations drawing their members from neighborhood areas did reappear after the war, in three forms. Some retained the old name, *chōkai* or *chōnaikai*. Usually found in former rural hamlets, these organizations undertook many activities associated with the prewar *chōnaikai*, such as shrine maintenance, fire protection, public works, police surveillance, and the promotion of general good will and harmony. A second kind was known as the *shōtenkai*, or business street association. Usually limited in membership to families that operated shops on specific commercial streets, such societies worked primarily to foster a climate of good will for business purposes. A third type of neighborhood association

15. A brief account of *chōnaikai* in English appears in Kurt Steiner, *Local Government in Japan* (Stanford, 1965), pp. 56–60 and 206–230. Helpful Japanese accounts are Takagi Shōsaku, "Tōkyō to-kusei to chōkai rengōkai [The Prefectural and Ward Administrations of Tokyo and the Neighborhood Association Liaison Council]," in Nihon seiji gakkai, ed., *Nihon no atsuryoku dantai* [Pressure Groups in Japan] (Tokyo, 1960), pp. 146–159; and Tōkyō to, sōmu kyoku, gyōsei bu, *Chōkai jichikai no jittai chōsa hōkokusho* [Report on a Survey of Neighborhood and Self-governing Associations] (Tokyo, 1956).

16. These comments are based on materials gathered in an interview with Arai Genkichi, mayor of Musashino between 1947 and 1963, on April 17, 1976, in Musashino.

also emerged after the war, often bearing the name *jichikai,* or society for self-government. As the name implies, members of such organizations wished to shed the image of the prewar *chōnaikai* and to replace it with a label connoting spontaneity, voluntarism, and self-help. Although *jichikai* varied greatly in their purposes, functions, and operations, many formed in the city's new *danchi* units and came to serve as organs to express political demands. Since many of these three types of associations were so loosely organized they were barely viable, data on their numbers are difficult to find. One quasi-official source published in the early 1960s indicates that Musashino had at least forty-seven such organizations, which at a rough estimate would have included only one-fourth of the city's households.[17]

Immediate postwar years in Musashino witnessed the maturity of a residential suburb dominated by white-collar workers and their families. Many lived in new physical surroundings, cramped together with thousands of others like them in small dwellings where they faced a wide range of common problems. In addition to common problems, they also shared a common background. Many had lived either in the ward area or in another large city before settling in Musashino. They were generally well educated, always securely employed, and often about the same age. Young, still ambitious, and increasingly optimistic about their future prospects, many of Musashino's new suburbanites also shared uniform political preferences, as we shall see after examining how Fuchū was affected by the end of war and the decade of reconstruction.

While Musashino approached maturity as a residential suburb, Fuchū evolved into a community of unbridled diversity. Less accessible to the downtown sections of Tokyo, Fuchū became a commuter suburb a decade or so later than Musashino. Having more space, Fuchū also offered better opportunities for industrial and agricultural endeavors. In contrast to the residential thrust that motivated Musashino's development immediately after the war, Fuchū thus experienced changes promoted by agricultural, industrial, and residential forces alike.

Fuchū's location deferred its development as a commuter suburb because this made a trip to central Tokyo long and taxing. In

17. Tōkyō to jichi shinkōkai, *Tōkyō to chōkai binran: 1962* [1962 Guide to *chōkai* in Tokyo] (Tokyo, 1962), p. 160.

Musashino, a commuter could hop the Chūō Line and ride directly to the central wards in perhaps forty minutes by the late 1950s. From Fuchū, one probably initiated the trip on the Keiō Line, which terminated at Shinjuku, where anyone going to the center had to transfer to another line. Demanding a quick hike up and down several flights of steps and a steady struggle with thousands of commuters rushing between stations, such transfers not only added ten to twenty minutes to a commute, they also exhausted the traveler. A commute from a home near Fuchū Station to Tokyo Station thus required as much as an hour and a half, producing a difference in commuting time—and attendant costs—that helps to explain why Fuchū was slower than Musashino to develop as a commuter suburb.

Whereas numerous commuters appeared in Musashino during the late 1930s and early 1940s, they did not arrive in force in Fuchū until the late 1950s. Nearly six in ten workers living in Musashino were already commuting in 1955, but only three in ten were in Fuchū, where almost 70 percent of the resident employed still worked in the city. Moreover, even among the small numbers of workers living in Fuchū who did commute, only 40 percent went to the center of the metropolis, while in Musashino the figure was 60 percent. As a result, only one in ten employed persons in Fuchū was exposed daily in 1955 to the problems, ideas, and attitudes that circulated in the center of the nation's capital, while in Musashino one in three workers gained such exposure. Such commuting patterns contributed to the relatively more cosmopolitan outlook of Musashino's residents, while they perpetuated the somewhat provincial atmosphere in Fuchū.[18]

In addition to its location, Fuchū's size also kept it a mixed industrial, agricultural, and residential community. The area of Fuchū *machi* was no larger than Musashino, but when Nishifu and Tama consolidated with the town to create a city in 1954, the area of the new city of Fuchū nearly tripled, to eleven square miles. Since the two villages were still essentially farm settlements, their consolidation added a vast amount of farm and forest land to the city total, as well as a large contingent of farmers, who formed the city's

18. Sōrifu tōkei kyoku, *1955 Kokusei chōsa hōkoku* [1955 National Census Report] (Tokyo, 1959), IV, no. 1: 172–183.

largest occupational group in 1954. The amalgamation thus carried the industrial and commercial town of Fuchū a step or two into the past, by fusing socially and politically conservative elements from the farm villages into a new community context.

Faring better than factories in Musashino, large industrial plants in Fuchū escaped the war without damage, but this was no guarantee of continued success. Most of the city's firms were buffeted by the unsteady economic winds that followed the war. The small-plane factory tried manufacturing radio cabinets and furniture, but had to dissolve and lay off its remaining 120 workers in 1949. Across the street, half the old Nihon Seikō factory was confiscated by Occupation authorities, who converted it to a vehicle repair shop called Victor Auto. They allowed Nihon Seikō to retain the rest of the factory, where that firm employed several hundred workers to make gas engines, threshers, and any other mechanical equipment for which they could find a market. Victor Auto employed about three thousand workers until the severe deflation of 1949, when its work force shrank to about twelve hundred, where it remained until the site closed in 1962 and reverted in its entirety to Nihon Seikō.[19]

The acute deflation of 1949, caused by policies that sharply reduced government spending, had deep effects at the Tōshiba factories, also. After trimming their work forces from nearly six thousand in August 1945, to only three thousand one month later, both local factories fared reasonably well for the next three years. One manufactured small electrical equipment and sold it to members of the American military. The other produced railroad and mining equipment, for which reconstruction activities created a steady demand. The firm had just received a large order from the Japan National Railway, in fact, when the national economic policies that caused the 1949 deflation went into effect, forcing cancellations of government orders. As a consequence, Tōshiba sought the retirement or forced the layoffs of 21 percent of its local work force, which shrank to less than twenty-four hundred by late 1950.[20]

Already skittish about threats of dismissal amidst constant inflation, workers were primed for protest, but to little avail. Tōshiba

19. *Fss,* II: 858–876.
20. Ibid.

employees had moved soon after the war to establish a collective bargaining organization and to employ it to seek better wages. By 1946 they had joined with some of the most militant segments of the postwar labor movement. For the next three years, as the Tōshiba enterprise faced intermittent problems of debt, low sales, and poor profits, workers challenged them to provide better wages and more security. Tensions ran high between the union and the enterprise when a new leader took the helm at Tōshiba in early 1949. Named Ishizaka Taizō, he later became a leading figure in Japan's major manufacturers' organization, Keidanren, possibly establishing his reputation with the tough stance he adopted toward Tōshiba unionists in 1949. Exploiting the pro-business atmosphere surrounding the deflation and the "red purge," he laid off over 4,000 workers in the firm as a whole, including 120 alleged Communists who had provided the core of the union's leadership up to then.[21]

As so often happened in Japan during the early 1950s, retained workers—who now enjoyed job security and the prospect of rising real incomes—turned docile. Within two years, Tōshiba employees severed their relations with the militant national organizations to which they had belonged and formed one large enterprise union. Two years later, they established ties to a liaison council of labor unions based on workers in the electrical industries, known in its shortened Japanese form as *Denki rōren*. With the passage of three more years and the formation in 1956 of the Liaison Council of Neutral Labor Unions *(Chūritsu rōren),* a strongly anti-Communist national federation with Socialist leanings, Tōshiba workers accompanied their industry union *(Denki rōren)* into this body. In one short decade, the formal ties of local unions, established by their most active leaders, had moved from one extreme of the labor movement to the other. By the late 1950s, the largest union in Fuchū had adopted a deferential, company-oriented attitude, which eschewed political extremism and promoted improved economic conditions. Most of the local membership, who had probably yearned for such a stance all along, found it a comfortable position.

Their response, which was duplicated many times over in Japan's

21. *Fss,* II: 870–874; Tōshiba Fuchū rōdō kumiai, *Kumiai undō shi* [A History of the Union] (Fuchū, 1955); and Tōshiba Fuchū rōdō kumiai, *Kumiai tōitsu jūshūnen kinen shi* [The Tenth Anniversary History of the Unified Union] (Fuchū, 1961).

small industrial communities during the immediate postwar period, was a logical reaction in Fuchū for two reasons.[22] Many of the factory laborers at Tōshiba were young men from small farm settlements. They were accustomed to the social mores of agrarian Japan, which still survived with some vitality in Fuchū as well. Moreover, in the factory itself, once economic conditions revived, workers were not anonymous cogs in an impersonal machine, or victims of a monotonous production line. The Tōshiba plants made large-scale electrical equipment, and workers labored in small groups that enjoyed substantial responsibility for their projects, whose success depended on effective teamwork. This built pride in craftsmanship and a sense of camaraderie, which workers carried outside the factory when they returned to their company dormitories and apartments nearby at night.[23] In time, as later discussions illustrate, the attitudes brought with them from rural Japan, which were reinforced by working relationships in the factory, led to distinctive forms of political behavior among the largest group of union members in Fuchū.

Economic dilemmas and Fuchū's locational disadvantages both influenced the pattern of population growth during this period. Moderate rates of growth at the Tōshiba factories and Fuchū's distance from the center discouraged any large influx of newcomers through the mid-1950s. But as land prices in the periphery rose, young couples wanting to build their own homes found Fuchū increasingly attractive, as did public housing agencies, because land in the periphery was becoming too dear for their budgets. Given ample room for expansion, population growth quickened perceptibly in Fuchū after the mid-1950s. Only twenty thousand newcomers entered in the decade before 1955, but another twenty thousand came within the next four years. By 1960, the city had a population exceeding eighty-two thousand, to which it was adding several thousand residents annually, and its rate of growth during the 1950s had slightly outpaced that of Musashino.

The migration patterns that shaped Fuchū's development differed from those in Musashino. Because Fuchū grew at a relatively slower

---

22. For a study of a similar case involving auto workers in small towns near Nagoya, see Allinson, *Japanese Urbanism.*

23. These observations are based on an interview with Kondo Katsuhiro, Secretary of the Tōshiba Labor Union in Fuchū, February 16, 1976.

rate during the early 1950s, newcomers made up a relatively smaller share of its populace. What share, we do not know, because proper demographic materials are not available. We do know that Fuchū residents were relatively less mobile than those in Musashino. In the latter, for example, in- and out-migration in 1957-58 involved the equivalent of 33 percent of the city's populace, while in Fuchū such migration affected only 20 percent. Fuchū's migrants also came from different places of origin. Musashino attracted in-migrants primarily from the ward area of Tokyo or from other large cities in the country. By contrast, Fuchū drew only a fifth of its in-migrants from the ward area; a majority came from other settlements in the Santama or from adjacent prefectures. As a result, while Musashino attracted many well-educated, white-collar workers during the 1950s, Fuchū was far more likely to attract younger persons of lower status and rural background moving directly from farm to city.[24]

While many of the newcomers carried with them from rural Japan emotional baggage for which they found Fuchū a congenial setting, they also brought with them a diversity of occupational skills appropriate to a suburban community. As late as 1950, more than a quarter of the workers in Fuchū were farmers, another quarter toiled in the city's factories, and the remaining half found work in the tertiary sector. The influx of newcomers during the 1950s appreciably changed this occupational distribution. The number of farmers declined by more than a third; they shrank from 26 percent of the labor force to only 8 percent. Over seven thousand industrial workers moved in, boosting employment in manufacturing to 35 percent of the total. And the largest group of newcomers, nearly twelve thousand, entered the tertiary sector, which employed 57 percent of the city's resident labor force in 1960. Although its occupational distribution had not reached the extreme already evident in Musashino, Fuchū had certainly assumed by 1960 the structural contours of a suburban city.[25]

However, the social tone and the attitudinal character of the community seemed to trail behind its structural changes, a claim

24. Tōkyō to, *Eisei toshi jittai chōsa sho* [Report on Survey of Satellite Cities] (Tokyo, 1952), pp. 55 and 158; and Tōkyō to, *Tōkyō to kushichōsonzei yōran: 1960* [1960 Survey of Conditions in Tokyo's Wards, Cities, Towns, and Villages] (Tokyo, 1960), pp. 64–65 and 70–71.
25. 1960 National Census, pp. 254–257.

that is best affirmed by examining its neighborhood associations. In marked contrast with Musashino, where vocal opposition prevented the reinstitution of *chōnaikai* after the war, Fuchū residents preserved such associations and even expanded and invigorated them. The driving force behind their preservation was city hall, which encountered a dutifully enthusiastic response from the local populace. Official stimulus and popular deference then produced a community virtually blanketed with neighborhood associations. The 1962 quasi-official report, which listed 47 organizations in Musashino for its thirty thousand households, enumerated 147 *chōnaikai* in Fuchū, enough to include virtually all of its twenty thousand households, at least nominally.[26]

One reason why Fuchū found it easier to retain and invigorate neighborhood associations is that local residents were accustomed to using them for important functions, some obligatory and administrative and others voluntary and social. For instance, in the Nishifu area, the rural equivalent of the urban *chōnaikai,* the *burakukai,* or hamlet associations, had collected taxes and disbursed funds to support public elementary schools in their hamlets from the 1890s through the mid-1930s. Their budgets were subject to review by the council of the administrative village *(mura),* but they obviously enjoyed the right to undertake a serious administrative function that town or village *(chōson)* officials discharged in most communities. The hamlet associations of Nishifu also engaged in a variety of other tasks, such as maintaining roads (for which purpose they levied corvée labor duties on local residents), repairing irrigation facilities, protecting against fire, and conducting official ceremonies, not to mention sponsoring *obon* dances and other festivals. Members of the hamlet associations organized these activities themselves and raised their own funds to support them. In the process, they relieved higher-level authorities (*mura* officials) of the financial and administrative burdens entailed by such work.[27]

In reinvigorating neighborhood associations after the war, Fuchū city officials adopted this historical pattern of relationships in a more official context.[28] The city urged residents to create *chōnaikai*

26. *Tōkyō to chōkai binran: 1962*, pp. 170–173.

27. Torigoe Hiroyuki, "Buraku dantai no tenkai katei: Tōkyō to, Fuchū shi, Yotsuya chiku no jirei o tsūjite [The Development Process in a Hamlet Organization: The Case of Yotsuya District in Fuchū City]," *Shakaigaku hyōron,* 23, no. 3 (December 1972): 51–70.

28. Ronald Dore's *City Life in Japan* (Berkeley, 1958) contains a vivid account describing the postwar revival of a *chōkai* in an area of downtown Tokyo near Ueno Park. It stresses the

in order to supplement its own administrative activities. It relied on them, for example, to transmit information from city hall on announcement boards *(kairanban)*, to organize fire and police protection squads at the neighborhood level, and to distribute information concerning health and sanitation. In return, the city government offered each cooperating association a small fund of assistance *(joseikin)*, income that supplemented revenues the associations themselves raised by levying nominal fees on member households or by managing property they owned. Sensitive to the complaint that *chōnaikai* were odious artifacts of the war period, city officials urged all local associations to abandon the term *chōnaikai* in the early 1960s and to replace it with *jichikai*, which had more modern, democratic connotations. Such public relations gimmickry did nothing, however, to alter the fact that Fuchū's neighborhood associations preserved functional relationships with local government and nutured social relations among members that were reminiscent of the prewar *chōnaikai*.[29]

The persistence of neighborhood associations in postwar Fuchū reflected a social and attitudinal climate different from Musashino's. Mindful of the sometimes arbitrary actions of *chōnaikai* during the war period, some residents in Musashino worked after the war to resist their reestablishment. Well-educated, white-collar workers and their wives, who often came from urban backgrounds, found such associations troublesome intrusions on their private lives. By contrast, long-resident farmers and older retirees from commercial and professional occupations in Fuchū felt that neighborhood associations were proper objects of community attention. Such older men were eager to please local authorities, and they were even more eager to foster a climate of harmony in their neighborhoods. They kept pace with the official duties assigned *chōnaikai* by city hall, and they also worked to recruit newcomers to their neighborhood into association membership. Less wary than locals had once been about *kitarimono* (or outsiders), the older men who led Fuchū's

---

informal and mildly corrupt relations between the influential men of the neighborhood and local police authorities that may well have characterized Fuchū's *chōkai* in the 1950s. See pp. 269–287.

29. Interview with Takano Shōsei, former chief of police and for many years the vice-president of the local Liaison Council of Self-governing Associations, in Fuchū, on March 12, 1976.

chōnaikai believed it preferable to smother newcomers in a blanket of duty and affection, especially in the postwar period, when many may have imagined that isolating a newcomer was an open invitation to socialism, communism, or worse.

Despite apparent nominal success, not all *jichikai* in Fuchū won the active participation of every newcomer to their neighborhood. But that was less important than two other facts. Local residents did work diligently to maintain a close-knit, cooperative community, and they did draw some share of newcomers into their local associations, not only for administrative but for social purposes as well. Since many newcomers to Fuchū were, as we have seen, young, low-status workers from rural backgrounds, they blended naturally into organizations reminiscent of their hometowns and congenial to their own outlook. Fuchū thus preserved a firm undercurrent of social conservatism, characterized by deference and solidarity, that would deeply affect its citizens' political behavior.

By the end of this period, Fuchū had assumed many of the characteristics associated with suburban development. It had a large population, which was increasing daily. By contrast with an earlier era, mobility into and out of the city had accelerated sharply, bringing in a far higher ratio of newcomers than ever before. Many worked at jobs in an occupational structure markedly different from the 1940s, when Fuchū was essentially a rural market town with a small industrial quarter set down in a sea of farmland. Having grown quickly during the 1950s, Fuchū had become a large, somewhat unruly suburban community — on the outside.

On the inside, it retained many features of the past that circumstances had swept away in Musashino. Despite Fuchū's many newcomers, more came from rural backgrounds and had less cosmopolitan experiences than newcomers to Musashino. They encountered a community where arable farmland in Tama and Nishifu offered bright prospects for future development. In the meantime, native families dominated the numerous residential clusters in the rural hamlets and the old town center, while newcomers, as usual, were obliged to find their housing at a distance. Some of them were nonetheless brought into neighborhood associations that functioned to express popular deference to official demands and to foster a social climate more akin to the rural past than the suburban future.

More than demographic and structural changes, this legacy of habit and custom defined the texture of local society in Fuchū during the 1950s, distinguishing it from Musashino and providing the social foundation for different patterns of political behavior.

COMPETING FOR POWER

The National Scene

Japan experienced recurrent political instability in the first postwar decade. Cabinets formed, dissolved, and re-formed at rates like those of the 1930s, when it was rare for a government to serve more than a year. Two things exacerbated political instability: inconsistent Occupation policies, and divisions among Japan's political leaders. The latter were reflected in factional bickering and party splits that beset both the right and the left of the political spectrum with fragmentation during the first postwar decade.

With the exception of one, nine-month period in 1947-48, when a Socialist coalition cabinet was in power, majority conservative parties or coalitions of conservative parties governed the country during the decade before 1955. The leading figure during that era was a former diplomat named Yoshida Shigeru, whose legendary "one-man rule" spanned more than seven years between mid-1946 and late 1954. Having tired of his arbitrary leadership by that time, a group of conservative adversaries worked diligently to unseat him as the first step in forming a united conservative party. So successful were they that the Liberal Democratic Party, to which they gave birth in late 1955, won every national election and formed every cabinet for more than two decades thereafter. Their most serious challenge came during the late 1950s, when the two wings of the Socialist movement joined for a brief five-year period of unity.

Although their successes in the national arena were limited, Socialist parties in Tokyo Metropolitan Prefecture continued after the war to enjoy the relatively strong position they had enjoyed before. In each of the seven Lower House elections held between 1946 and 1958, Tokyo elected more Socialist representatives to the Diet than any other prefecture. As before, the ward area was an especially strong base of Socialist support. In 1952, for example, the six districts within the twenty-three-ward area returned twenty-seven Diet members, fourteen (or 52 percent) of whom were Socialists, although they won only 42 percent of the popular vote.

Their fortunes continued to rise through 1958, when Socialists captured fifteen (56 percent) of the Diet seats contested in the ward area with 47 percent of the vote.[30]

Obviously, any party that could attract nearly half the vote in Tokyo's central districts was drawing considerable support from older voters. The rise in its fortunes implied that it was also attracting a growing share of new entrants into the electorate. Because the basic strength of the Socialists in Tokyo and their ability to attract new voters during the 1950s had major implications for partisan change in the Santama region, it is important to attempt an explanation for Tokyo's Socialist strength before turning to discuss electoral trends in the Santama itself.

We must recall, initially, that the Socialists had already developed a substantial following in Tokyo before the war. They drew more votes and elected more Diet members from the metropolitan prefecture in 1937 than from any other in the country. Many of their prewar supporters were still alive in the 1950s and continued their loyal allegiance to Socialist candidates with whom they had established ties during the 1930s and 1940s. Personalistic, idealistic, and programmatic factors motivated those ties originally; the same factors worked to perpetuate them after the war. A prewar legacy of Socialist allegiance thus provided one portion of the electoral strength enjoyed by Socialists in Tokyo during the 1950s.

A second explanation for Tokyo's progressive strength rests on what might be called progressive visibility. Progressive parties, and especially the Socialists, treated Tokyo as the focus of their political efforts, as well they might have. It was the site of the nation's government and therefore a crucial arena in which progressive parties could publicize their views. It was the center of the nation's cultural life and thus attracted many intellectuals, a large share of whom had progressive leanings and wrote incessantly for the wide range of progressive-oriented weekly and monthly magazines that were published there. Tokyo was also the media center of the country, with several large, daily newspapers that often echoed the views of progressive parties and politicians. Finally, the national headquarters of the progressive parties themselves were situated in Tokyo, a circumstance that probably had more symbolic than organizational

30. Kōmei senkyo renmei, ed., *Shūgiin giin senkyo no jisseki* [Results of General Elections for the Lower House] (Tokyo, 1968), pp. 74–104 and 144–156.

importance. By contrast with isolated rural villages, where Socialists were anathema, Tokyo was the scene for constant propagation of progressive policies, programs, and personalities, one consequence of which was the relatively great electoral strength of the progressives.

Postwar changes in Japan's educational system also help to explain the increasing strength that progressives enjoyed among younger voters. A new curriculum that emphasized democratic ideals, implemented by teachers who themselves were imbued with such values, produced new attitudes among voters who began entering the electorate in the late 1950s. The very political atmosphere of the schools also had an effect in conditioning some younger people to favor the Socialists once they began to vote. To resist government efforts at restoring prewar courses and methods, teachers organized a militant union whose own adversary behavior provided a suggestive model for many students.[31] While the full effects of this changed educational system were not felt until the 1960s and later, some students were exposed to it during the 1940s and 1950s, and the political orientations they developed contributed to growing progressive strength among young voters by the late 1950s.[32]

Finally, despite its elusive, subjective quality, what might be called the spirit of the time must also be mentioned as a factor underwriting Socialist strength in Tokyo during the 1950s, especially among younger persons. By the late 1950s Japan's citizens had cause for some optimism. They had completed the task of reconstruction and were in the initial stages of a period of rapid economic growth. Material circumstances were better than they had been for two decades. Jobs were usually plentiful and prospects generally optimistic. In pace with the nation's economy, the fortunes of the Socialists were rising at a steady rate. Largely free from blame for the war, and the primary advocates of competitive democracy, the Socialist parties seemed destined to assume power in a short time. For many young voters during the 1950s, the Socialists alone merited the support that would fulfill the promise of a politically new Japan.

31. On this subject, see Donald Thurston's informative account of *Teachers and Politics in Japan* (Princeton, 1973).
32. For an insightful account of the effects of the postwar educational system on a group of students active in the 1960 Security Treaty demonstrations, see Ellis Krauss, *Japanese Radicals Revisited* (Berkeley, 1974).

Some of these factors, such as the spirit of the times, obviously benefited Socialists in other parts of Japan, but their combination in the special setting provided by the metropolitan capital gave them added influence there. Having already enjoyed a large base of support before the war, Socialist parties after the war benefited from progressivism's visibility in the capital and also from the changes implemented in the postwar school system. By the late 1950s, many young voters entering the Tokyo ward-area electorate for the first time were lending their support to the Socialist parties, a trend that would have significant political consequences for the Santama and its suburbs.

Tables 9 and 10 report voting results for six Lower House elections after the war and the victorious candidates by party in the Tokyo Seventh, or Santama, District. It is apparent once again that conservative parties fared very well at the ballot box and even better in the Diet. They captured a majority of the district's votes in all six elections, as well as 60 percent of its seats on all but one occasion. Although progressive forces continued to nibble away at their dominance, conservative parties and their supporters in the Santama continued to enjoy both relative and absolute superiority in national elections throughout the 1950s.

Before assessing relative changes in party power, it is necessary to clarify trends obscured by the data presented in table 9. Although Socialists, Communists, and other opposition parties did better in the elections of 1947 and 1949 than they would do thereafter at the

TABLE 9. *Lower House Election Results, Santama or Tokyo Seventh District, 1947–1958 (in number and percentage)*

Year	Total Votes	Conservatives	Progressives	Unaffiliated
1947	254,270 (100)	129,526 (51)	116,167 (46)	8,577 (3)
1949	287,377 (100)	171,845 (60)	107,844 (38)	7,688 (2)
1952	353,626 (100)	222,807 (63)	108,800 (31)	22,019 (6)
1953	348,388 (100)	213,549 (61)	116,480 (33)	18,359 (6)
1955	401,735 (100)	237,349 (59)	141,496 (35)	22,890 (6)
1958	474,240 (100)	252,999 (53)	195,276 (41)	25,965 (6)

SOURCE: Shūgiin jimukyoku, *Shūgiin giin sōsenkyo ichiran,* nos. 23–28 (Tokyo, 1948–1958).

TABLE 10. *Victorious Candidates for the Lower House, Santama or Tokyo Seventh District, 1947–1958*

Year	Conservative Representatives			Socialist Representatives		Others
1947	Kuriyama	Namiki	Yatsunami	Matsutani	Yamahana	
1949	Kuriyama	Namiki	Fukuda		Yamahana	Dobashi, Matsutani
1952	Kuriyama	Namiki	Ōkubo	Nakamura	Yamahana	
1953	Tsugumo	Namiki	Fukuda	Nakamura	Yamahana	
1955	Kizaki	Namiki	Fukuda	Nakamura	Yamahana	
1958	Hosoda		Fukuda	Nakamura	Yamahana	
				Hōjō		

SOURCE: Same as table 9.

national level, their national pattern of success and decline does not explain the drop in their fortunes locally between 1947, when progressives won 46 percent of the Santama vote, and 1952, when they won only 31 percent. This disparity is explained by the behavior and party ties of one exceptional candidate.

When she first won a Diet seat in the 1946 election, Matsutani Tenkōkō was the twenty-six-year-old chairman of the Starvation Prevention Alliance. A former employee of the Navy Ministry and a graduate of Waseda University, she was a woman of vivacious personality and excellent public-speaking skills who parlayed early postwar enthusiasm for the new political role of women and for the revived Socialist parties into a successful Diet campaign. She won reelection in the 1947 election and was just beginning to establish her political credentials when the Socialist party expelled her for differing with its budget policies. Undaunted, she entered a conservative labor-farmer party (the *Rōdōsha nōmintō*) and ran on its ticket in 1949. Although she lost nearly thirteen thousand supporters as a result, she still won a seat. By the time she stood for reelection in 1952, however, she had married a Diet member from the Kaishintō (one of the conservative parties) and was running under its endorsement. Suffering the loss of another thirteen thousand votes when the local party decided to back another Kaishintō candidate, she lost her seat in 1952. Although she ran again three times and attracted a steady twenty thousand votes or more on each occasion, she was never able to regain her early postwar popularity and left the political scene after her fourth straight defeat in 1958.[33]

Matsutani Tenkōkō poses difficult problems for anyone trying to understand the Santama's postwar electoral history, because in the interests of consistency one must decide whether she attracted primarily conservative or progressive votes. One could argue that the sharp drop in support following her expulsion from the Socialist party affirmed that she won many votes from the labor movement in 1947. But one must also note that she had many conservative party supporters as well, if she could attract over twenty thousand votes as an endorsed conservative candidate. If we accept the latter

---

33. Rōyama Masamichi, ed., *Seiji ishiki no kaibō* [An Analysis of Political Consciousness] (Tokyo, 1949), p. 184; and Rōyama Masamichi, et al., eds., *Sōsenkyo no jittai* [A Case Study of a General Election] (Tokyo, 1955), p. 149.

claim and treat Matsutani's votes as votes drawn primarily from the conservative camp, then the apparent inconsistencies in table 9 disappear. Revisions would give the conservatives 70 percent of the vote in 1947 and 73 percent in 1949, with the progressive share falling to 27 percent in the former year and 25 percent in the latter.

These revisions cast a different light on the trends of partisan change in the Santama District during the 1940s and 1950s. They suggest a long-term consistency of partisan divisions that can be traced back at least to 1942, when candidates of the established, conservative parties captured 75 percent of the district's vote and two Socialists captured the remaining 25 percent. The election of 1947 reflected those divisions almost exactly. Conservative support remained strong thereafter, but it suffered a relative decline in each election from 1949 onward, despite an absolute increase. If Matsutani's votes are treated as conservative ballots, then 75,000 voters joined the ranks of the conservatives in the Santama between 1947 and 1958. But at the same time, over 128,000 others — 63 percent of all new voters — were entering the ranks of the progressive parties. The political inclinations of this second, larger group suggest very strongly that newcomers from the ward area who began moving to the Santama region after the war boosted the fortunes of progressive parties.

A comparison of Lower House election results in Musashino and Fuchū refines and affirms this assertion. Tables 11 and 12 present the official results of the 1947 and 1949 elections according to the candidates' parties. If revisions are made for Matsutani, then con-

TABLE 11. *Lower House Election Results, City of Musashino, 1947–1958 (in number and percentage)*

Year	Total Votes	Conservatives	Progressives	Unaffiliated
1947	18,291 (100)	6,742 (37)	10,864 (59)	685 (4)
1949	22,499 (100)	11,653 (52)	9,742 (43)	1,104 (5)
1952	28,547 (100)	15,759 (55)	10,621 (37)	2,167 (8)
1953	28,090 (100)	14,887 (53)	10,773 (38)	2,430 (9)
1955	35,018 (100)	18,068 (52)	13,776 (39)	3,174 (9)
1958	42,106 (100)	19,300 (46)	22,273 (53)	533 (1)

SOURCE: Same as table 9.

TABLE 12. *Lower House Election Results, City of Fuchū, 1947–1958 (in number and percentage)*

Year	Total Votes	Conservatives	Progressives	Unaffiliated
1947	12,630 (100)	6,171 (49)	6,116 (48)	343 (3)
1949	14,409 (100)	7,510 (52)	6,823 (47)	76 (1)
1952	18,067 (100)	10,979 (61)	5,373 (30)	1,715 (9)
1953	17,143 (100)	10,008 (58)	5,981 (35)	1,154 (7)
1955	20,829 (100)	11,300 (54)	8,146 (39)	1,383 (7)
1958	25,155 (100)	13,478 (54)	11,192 (44)	485 (2)

SOURCE: Same as table 9.

NOTE: These results report the combined totals for Fuchū *machi* and Tama and Nishifu *mura* for the elections between 1947 and 1953.

servatives took 65 percent of the Musashino vote in 1947 and 67 percent in 1949. In Fuchū, they took 67 percent and 75 percent, respectively, largely because Matsutani's 1949 candidacy on Yabe Jingo's old party ticket brought her an additional thousand votes from the village areas of Fuchū. These figures also coincide closely with prewar trends. As before, Musashino was more progressive than the district as a whole, and it moved steadily into the Socialist-Communist camp as the 1950s progressed. Still more conservative than Musashino, Fuchū nonetheless had become slightly more supportive of progressive candidates than the district.

The relative rates of change in Musashino and Fuchū are explained in large part by reference to the migration patterns described in the first part of this chapter. Drawing its newcomers primarily from the ranks of well-educated, white-collar workers who formerly lived in the ward area, Musashino saw progressive candidates attract nearly 70 percent of the additional votes in the community between 1947 and 1958. By contrast, in Fuchū, where many of the city's newcomers in the early 1950s came directly from other Santama communities or from rural towns and villages, conservative forces added many voters to their camp. As more commuters moved from the ward area to Fuchū in the late 1950s, however, the city's progressive fortunes rose, and 60 percent of the additional voters by 1958 had entered the progressive camp.

Before we examine the consequences of this expanding progressivism at the prefectural and municipal levels, a closer look at some of the individual candidates who accounted for these partisan changes is necessary. A glance at table 10 indicates that many politicians who served the district after the war were newcomers to the local scene. Occupation policies and age account for the appearance of so many unfamiliar faces. Sakamoto Ikkaku, the long-time Seiyūkai candidate who had represented the Minami Tama area, died in 1947. His old Minseitō adversary, Yatsunami Takeji, had reached his late sixties by war's end and retired from active political life. Those not removed for natural reasons were the victims of a purge of wartime officials, initiated by Occupation forces in early 1947 and continued in force through early 1952. Both the Seiyūkai politician Tsugumo Kunitoshi and the Socialist Nakamura Takaichi were obliged to leave political life for five years because of this policy. As a result, all parties had to recruit new candidates to stand for the Diet.

Conservative parties preferred candidates with prestigious educational and career backgrounds. Kuriyama Chōjirō, a victorious Jiyūtō candidate four times between 1946 and 1953, held an undergraduate degree from the University of Utah and had done graduate work at Harvard University. His career as an administrator for the *Mainichi shimbun,* one of the nation's largest newspapers, imparted a tone of intellectualism to his candidacy as well as a certain popular touch. Namiki Yoshio held a law degree from Tokyo University and had gained experience in New York and Manila while working for a Japanese trading firm. Fukuda Tokuyasu also was a Tokyo University graduate; he had served as a private secretary to Prime Minister Yoshida Shigeru following a career in the Ministry of Foreign Affairs. All three of these men thus offered an extra advantage—foreign experience—to an electorate that might have prized such a trait during a period of foreign occupation.

Other conservative victors—Hosoda Gian, Ōkubo Tamejirō, and Yatsunami Tatsuo (nephew of Takeji and a Diet victor in 1946 and 1947)—were also college-educated men who had pursued careers as lawyers, teachers, and civil servants before turning to politics. Only Kizaki Shigeo, scion of a powerful political family in Naruki Village and a farmer, mayor, and prefectural assemblyman before his Diet victory in 1955, departed from this conventional, conservative pattern. But even he had graduated from an agricultural college.

Parties on the other side of the political spectrum were less anxious about the pedigree of their candidates, and thus provided an opportunity for men of humble background to pursue a political career. Left-wing Socialists did this for Yamahana Hideo, an elementary school graduate from the Kobe area in western Japan who had gone to work in a rubber factory at sixteen and been active in the labor movement since 1921. When he ran for a Diet seat in 1947, Yamahana was a union official living in the industrial quarter east of Tokyo Station, where he organized workers in the construction and rubber industries. He did not establish residence in the Santama District until he bought a home in Chōfu, east of Fuchū, in 1954, by which time he had already represented the district for four years. A one-time Communist victor during this period, Dobashi Kazuyoshi, was also a union official. Although he held a law degree from Meiji University, Dobashi enjoyed a reputation as a folksy, popular politician, perhaps because of his role as a leader of the postal and communications union.

Death, retirements, and the purge thus created an opportunity for parties in the Santama to recruit new candidates for national leadership after the war. Conservative parties responded by seeking men born in the district who had good educations and who had pursued careers in government, business, and the professions. Opposition parties were concerned neither about a man's place of birth nor about his educational background. They valued his commitment to the goals and organizations embraced by Socialism and Communism. Men with credentials as union organizers, like Yamahana and Dobashi, were prized candidates.

It may appear on the surface that postwar political changes facilitated recruitment of leaders from a broader spectrum of Japanese society. To the limited extent that Socialists and Communists began to promote men with union experience as political candidates, this observation is true. But, in large measure, new avenues of recruitment stopped there. In the absence of open, preferential primaries, leading party figures at the national or the prefectural level, or both, retained, as they had during the prewar period, ultimate authority over the choice of candidates. While this often resulted in the selection of men with fine qualifications, it precluded any public role in candidate selection and it obviously obstructed the successful candidacy of self-made men who did not enjoy access to the center of power. In time, also, men at the center became wedded to certain criteria; those on the right preferred officials and businessmen, those on the left, union leaders. This caused little difficulty during the 1950s, but the intractability of this selection process was giving root to anomalies and dissatisfactions that would rebound on the parties in later years.

Since, with the exception of Tsugumo and Nakamura, neither Matsutani Tenkōkō nor her male colleagues had spent their adult careers in the Santama region, it was necessary for most of them to build new electoral bases after the war. In doing this, conservative candidates resorted to time-tried practices: they divided the district geographically. The Jiyūtō candidate Kuriyama relied on the Kita Tama area for 80 percent of his support, with about 20 percent coming from Minami Tama. He avoided Nishi Tama, where Namiki Yoshio possessed a secure base of about twenty-five thousand voters. They were enough to elect him through 1949, but as more of the district's electorate settled in Kita Tama, he had to draw support from that area as well after 1952. Namiki might have avoided expansion into the north, had he been able to attract a larger share of the vote in Nishi Tama. But two other candidates, Tsugumo Kunitoshi and Fukuda Tokuyasu, both born in Nishi Tama villages, also enjoyed support from the still strongly conservative voters in that section. They, too, found it necessary to expand into Minami and Kita Tama in order to accumulate enough votes to best their rivals.[34]

Conservative candidates continued to rely on appeals of a type that had served them well during the prewar period. This was especially so in the Nishi Tama area, where as late as 1958 conservatives commanded 77 percent of the vote, with almost a third controlled by Tsugumo Kunitoshi alone. It was also true of farm villages in other parts of the Santama, as well as former rural neighborhoods even in the most dynamic suburban cities. In such places conservative candidates could count on voters who were motivated by long-standing personal ties with individual candidates or the parties they represented, or both, as a group of political scientists studying

34. The ensuing discussion of *jiban* in the Seventh District between 1947 and 1958 is based on Shūgiin jimukyoku, *Shūgiin giin sōsenkyo ichiran*, for the twenty-third through the twenty-eighth general elections (Tokyo, 1948–1958).

Fuchū during the 1949 election discovered. When asked why they voted for a given candidate, many responded to this effect: "This household has voted for the Minseitō [i.e., Yatsunami Takeji] for generations so we supported the Minshutō [i.e., Takeji's nephew, Tatsuo] this time."[35] Among some conservative supporters, therefore, voters who established an identity with a party and its candidate in one period passed their loyalties on to succeeding generations.

Other electoral practices also persisted into the postwar era in the Santama, as the political scientists also discovered.

One can see that a feudal character is deeply rooted. . . . The people of the village understand very well whom the organization chairmen and local influentials support. Before the election, every organization held a nominal meeting of some kind, but even if such meetings had not been held to seek further support, the people of the village would have known whom this organization chairman or that village councilman or hamlet chief was supporting and gone along accordingly. As an older man, who was active during the so-called "Santama *sōshi* period," put it, "In this village, if Mr. X (an organization chairman) supports Mr. O, then everyone from top to bottom does so."[36]

Perhaps in his anxiety to please, their informant exaggerated the power of Mr. X, because electoral returns from the village of Nishifu that he was describing indicate that only one candidate— the conservative Kuriyama—commanded as much as 33 percent of the vote in 1949. Nonetheless, there is enough truth in his assertion to warrant the claim that the same kind of cross-stratal support based on residential hamlets and mobilized by men of influence that served conservative candidates before the war served them after as well, although in a considerably attenuated fashion.

Time-tried loyalties within kin groups and the efforts of men of influence in rural hamlets were indispensable to the success of conservative candidates in the rural areas of the Santama, but they needed different techniques in the more dynamic suburban zone of the northeast, where conservatives found it difficult to penetrate the ranks of newcomers. Since Nishi and Minami Tama together embraced barely a third of the Santama's electorate by the 1950s, it was suicidal for conservative candidates to confine their campaign ef-

35. Rōyama, *Seiji ishiki,* p. 196.
36. Ibid, p. 202.

forts there. They had to achieve some method of contacting the newcomers who were not integrated into the existing networks of family and hamlet association on which Seiyūkai supporters had relied for their prewar support in Kita Tama.

One method adopted by many conservative politicians in the Santama, as well as in the rest of the nation, was the creation of personal support groups, or *kōenkai*. Organized by campaign operatives in much the same way prewar electoral networks had been, a chief difference between the postwar *kōenkai* and the prewar *jiban* rested on the affiliations of their supporters. Before the war, residential units at the subvillage level—hamlets, or *buraku*—had been the building blocks of conservative campaign organizations. In rural districts after the war, hamlets continued to function in the same way, although as the Nishifu case illustrates, in a more attenuated fashion. In urban districts after the war, candidates sought to use, as the base for their campaigns, functional organizations that drew together people engaged in common economic or recreational activities. Conservative candidates in the Santama who began building formal *kōenkai* in the late 1950s sought, as did Fukuda Tokuyasu, to attract support, for example, from the Fuchū Association of Fire Squads, the Musashino Restaurant Owners' Association, the Koganei Traditional Dance Club, the Mitaka Junior Chamber of Commerce, and so on. In this way it was at least partly possible for a conservative candidate to establish indirect contact, mediated by a campaign organization, with potential supporters.

Some candidates in the district resorted to the even more demanding task of contacting voters directly. The conservative Namiki Yoshio developed a legendary reputation for his efforts, which paid off handsomely from 1947 to 1958. Namiki was, to use the American phrase, very good at "pressing the flesh." He often commuted from his base in Nishi Tama by Chūō Line to the Diet Building in Chiyoda Ward. Boarding the train at the rear, he would walk its entire length in the course of his journey, shaking hands with all the riders and introducing himself as their legislator. During campaigns he rolled out early in the day attired in unpressed pants and tennis shoes to greet voters personally. His generally light-hearted manner was also effective on the speaker's platform, where he delighted in making puns that derided Yoshida Shigeru, while Yoshida's stodgy cohort Tsugumo Kunitoshi glowered disapprovingly. Unfortunately for Namiki, this energetic approach eventually lost its effect, perhaps because is was out of keeping with the aloof reserve expected from men of power in Japan.[37]

The sometimes short tenures experienced by Santama conservatives during this period were attributable less to their method of mobilizing voters and more to their method of choosing candidates. To put it simply, the conservative parties, rent by both inter- and intraparty disputes in the first postwar decade, found it difficult to regulate candidacies. In 1949, seven candidates ran with endorsements from conservative parties, for only five seats. Such multiplication of candidacies reduced the number of votes needed to win and tended to benefit progressive candidates, who had small bases to work with. Even in 1958, after the LDP had formed, the legacy of factional disputes resulted in the candidacy of five conservatives in the Santama, at a time when they could have won only four seats at best. With the retirement of older politicians, like Tsugumo, and a stronger effort to control candidacies by the national party, however, the LDP eventually learned to manage effectively the constantly shrinking electoral base at its disposal. But factional disputes and party splits aborted efficient electoral management during the 1950s and produced uncharacteristic instability among conservative *jiban*.

Their instability is only highlighted, of course, by the relative security of Socialist bases in the district after 1952. Freed from the strictures of the purge by the peace treaty of 1952, Nakamura Takaichi stood for his old Diet seat in the October election and won handily, finishing first in the district with more than sixty thousand votes. It is noteworthy that he drew his support from virtually the same parts of the district that he had drawn it from in 1942. In the latter, wartime election, Kita Tama voters had provided 48 percent of this support, while those in Minami and Nishi Tama had added 32 percent and 20 percent, respectively. In 1952, the same areas provided 54 percent, 29 percent, and 16 percent, respectively. Obviously, many of Nakamura's loyal supporters during the war easily rekindled their support for him one decade later, underwriting his successful campaigns throughout the 1950s.

Although his base in 1952 was geographically similar to his 1942 base, it differed in one important respect: it had nearly four times as

37. On Namiki, see Rōyama, *Seiji ishiki,* p. 185; Rōyama, *Sōsenkyo,* p. 148; and *Ms,* II: 22–23. Also, interview with Nakamura Takaichi, in Musashino, April 16, 1976.

many voters. The increase was drawn from three groups. Some came from the wives of men who had previously supported Nakamura, since in the early postwar period wives strongly tended to support the party of their husbands. Another part of the increase was drawn from middle-level, white-collar workers moving from the ward area into such suburbs as Musashino, where Nakamura attracted more votes in 1952 than any other candidate. Accustomed to the appeals of the Socialists and perhaps even being loyal Socialist voters already, most newcomers, as was noted previously, were potential Socialist supporters. The third part of the increase was drawn from those unions within the labor movement associated with its right wing, such as the Tōshiba unions in Fuchū, where Nakamura won 18 percent of the vote in 1952. As a moderate, if not conservative, figure within the Socialist movement, Nakamura relied heavily on the middle-ranking, white- and blue-collar *kitarimono*—newcomers to the Santama region—for his support.

His Socialist cohort Yamahana Hideo represented the other wing of the Socialist movement and drew most heavily on union voters for his support. In the Santama region, as in most of Japan, labor unions in private corporations were often more conservative than their counterparts in the public sector, and they tended to support right-wing Socialists such as Nakamura. The public unions, on the other hand, as well as those corporation unions aligned with the left-leaning national federation Sōhyō, gave their support to Yamahana, at least officially. As he himself noted, even when workers were "drunk on democracy" in the immediate postwar period, an official who told his workers to support a Socialist candidate might expect only 70 percent to do so. But even if 70 percent of all public union members in the Santama had supported Yamahana in the 1950s, they could not have elected him. Like Nakamura, he also drew support from the nonunion newcomers to the district who had grown accustomed to supporting Socialists while living in the ward area.[38]

It is necessary to remark once again on the organizational efforts undertaken by Nakamura and Yamahana. Neither man organized the kind of personal support group *(kōenkai)* that was the mainstay of LDP politicians after 1955. Rather than a tightly organized team of

38. Interview with Yamahana Hideo, at his son's campaign headquarters in Chōfu, on February 10, 1976.

campaign workers contacting operatives in each city, town, village, and hamlet in the district, both Nakamura and Yamahana relied on two other modes of mobilization: idealistic appeals, in the prewar tradition, and contacts with union leaders. The idealistic appeals were apparently effective with many newcomers entering the district after the early 1950s. They were conditioned to Socialist candidates and successes in the ward area; they were young and optimistic; and they felt that Socialist victory was assured, if only they were patient and loyal. Contacts with union leaders also resulted largely in idealistic appeals, directed mainly at union members and their immediate families. Union personnel were mobilized to encourage other union members to vote, but they were not sent onto the streets to persuade other voters to support their candidates. Again, it was simply taken for granted that Japan's growth as an industrial economy would create a labor force composed mainly of union workers who would inevitably support Socialism. These two optimistic strains running through the Socialist movement during the 1950s found ample support in the electoral trends of the Santama during that decade and thereby encouraged a complacent attachment to ideals the future would treat harshly.

But even in the 1950s, not all of Yamahana's and Nakamura's natural supporters were committed Socialists. Witness the comments of a young man who belonged to the national railway union, when asked in 1949 for whom he planned to vote.

It's often said that in this election people will vote more for the man than the party. However, as far as we laborers are concerned, we'd like to make a choice on the basis of the party. I'm basically in agreement with the Socialist platform where workers are concerned. But when I think about Japan's present circumstances, I realize it's going to be difficult to establish Socialism right away, and, besides, I have some doubts about it anyway. So, as an individual, I'm voting for the Liberal Party.[39]

The reserve inherent in these remarks by a union member who should have been a logical Socialist supporter introduces a note of skepticism. He contradicts the idealistic notions that Socialist leaders harbored in the 1950s about their party's destiny, and his remarks provide a suitable note on which to begin analysis of electoral changes at the prefectural and municipal levels between 1945 and 1960.

39. Rōyama, *Seiji ishiki,* p. 190.

The Local Scene

Although residents of the Santama had been voting for representatives to a prefectural assembly since the 1870s, they had never participated in electing a governor for Tokyo Metropolitan Prefecture before 1947. True to their nature, they offered the bulk of their support to the candidate endorsed by conservative parties, Yasui Seiichirō. Yasui was Tokyo's last appointed governor (he served from 1946 to 1947) and also its first elected governor. Running in 1947 and 1951 against former Socialist Diet members who were well known in the industrial quarters they represented but little known outside, Yasui won election easily. He faced stiffer competition in 1955, when the progressive parties endorsed Arita Hachirō as their candidate. A former Minister of Foreign Affairs with impeccable credentials, Arita could challenge Yasui on his own conservative grounds. Although Arita outpolled the former Socialist candidate in every part of the prefecture, he still failed to unseat Yasui, who completed his third, four-year term in 1959.[40]

Encouraged by Arita's showing in 1955, progressive parties backed him again in 1959, when the conservatives endorsed Azuma Ryūtarō as their candidate. Azuma was a former professor at Tokyo University and a former president of a nearby prefectural university. He enjoyed a reputation as a man of culture befitting the nation's capital, but he also enjoyed an added advantage: he was a sports enthusiast who had been on the International Olympic Committee since 1946. Already feverish in their enthusiasm for an Olympic competition, Tokyo's voters could hardly have asked for a better candidate. Although he had a tight battle in the Santama area, Azuma defeated Arita easily and took office at age sixty-six in 1959.

Table 13 illustrates the partisan preferences of Santama voters in gubernatorial contests after the war. A comparison with Diet results indicates that nominal progressive candidates for the national legislature outpolled the progressive gubernatorial candidate in 1947 and 1951, a finding that bespeaks Yasui's strength in the Santama. By 1955, however, the progressive candidate for governor pulled abreast of his conservative opponent in the district and clearly out-

40. For information about Yasui, see Nihon jihō sha, comp., *Yasui Seiichirō den* [A Biography of Yasui Seiichirō] (Tokyo, 1967).

TABLE 13. *Vote for Major Progressive Candidate for Governor, Tokyo Metropolitan Prefecture, 1947–1959 (in percentage of total vote)*

Year	Prefecture	Santama Area	Musashino	Fuchū[a]
1947	42	40	47	48
1951	34	28	32	36
1955	45	41	51	48
1959	46	48	53	48

SOURCE: Official reports of the Tokyo Election Management Commission [*Tōkyō to senkyo kanri iinkai*].
[a]The figures for Fuchū include the returns from the villages of Nishifu and Tama in 1947 and 1951.

TABLE 14. *Vote for Progressive Candidates for Prefectural Assembly, Tokyo Metropolitan Prefecture, 1947–1959 (in percentage of total vote)*

Year	Prefecture	Santama Area	Musashino	Fuchū
1947	29	32	NA	NA
1951	22	NA	39	NA
1955	27	24	57	29
1959	33	34	57	25

SOURCE: Same as table 13.

distanced his progressive allies running for the Diet. Recognizing that their loyal supporters were still a minority in the Santama (as well as the ward area), Socialist leaders promoted Arita Hachirō precisely because he could draw otherwise conservative voters to the Socialist cause, as he obviously did in the Santama, in Musashino, and in Fuchū, in 1955 and 1959.

Turning to the results of prefectural assembly elections, we find enthusiasm for progressives beginning to wane. The poor quality of existing records makes comparisons in 1947 and 1951 difficult, but it is evident that a wide disparity existed by 1955 between progressive support in Diet and gubernatorial elections and such support in prefectural assembly elections. With the exception of Musashino, which will be discussed shortly, progressive candidates for the prefectural assembly drew discernibly less support than their cohorts in

Diet elections. As a consequence, the Santama delegation to the prefectural assembly was always dominated by a majority of conservatives in this period.

A note of caution is necessary, however, because partisan affiliations in the prefectural assembly remained somewhat vague through the 1955 election. Although most candidates were clearly identified with one side of the political spectrum, if not a specific party, they often ran as unaffiliated *(mushozoku)* candidates. This muted partisan divisions in election campaigns and made it possible for men in one camp to appeal to voters in the other. In 1955, fourteen successful candidates ran unaffiliated, eleven conservatives and three Socialists. They made up about 12 percent of the assembly's 120 delegates. After 1959, however, virtually every candidate for the Tokyo Prefectural Assembly declared his party affiliation, and assembly contests became embroiled in the same partisan divisions that had characterized Diet campaigns for decades.

The presence of unaffiliated candidates accounts for some of the disparity between progressive support at the Diet and assembly levels, but only a small part of it. A closer examination of the Fuchū case helps to explain the disparities more fully. Socialist parties paid relatively little attention to elections below the national level in the 1950s. Very nearly obsessed with national and international issues, they focused their attention on the Diet and eschewed the demanding task of electoral competition at the local level. Consequently, Socialist assembly candidates got little financial or organizational backing from their party, unless it happened to be quite strong locally owing to the presence of an active, well-financed union. Local Socialists did not even field a candidate in 1951, and the ones who did run in 1955 and 1959 drew their support almost exclusively from union workers and their wives, a base too small to win a seat. From 1947 through 1961, therefore, a former schoolteacher affiliated with conservative parties represented Fuchū in the prefectural assembly, his victories aided by Socialist party indifference to prefectural assembly contests.

Implicit in the foregoing discussion are two other explanations for disparity: organizational weakness and the method of mobilization. Although there was a branch of the JSP in Fuchū during the 1950s, it was an avocational affair involving a handful of men from local unions. Without a large membership, they had few if any funds and only the time they could find after work to organize a campaign. Even if they overcame these obstacles, as they did to some extent by relying on the good services of union members, they were still stymied by the techniques they used to mobilize voters. These consisted mainly in telephoning other union leaders and activists, appealing for their candidate, printing a few handbills, and hoping for the best. Although union members were growing in number in Fuchū during the 1950s, they were still too few to return a candidate to the prefectural assembly with their support alone.

While party policies, organizational weakness, and mobilization techniques produced meager results for prefectural assembly candidates in Fuchū, progressives fared better in Musashino, their vote actually outstripping support for progressives at the national level. This disparity is explained, as it was in Arita Hachirō's case, by reference to an individual. Running for the first time in 1951 as a known progressive but an unaffiliated candidate in a crowded field with five others, Jitsukawa Hiroshi captured an assembly seat by winning only 28 percent of the vote. In his early forties at the time, Jitsukawa had come to Musashino in 1927, where he taught in local elementary schools for two decades before becoming a principal in nearby Hōya. Disturbed by the poverty he witnessed among his students in the early postwar period, and upset by the callousness with which local landlords responded to his pleas for help, he decided he could be more effective as a politician than a teacher. Squeaking into office in 1951, he quickly established his power and won reelection in 1955 and 1959 with large pluralities.

Like Arita, Jitsukawa was a strong progressive candidate because he appealed to conservative voters, though in a different fashion. Having taught in the prewar school system for many years, he had—like most Japanese *sensei*, or teachers—cultivated bonds of friendship with many former students, who felt an implicit sense of obligation toward him. When he ran for the assembly after 1951, they at last had a tangible means of repaying their obligations; they could organize his supporters and vote for him. Even though many of them were merchants, farmers, factory owners, and businessmen who would normally vote conservative, Jitsukawa's former students nonetheless felt duty bound to their *sensei* and offered him essential electoral and organizational support. When combined with votes from union members, their wives, and incoming Socialists from the ward area, the votes Jitsukawa won from his former students enabled him to secure a stranglehold on Musashino's prefectural assembly seat. He won election for the eighth time in 1977.

The social characteristics of his supporters enabled Jitsukawa to perceive his position and discharge his duties in special ways, which deserve our attention. Jitsukawa preferred to think of himself primarily as a *tomin daihyō*, or a representative of all residents of the prefecture. Rather than being a spokesman for a particular pressure group or social class, he was open to demands and requests from all constituents, which he apparently handled with ease and effectiveness. This general posture was further affirmed by his own hazy understanding of his constituency. Although supporters organized a *kōenkai* for him, he had little to do with it himself and had only the weakest conception of the areas and groups within the city that contributed to his electoral support—save for his former students. Jitsukawa actually sought this kind of situation. In explaining his public declaration as a Socialist in 1955, he said that the policies of the Socialists, to which he paid no attention, were not an inducement. Rather, the Socialists provided a suitable base because they were so loosely organized and exercised such weak control over their members. Not surprisingly, in view of such perceptions, Jitsukawa was regarded as a moderate to conservative Socialist in Musashino, who drew support from the left, the center, and the right of the political spectrum as he pursued policies aimed at placating the majority of the populace, regardless of political allegiance.[41]

These observations prompt one final comment concerning the nature of Jitsukawa's electoral base, Socialist organization in Musashino, and the strength of voter identity with the JSP. It is often alleged that prefectural assemblymen possess *jiban* they can mobilize in their entirety for senior colleagues running for Diet seats. This was assuredly not the case in Musashino, first, because Jitsukawa's base was not so tightly organized that he could "deliver" it to a Diet candidate, and second, because some of his supporters voted for him as an individual in spite of his party ties. Just as Jitsukawa had supporters he could not mobilize to vote for Nakamura, so also did Nakamura have supporters who would not vote for Jitsukawa. Had the Socialists been linked to executives at

41. Interview with Jitsukawa Hiroshi, in Musashino, April 25, 1976.

the local and national levels who were in strategic positions to provide benefits to constituents, the party might have been able to elicit a firmer sense of identity from some of its marginal supporters, such as the businessmen who were Jitsukawa's former students or the small farmers who were Nakamura's former tenant union associates. But in the 1950s there was no effective link between Musashino's Socialist legislators and Socialist mayors or cabinet ministers. The absence of such a link seriously impeded the party's ability to establish strong bonds to its supporters and thereby encouraged voters to retain firmer identification with individual candidates than with the party itself.

The difficulties encountered by progressive parties as they aspired to gain power are highlighted by analysis of mayoralty and council elections in Musashino and Fuchū between 1947 and 1959. Although progressive parties cut deeply into conservative strength at the national level and even achieved some gains at the prefectural level, their efforts floundered at the municipal level, which remained a firm conservative stronghold. In both communities, victorious conservative candidates for mayor always secured half or more of the vote and ran in virtually every case against another conservative. Socialists could not even muster a major challenger to run against Fuchū's conservative mayors, and although they tried in Musashino, they could not unseat the incumbent. Consequently, conservatives monopolized the mayoralty in both Fuchū and Musashino throughout this period.

Making even more comfortable the already secure position of conservative mayors were the conservatives who dominated city councils, whose strength is illustrated in table 15. If partisan affiliations were slow in penetrating to the prefectural level, they were even slower in reaching the municipal level. Socialists and Communists began declaring their party affiliations in Musashino and Fuchū in 1955, but as table 15 indicates, most conservatives continued to run as unaffiliated (*mushozoku*) candidates through the 1950s. They intentionally avoided public identity with a party in order to muffle partisan divisions within their communities, which they sought to protect from political divisiveness. This accorded with a psychological stance that valued solidarity at the local level at the same time it embodied practical wisdom. When most higher-level authorities were conservatives, it was sensible to deal with

TABLE 15. *City Council Election Results, Musashino and Fuchū, 1955 and 1959*

City	Percentage of Vote by Party					Partisanship of Victors		
	NP[a]	Cons.	JSP	JCP	Total	Cons.	Prog.	Total
Musashino								
1955	72	4	18	6	100	27	9	36
1959	59	12	24	5	100	24	12	36
Fuchū								
1955	89		8	3	100	27	3	30
1959	91		7	2	100	28	2	30

SOURCES: Official election returns, Musashino Election Management Commission and Fuchū Election Management Commission.
[a]NP = unaffiliated (*mushozoku*) candidates.

them on their ground and to avoid identity with the progressives or even a factional adversary. Therefore, unaffiliated candidates, most of whom were conservatives, dominated the city councils in Fuchū and Musashino before the 1960s.

In view of the electoral support retained elsewhere by conservatives, their dominance on city councils should not be surprising, but their strength is. At virtually the same time that Musashino voters were casting 53 percent of their ballots for Socialists and Communists in Diet elections they gave less than 30 percent to council candidates from those parties. In Fuchū the disparity was even greater: 44 percent of the vote for Diet progressives, 8 percent for council progressives. A full explanation for these disparities rests on factors mentioned above, as well as several others.

Progressive party policies, organizational skills, and patterns of participation all contributed to the weak showing of progressive council candidates in Musashino and Fuchū. Demonstrating little interest in council elections, the Socialist party could hardly expect its few card-carrying members to undertake enthusiastic candidacies without party backing. The absence of any strong organizational apparatus at the local level was a further discouragement to individuals who faced the prospect of raising their own funds and doing all their own work. Union members did offer a source of funds and manpower, and a few Socialists and Communists elected in the two cities owed their victories primarily to union efforts. High rates of abstention, which kept as many as four in ten voters from the polls in Musashino, also hampered the progressive cause. Although residential requirements were loosened after 1950 to permit residents of three months' standing to vote in local contests, rates of abstention remained high among newcomers.[42] Quite likely to vote progressive, by staying away from the polls they allowed loyal conservative voters an opportunity to cast ballots out of proportion to their true strength in the total electorate.

Another explanation for the disparities under discussion rests on the way in which candidates mobilized support in council elections. Most council candidates marshalled votes from a territorial base focused on their residence, because they were best known in the area where they lived and, often, worked. Since neighborhoods in Japanese suburbs were not nearly so homogeneous as those in America, a given district within a city was likely to contain a cross section of all groups in Japanese society, rich and poor, farmer and laborer, conservative and progressive. Someone representing such a district tried to mute partisan differences as much as possible in order to appeal to voters at all points along the political spectrum. This structural imperative muffled even more the already nonpartisan tendencies of municipal politics.

Strong progressive candidates who could accept the sacrifices incumbent upon local public office were difficult to find. A city council position in the 1950s was a low-paying, part-time job. The kind of men who could afford to accept such a post were farmers, shopkeepers who could find someone to tend their business while they were absent, or real estate agents, contractors, and self-employed professionals for whom it was an integral part of their work. By contrast, young salary men commuting outside the city each day could afford neither the time nor the money that council service required. Since such men formed the largest group from which the Socialists might have recruited candidates, the lack of viable candidates also exacerbated Socialist difficulties at the municipal level.

Further reinforcing the already apathetic tendencies at work was the manner in which major newspapers treated local politics. For the

42. Musashino shi senkyo kanri iinkai, *Musashino shimin no seikatsu to sansei taido* [Social and Political Attitudes of Musashino Citizens] (Musashino, 1956), p. 45.

most part, they ignored them completely. Sometimes the results of a mayoralty election were published, with perhaps four lines of commentary. Reports of council election results seldom appeared in the major metropolitan dailies in the 1950s, even in the sections dealing with local matters. And little attention was given to the formal political affairs of local communities, unless a sensational event transpired or a local issue assumed national or international importance, as sometimes happened when disputes arose in cities with American military bases. By and large, the newspapers and other media during the 1950s seemed to feel that the nonpartisan character of local politics deserved only their indifference.

The large gap between the progressive vote in Diet and council elections is thus explained by a complex combination of factors. Party policies adopted by the progressives played a major role, by demeaning the importance of local elections. The low prestige and high personal costs that accompanied the position of council member discouraged many progressives from running. General apathy conveyed by party policy was reinforced by the indifference of the media toward local politics, and this in turn discouraged key progressive supporters from participating. The product of these varied factors was a poor showing by progressive forces at the municipal level in both Musashino and Fuchū throughout the immediate postwar period.

In the face of this weak progressive challenge, conservatives found it easy to dominate local politics according to patterns with deep historical roots. The mayor of Musashino in the period between 1947 and 1963 was Arai Genkichi. Scion of a Kichijōji gentry family in its thirteenth generation, Arai rose to office in the steps of his older brother, who had been mayor for a year in 1946-47, and of his father, who had served on the prewar council. Arai himself had worked at two administrative jobs after graduating from Keiō University in 1930, before returning to enter town hall in 1938. He was serving as city treasurer when the first popular election for mayor was held.

The 1947 mayoralty race in Musashino was an untidy affair befitting the city's chaotic character at the time. Initially, four candidates declared: Arai, two other conservatives, and a young lawyer aligned with the Socialist party. Only two candidates were of any consequence, Arai and another member of the Kichijōji gentry named Takahashi Shinzō. Son of a former mayor, Takahashi felt he had a customary claim on the conservative candidacy, both because his father had once been mayor and because it was now time for a man from Kichijōji to serve, since Sakai politicians had been in office for two decades. Moreover, as Arai's former teacher, he thought he had a claim on Arai's deference. Most conservatives felt differently, contending that Arai would be a far stronger candidate. When they failed to persuade Takahashi to withdraw, Arai himself bit the bullet. While confirming his feelings of deference to his former teacher, Arai also pointed out that a Socialist would win if they both ran. Takahashi deferred, and with the active support of many young officials in city hall, Arai plunged on. Promoting himself as a *kakushin* or reformist candidate, Arai drew on Takahashi's retinue and his own in Kichijōji, besting the other conservative from the Sakai area by winning 53 percent of the vote. In three following elections, he turned back his challengers by winning, in sequence, 51 percent, 56 percent, and 58 percent of the vote.[43]

Arai faced serious challenges in his first years as mayor. The city's extremely rapid growth during the wartime period stimulated the need for a wide range of services not attended to by prewar mayors, who took more pride in their balanced budgets than in their civic accomplishments. When the war ended in 1945, Musashino had no garbage collection services, no public library, virtually no sewers, few paved roads, minimal water services, and a crowded school system.

Arai attacked some of these problems head on while dealing with others as well. He was a stocky man with a commanding presence who moved with decisiveness and authority. These qualities must have appealed long before 1947 to the city workers who supported him that year. He responded to some of their needs by rationalizing the administration of city hall, and by introducing modern filing systems and managerial techniques. He established a new public library, and he turned his attention to the construction of new schools and roads. His quick, forthright manner, and the special self-confidence that only a member of the local gentry could bring to

---

43. Interview with Arai Genkichi, in Musashino, April 17, 1976. See also *Mss*, p. 798.

office, must have pleased the conservative politicians and businessmen of the city who were setting about the task of reconstruction.

In some respects, Arai may have been in advance of his times. He promoted a range of innovations that were designed to bring government and its beneficiaries into closer contact, including chats with the mayor, discussion sessions between local women and city administrators, and suggestion boxes to elicit citizens' ideas. He established a fruitful relationship with public administration specialists at Seikei University and from other schools, which brought professional advice inspired by democratic principles into city government. He relied on these advisers to conduct surveys of public opinion to determine where the city should direct its efforts and resources.

Despite the appearance of genuine sincerity, Arai did not respond effectively to the demands expressed by Musashino's citizenry. The surveys of public opinion illustrated a strong desire for attention to a sewer system, but his last two budgets contained no special allocations for that purpose. Although more and more of the city's newcomers had to settle in Nishikubo and Sakai, he continued to pour city funds into road and school projects in the Kichijōji region, his home area. In time, newcomers grew disillusioned. They found his authoritative manner blustery and his decisiveness a mark of arrogance. Behind his energetic, democratic demeanor there did indeed lurk a hint of condescension, a controlled irascibility with others not as bright as he, and a thinly veiled sense of noblesse oblige that inheres in politicians of his station. In the end, he may have succeeded too well, by inspiring a popular desire to participate and make demands which he lacked the dedication and the city the resources to fulfill. His service was appropriate to his era, but his departure is the tale of a later time.[44]

Arai's conservative colleagues in Fuchū faced the same dilemmas he faced after the war, and they dealt with them amidst the same factional squabbles that had divided the city's politicians since the 1870s. Still anxious about Fuchū's ability to live up to its potential for growth, leaders of the prewar Minseitō-Seiyūkai reform coalition persuaded a new man to stand for mayor in 1947. Born in

44. See *Ms*, III: 29–86, and *Mss*, pp. 1120–1121.

Fuchū and the brother of a well-known merchant and former council member, Moriya Senzō was a graduate of Waseda University and had long managed the business office of the Tokyo Prefectural Assembly. With his experience in Tokyo and his understanding of administrative duties, he seemed a logical candidate to provide the leadership that reformists felt the city needed. Moriya relied on indispensable support from former mayors Yajima Kenkichi and Ōtsu Shōji, from a number of council members, and from other, behind-the-scenes activists, some of whom had been associates of Yabe Jingo. His opponent in the 1947 race was a staunch Seiyūkai veteran who operated an inn on the Kōshū Road, Akimoto Hideo. Advantaged by the brief democratic euphoria that followed the end of war, Moriya won the election and set about to reorganize town hall.[45]

Like Arai in Musashino, Moriya quickly discovered that Fuchū had barely kept pace with the public needs created by its wartime expansion. The city had no hard-surfaced roads, its schools were overcrowded and outmoded, its recreational facilities were insufficient, and its police force needed a station. Recognizing that even faster growth was only a matter of time, Moriya began to float bonds for new projects. In a conservative community where the mere thought of debt struck fear in men's souls, this proved his undoing. Akimoto and his cohorts began spreading rumors that Moriya was driving the town to the poor farm, that increased taxes were just around the corner, and apparently for good measure, that Moriya was a drunk.

In the 1951 mayoralty election, Akimoto and his former Seiyūkai associates promoted the candidacy of Kobayashi Moichirō. An insurance salesman who was the descendant of an old-line Seiyūkai family from the center of town and the chief of Fuchū's volunteer fire department, Kobayashi brought little talent and no political experience to the job. Nonetheless, Akimoto's smear campaign and the town's renascent conservatism were sufficient to unseat Moriya, who could only attract 39 percent of the vote. Kobayashi settled in with 55 percent. (A Socialist captured the remaining 6 percent.)

45. The most informative account of early postwar politics in Fuchū is by Moriya's assistant mayor, Kuroda Kaname, *Shūsengo no Fuchū chō to watakushi* [Fuchū and I in the Postwar Era] (Fuchū, 1972). I am also indebted to an interview with Yabe Takaji, an official in city hall from 1930 onward, for some of the observations related here, in Fuchū, on February 13, 1976.

When the town became a city in 1954, Kobayashi stood for reelection and won again, this time defeating the old Seiyūkai nemesis, Yajima Kenkichi himself. Voters in the two villages that joined Fuchū that year, where the Seiyūkai had possessed powerful *jiban* before the war, undoubtedly added to Kobayashi's edge over Yajima and aided the rejection of Fuchū's reformist coalition. Kobayashi won office for a third time in 1958, by taking 54 percent of the votes.

Kobayashi's major contributions to Fuchū's political history were his neglect of administrative duties and his mere presence as a conservative figurehead. The former made it possible for capable young officials in city hall to implement many of the plans Moriya had conceived during his brief tenure. This opportunity proved a valuable lesson for one of them, Yabe Takaji, who would put the training to work in his own right once Kobayashi left the scene. His continued presence, meanwhile, vested authority in those who valued such groups as *chōnaikai,* fire squads, and police protection leagues. By nourishing an environment in which such bodies could be reinvigorated, Kobayashi helped perpetuate the conservative political subculture that identified his city.

Despite the penetrating nature of postwar political changes, men from the parties that had governed before the war retained a firm grip on power in the Santama region, in Musashino, and in Fuchū during the first fifteen postwar years. They benefited from the continuity of partisan identities and techniques of voter mobilization that had elected conservative Seiyūkai candidates in the towns and villages of the region since the 1890s. They also benefited, especially at the prefectural and local levels, from the policies adopted by their progressive opponents and from the inability of the latter to organize or mobilize their prospective supporters.

The persistence of conservative power was also a product of the age structure of the electorate. Young people exposed to the democratic ideals of the postwar educational system and conditioned to the competitive partisan politics that arose in the 1950s began to enter the electorate only in small numbers before 1960. Older people constituted the bulk of the electorate. Educated in the prewar school system, aligned with conservative politicians, and accustomed to the relatively consensual politics of the 1920s and 1930s, they were likely in six or seven of ten cases to favor conservatives in office.

The core of conservative support provided by these older voters was indispensable protection against a progressive landslide, even in a community like Musashino, where Socialists were already strong in 1942 and where their strength grew rapidly thereafter. The simple mechanics of demographic change preserved conservative influence. Beginning, for example, with an electorate numbering sixty thousand, where forty thousand voters were conservatives and twenty thousand progressives, a community that witnessed the arrival of sixty thousand more voters—forty thousand progressives and only twenty thousand conservatives—still had an electorate in which conservatives retained an even 50 percent of the votes. Precisely by this process did conservatives manage to retain power in Musashino during a period when the electorate added large numbers of new voters, most of whom (nearly seven in ten) were progressives. When many of these younger progressives failed to vote during their first years in a new community, they merely magnified further the strength of the older conservatives in the electorate.

In time, however, progressive newcomers began to play a role in the political process. More of them began to vote, and they took a greater interest in local affairs. In addition, by the late 1950s a booming economy forced many of them to identify problems they might earlier have tolerated indifferently, and to make choices they would formerly have left by habit to men of influence. The *danchi* dweller who used flush toilets and walked on paved sidewalks at his downtown job by day grew irritated with backyard cesspools and muddy paths he encountered when he arrived home at night. Despite the litany of poverty to which he had been subjected since birth, rehearsing the refrain that Japan was too poor for such amenities, this hypothetical *danchi* dweller and many others like him during the late 1950s came to realize that resources *were* available to deal with their problems, if only they were properly marshalled. Since incumbent conservatives were not doing the job, they hoped for satisfaction from the Socialists, perhaps with some measure of desperation.

Multiple Socialist candidacies provided voters ample opportunity to express their intentions in national elections, but progressives often failed them in prefectural and local contests. Eschewing such campaigns, the Socialist parties of the 1950s left their partisans adrift in an arena where they could well have benefited from direction and support. Communities throughout Japan, and especially in the Santama, faced a broad range of problems calling for choices among priorities and resources, but Socialists turned their backs on such problems, enthralled as they were with national and international issues. They neglected the opportunity to build an integrated organization of supporters that would translate their ideals into policies at all levels of the political system. This prevented electoral successes in the cities and towns experiencing the greatest social and partisan changes, and it undercut the chance to produce tangible benefits for Socialist supporters.

Their proclivity for bold rhetorical positions and their singular efforts to acquire power in the national Diet damaged the long-term prospects of progressive, and especially Socialist, parties. Obviously, if they wished to govern the nation, they had no choice but to concentrate party energies on national campaigns. But their prospects for success were diminished by the widespread strength of conservative support in the country's rural areas. In rapidly growing suburban towns, however, where progressive support was nearing parity with conservative, Socialists could have concentrated efforts on electing mayors who played a decisive role in determining municipal policies. Perhaps it is unrealistic to think that Socialist mayors could have pursued new programs at a time when national leadership remained in firmly conservative hands. And it may be unrealistic to think that even progressive suburbs were ready for Socialist mayors, although some, like Musashino, were fully capable of returning Socialist legislators in the same kind of plurality contest that shaped mayoralty campaigns. Whether realistic or not, it is essential to note that by their failure to put local executives in office during the 1950s, the Socialists prevented themselves from exercising power at any level in Japan's political system.

Conservatives, by contrast, exercised power at every level of the political system, and they monopolized the most important positions of prime minister, governor, and mayor. They could offer their followers both the spoils of office and the benefits of programs. The LDP was therefore able to nurture a stronger identity between itself and its supporters than other parties were able to do, by relying on instrumental returns. Despite factional strife within, despite its inability to penetrate the ranks of suburban newcomers, and despite a growing remoteness from some segments of its loyal constituency, the LDP during the 1950s elicited firm loyalties from many supporters and built a solid electoral base in part because it could offer its adherents political returns—or at least appear to.

Throughout the 1950s Socialists were frustrated on this count. Their inability to capture executive positions left them open to conservative ridicule for being unable to achieve power. And, perhaps more important, it also prevented them from being able to reward their partisans with appointments or policies. This highlighted the already anemic organizational capacities of the party, and must have stirred doubts, even among the most avid Socialist supporters, concerning the ability of their movement to achieve concrete goals. Such an undercurrent of self-doubt, nascent among the largest group in the opposition during the 1950s, was a fragile foundation on which to seek expansion of opposition power.

five

THE SURGE OF SUBURBAN GROWTH

This chapter has three complementary purposes. One is to illustrate how the segmented polity that arose in suburban Tokyo after the 1960s was fittingly enmeshed with the diverse society that had evolved by then. A second is to argue that, in order to understand political change in that society, we must employ a variety of techniques in addition to survey research. And the third is to demonstrate that suburban voting patterns led to unexpected partisan policies, at least at the municipal level in Musashino and Fuchū. The first part of the chapter depicts the diversity of suburban society by addressing changes in social structure, attitudes, and behavior in the Santama and two of its cities. The second part relates these changes to new partisan alignments, politicians, and policies. And a concluding segment highlights the observations with sketches of two hypothetical voters and the significance of their choices.

AN ENDURING SOCIAL VARIETY

The Santama Region

In pace with the remarkable economic boom that Japan enjoyed during the 1960s, the population of suburban Santama swelled dramatically. In one short decade it nearly doubled, rising from 1.3 million to 2.5 million. Growth slowed in the early 1970s, owing to unsettled conditions in both the domestic and the international economy, but yet another half million residents had appeared by 1975. Of the 2 million new residents added to the metropolitan prefecture in this fifteen-year period, more than eight in ten settled in the Santama, which had become one of the most populous and burgeoning regions in all Japan.

The surge of growth transformed its settlements into large suburban cities. Only thirty years before, virtually all the communities in the Santama had been farm villages or market towns of less than 10,000 people. But over the next four decades, fourteen communities grew beyond 40,000, another ten expanded beyond 100,000, and two cities in the region rose above 250,000. Although questions might arise concerning the urban qualities of some settlements, the cities of the Santama had certainly passed a demographic threshold on their way to suburban development.

The process of growth after 1960 was reminiscent of previous patterns. As before, Fuchū attracted most of its in-migrants from other parts of the Santama or from the central wards of Tokyo, while Musashino drew primarily on former ward dwellers or prefectural outsiders, who also made up every four in ten of the new arrivals to the Santama region and included both young people from rural Japan and older people with families from other cities in the country. The majority of the newcomers, however, about six in ten, moved to the Santama from the ward area of Tokyo Metropolitan Prefecture. In fact, so great did the exodus from the center wards become that they actually began to suffer a net decline in population after 1967. This unprecedented trend continued into the 1970s as more and more Tokyo residents sought housing in the suburban areas beyond the periphery.[1]

Although the growth of Tokyo's suburbs produced a net decline in the residential population of the wards, Tokyo's postwar suburbanization did not repeat the American experience. After World War II, the growth of suburbs in the United States occurred in large part at the expense of central cities. As new housing tracts, shopping malls, entertainment facilities, and corporate headquarters rose in the suburbs, both residents and workers fled the central cities, which have suffered—and continue to suffer—an apparently irreversible decline. The pattern of metropolitan change in Toyko after 1960 differed sharply from the American pattern, however. Despite a drop in their residential populations, the central wards witnessed con-

1. Sōrifu tōkei kyoku, *1970 Kokusei chōsa hōkoku: Tōkyō to* [1970 National Census Reports: Tokyo Metropolitan Prefecture] (Tokyo, 1972), pp. 142–156. Hereafter, 1970 National Census.

tinual growth in employment and affluence. Between 1955 and 1970, for example, the twenty-three-ward area added 2.6 million workers to its labor force of 3.3 million.[2] About one in four of the new job holders found housing in the ward area itself, but the other three in four were forced to settle in the suburbs beyond. Therefore, rather than decay of the metropolitan center, *growth* in the center and periphery—of job opportunities, commercial districts, office buildings, and government agencies—sped Tokyo's suburbanization.

The attitudes and processes underlying Tokyo's suburban expansion thus differed in significant ways from those that accompanied suburban growth in the United States after World War II. In the rapidly growing Santama region, housing, jobs, and the environment were the primary attractions for new in-migrants, some of whom explained their reasons for moving in a 1972 survey so instructive it deserves a moment's attention. In declaring their motives for migration, newcomers mentioned housing (42%), job considerations (23%), changes in marital status (15%), desire for a better environment (14%), and schools (3%). Most (59%) of those seeking housing came because their former dwellings were too small; some (15%), because their rents were too high. Job considerations affected primarily college graduates going to work for the first time and older workers being transferred. Most of those moving because of changes in marital status were young newlyweds, while those mentioning environmental reasons cited access to more sun and breezes (high priorities for people whose homes are not centrally heated or cooled), the desire for a quieter neighborhood, and an easier commute as their reasons for entering the suburbs. Schools were a consideration only for migrants in their late teens and early twenties, and for students seeking cheap rooms or apartments during their college days.[3]

These explanations for moving to suburbia are especially illuminating by contrast with the American case. Although new, spacious, readily financed housing has been a powerful lure for many suburbanites in the United States, many were also pushed, consciously or unconsciously, by subjective considerations rooted in anxieties about inner-city crime, race relations, and educational quality. None of these anxieties influenced Japanese suburbanites.

2. 1970 National Census, Vol. 6, no. 1, Part 2, pp. 575–588.
3. Tōkyō to, rōdō kyoku, *Tōkyō no rōdō* [Labor in Tokyo] (Tokyo, 1975), pp. 17–32.

The Tokyo area—center, periphery, and suburbs alike—enjoyed the lowest crime rates in the world for a metropolis its size. The problem of race was virtually nonexistent, and satisfactory educational options were available for most people irrespective of their place of residence. Released from the implicit demand to settle in a "safe" community with "good" schools, the Japanese suburbanite chose his dwelling on the basis of practical considerations: the price and availability of housing, its proximity to his work, and the physical—not the social—features of the neighborhood.

Although they were not intent on forming socially homogeneous communities of one type, Tokyo's suburbanites did promote social homogeneity of another type. By 1975 so many middle-level, white-collar workers had arrived that the occupational structure of the Santama was virtually identical to that of the ward area, with about four in ten resident workers in manufacturing and the other six in the tertiary sector. There were some differences. In the Santama (in 1970) forty thousand farmers still worked land and made up 4 percent of its labor force, while in the wards there were only twenty thousand farmers, less than 1 percent of the work force. As commercial centers, the wards had relatively more retail clerks and sales personnel, while the Santama had a larger contingent of technical and managerial workers, the white-collar commuters who jammed the Chūō Line and private commuter railways each day. In broad terms, however, the occupational structure of the Santama was virtually indistinguishable from that of the ward area by the 1970s, one mark of its maturity as an urban area.[4]

The Santama region matured in other ways also after 1960. Having emerged from a lengthy period in which residential development was the force behind expansion, its economy was relatively weak in 1960. Although it embraced 14 percent of the prefecture's population, the Santama had only 7 percent of its factories, 7 percent of its retail shops, and 12 percent of its service establishments. During the 1960s its industrial stature rose, as many large firms manufacturing automobiles, tires, and electrical products built factories. By 1970 the region still had only a tenth of the factories in the prefecture, but they employed almost a fifth of its industrial workers and they produced over a fifth of its industrial output. During the 1970s the commercial stature of the Santama increased, as many supermarket

4. 1970 National Census, pp. 181 and 378.

and discount chains, exclusive boutiques, small retail shops, and giant department stores all opened for business. Although these elevated the Santama's relative status only slightly, since the ward area also experienced marked commercial expansion, these establishments did sharply enhance the value of commercial activity in the region by introducing affluent consumerism to the suburbs for the first time.[5]

Rapid growth also introduced another feature of urban life: high land values. We noted earlier that Tokyo's costliest land in the 1930s was in the commercial district of Nihonbashi. Shifts in settlement and transportation patterns after the Pacific War reduced Nihonbashi's importance and enhanced that of the Ginza area near Tokyo Station, but, more dramatically, that of Shinjuku, a commuter mecca on the western edge of the center. In 1976, Tokyo's costliest land sat at the foot of the Takano Fruit Parlor, across from Shinjuku Station; it was valued at ¥2,560,000 per square meter (about $8,500 per square yard). Expensive as such land was, it is the narrow gap between its value and that of suburban land that is most surprising. In the 1930s, Kita Tama property was worth barely 1 percent the value of Nihonbashi land. In 1976, Kichijōji real estate was 35 percent as valuable as that in Shinjuku, yet another sign that the suburbs were closing the socio-economic gap between them and the center of Tokyo.[6]

One should not press too far, however, the apparent similarities between the wards and the suburbs. They did possess similar social and occupational structures, they did share (in settled areas) a similar physical appearance, and they were approaching an economic equilibrium. But it is also true that beneath such similarities lay marked diversity, both between the Santama region and the ward area and among the cities of the Santama itself, as the following sketches of Musashino and Fuchū suggest.

Musashino

Kichijōji is the first stop in Musashino for commuters arriving from central Tokyo; it is also the gateway to the suburbs of the Santama. First opened in 1889, it was an anonymous station on the Chūō Line for three decades, until the first spurt of suburban growth

5. Tōkyō to, *Tōkyō to tōkei nenkan* [Tokyo Metropolitan Prefecture Statistical Yearbook] (Tokyo, 1976), pp. 86–89.

6. *Asahi shimbun*, February 11, 1976, p. 17.

attracted commuters to nearby communities. Kichijōji's importance rose in 1934 when it became the terminus for the Inokashira Line, a commuter route originating in Shibuya. After the war the station attracted steadily increasing numbers of people, serving as a mecca for commuters during the week and for park visitors during weekends. By the mid-1970s over 250,000 students, workers, and housewives bustled through the station daily, hurrying to shops, offices, factories, and schools.

Alert to the commercial opportunities they created, businessmen, developers, and even Musashino's progressive mayor strived to make the business district near the station a magnet for shoppers and other visitors. By the early 1970s their efforts had borne fruit. They had methodically replaced the warren of tiny shops that had infested the area north of Kichijōji Station with multi-storied emporiums housing some of the nation's major department stores as well as many of its most exclusive boutiques. Shoppers drawn to the business style of the Kansai merchant could browse through the spacious new Kintetsu Department Store, built and operated by a private rail firm from the Osaka area. Former residents of the Shinjuku and Nihonbashi areas may have preferred the new orange symbol of Isetan, a Tokyo department chain that began exploiting the suburban market with its branch in 1971. And those from the Shibuya area who had grown accustomed to the hearty blue of the Tōkyū chain could satisfy their wants at its elegent new store around the corner from Isetan. Lingering along the way, a shopper might stop at one of many coffee shops, have a sweet at Dunkin' Donuts, a pizza at Shakey's, a sandwich at MacDonald's, or a cone at the Dairy Queen. Capstones of Kichijōji's maturity as a commercial district, such shops were a powerful lure for thousands of young strollers and middle-aged shoppers who were gradually converting the area to the commercial hub of Tokyo's western suburbs.

In exchange for its new status, its posh shops, and its modern flavor, Kichijōji's commercial district sacrificed a measure of community spirit. Merchants had once lived above or behind the small shops they operated north of the station, their children a permanent feature of the street, squatting in mud puddles, bouncing balls, riding tricycles, eating candy. With the renovation of the district, land values rose so sharply that every inch of property had to be exploited for business purposes. Moreover, many merchants were obliged to set up new shops in the basements of the large department stores, where there was no provision for housing. Forced to relocate elsewhere, over seven hundred families left the area in the late 1960s, and the merchants who had once passed both their working and their leisure hours in this neighborhood now returned only during work hours. With their permanent departure, the area lost those intangible associations that led to mutual assistance in times of need, street dances during festival seasons, and networks of political support for city council candidates. Commercial renewal had curtailed warm social relationships in the neighborhood and replaced them with the cold impersonality of a modern shopping center.

Strolling along the covered arcade that leads through the main shopping district to the Itsukaichi Road, we eventually enter the quiet, residential neighborhoods that are the hallmark of Musashino. To the north, east, and south of the commercial district, they present a common appearance. Many new, two-storied houses huddle together, peering cautiously above the high stucco walls defending them against inquisitive viewers. Some walls hide only long rows of rental flats, where young salesmen and clerks have settled before marriage and children oblige them to consider other housing. But most walls protect more spacious dwellings, the products of later years when the executives, professors, physicians, lawyers, and others who own them have had the money necessary to build the home of their dreams, and the good luck to find land at a price they could afford. While a tour of the Kichijōji residential district might lead one to think the homes owned by such families predominate, they actually account for barely a third of the city's housing units, although they set the affluent tone of the city's eastern quarter.

Moving westward along the Itsukaichi Road, we pass through an older shopping district behind which are many of the staid homes built near Seikei University, whose entrance soon greets us on the right. Sheltered in the lush green of its majestic Zelkova trees, the Seikei campus stretches northward to occupy nearly a full sub-ward of the city's area. Spacious lawns surround the cluster of university buildings in the center, skirted by gyms and an elementary school on the east and a junior and senior high school on the north, where the track, the baseball fields, and the tennis courts extend almost to the city's northern border with Nerima Ward. Ringed with tall trees, this calm, open setting is a luxury seldom encountered in Japan's densely inhabited cities.

Continuing westward, we soon enter a kind of official quarter. To the left is the once-proud town hall, built to endorse the community's rise to urban status in the 1920s. A half-century has not been kind to it. Sagging floors, high ceilings, and drafty windows afflict with constant winter colds the city workers unlucky enough to be assigned there. Most of the city's thousand-odd officials fare better, however, because the old building is surrounded by newer temporaries to house the functions that have outgrown it. For years the city's fathers have chosen to use their resources for other purposes, avoiding the monumental display so contagious among cities in Japan. But Musashino has had to succumb, too, and will soon begin building a new, high-rise structure to house its municipal offices.

Other public sites range themselves along the road traveling north from city hall. The town library, built with haste and economy in the 1950s, is haunting testimony to that carelessness today. Its sagging roof, peeling walls, and cracking foundations offer a grim invitation to residents who might travel to its awkward location to borrow books. Greater sources of pride are the expansive recreational facilities situated north of the library: a track and field site (a legacy of the Nakajima firm), a municipal swimming pool, baseball diamonds, and tennis courts.

Heavy users of these facilities are the citizens who live across the street, residents of the Midori Machi Danchi. Now more than twenty years old, the *danchi* exudes a sense of hard times. Walls and floors separating apartments are so thin that residents claim to know the affairs of neighbors on both sides and above as well. Dripping ceilings, peeling plaster, and crowded parking are pressing problems, as is the narrow space in most apartments. The three-room setting that sufficed for parents and a small baby in the 1950s pinches them and their two high schoolers today.[7]

The anomalous quality of such housing in a society so affluent must be a source of anxiety for many *danchi* residents. Having entered when they were young and aspiring, many of the heads of households in Midori Machi were by 1975 middle-ranking managerial or supervisory personnel. They had always thought they would move into something larger once the children got older, but they have not been able to, and consequently they harbor ambivalent

7. *Asahi shimbun*, July 25, 1975, p. 15.

feelings about their entrapment in the *danchi*. Familiar, homey, and cheap, it is a source of emotional and financial satisfaction. But dilapidated, crowded, and noisy, it is a snare they would happily escape. Even though it seems their comfortable incomes should permit their flight to better quarters, land prices, construction costs, and commuting demands prevent it. Midori Machi today conveys a mood of confounded malaise.[8]

Many of Musashino's other public housing units are located in this area of the city. Beyond the former site of the navy factory is a large complex of tiny apartments built by the prefecture. Another prefectural development sits between the navy site and Midori Machi's *danchi*. A third sits across the Itsukaichi Road to the south. Although public units like these house only a tenth of the city's families, they help to account for the fact that nearly half the city's households live in dwellings of two rooms or less. Having left behind the residential areas of Kichijōji, where we are most likely to find the one in three families in the city that has four rooms or more, we are now in the late-developing western reaches, where, despite the general affluence of the Japanese economy and of the residents of this very city, housing remains exceedingly small and crowded by American standards.[9]

Many residents could probably afford better housing if the house itself were their only problem. A survey of new home builders in 1974 found the average income of the middle-aged head of a household who acquired a mortgage for construction was ¥3.1 million (or about $10,000). Construction costs averaged ¥8.6 million (about $29,000), and after putting down 30 percent, the new owner's annual mortgage absorbed 22 percent of his salary. Although this was 10 to 15 percent less than his average American counterpart was having to spend for new housing in 1977, the Japanese homeowner still felt himself hard pressed in eight cases out of ten. Half had cut down on holiday excursions since buying, and a quarter had assumed extra jobs to keep up with costs. Assuming that taxes rise at slower rates than income, most of these homeowners will probably

8. For a study that provides survey findings to support these assertations about the conflicting emotions common in the 1970s among suburbanites in public housing, see Kokumin seikatsu sentaa, ed., *Toshi no seikatsu kankyō: Sono jittai to ishiki* [The Urban Living Environment: Reality and Consciousness] (Tokyo, 1975), esp. pp. 50–90.

9. 1970 National Census, pp. 595, 654, and 694.

feel less pinched with the passage of five to ten years, provided they have been able to solve the other half of the housing problem: land.[10]

Figures mentioned earlier in this chapter illustrated the high cost of land in the Kichijōji commercial district. Just as the gap between commercial land values in the downtown areas and the suburbs had narrowed between 1939 and 1976, so had the gap in average land prices. Land in the center was nearly one hundred times more expensive than Kita Tama land in the 1930s, but it was only four times more expensive by 1976, when it cost ¥85,000 (about $283) per square meter. Even though the average new suburban home was only twenty by thirty feet, someone purchasing even a very small lot to build in the Kita Tama area would have needed over $40,000. The best ways of economizing were, first, to inherit land, second, to buy a smaller parcel, or, third, to buy in Minami or Nishi Tama (where prices were 30 to 50 percent lower). Most young families had to adopt the third alternative, which explains in part why distant cities such as Hachiōji and Machida grew so rapidly during the 1960s and why Musashino's growth essentially stopped.[11]

Our tour through the city of Musashino, which began at the commercial district north of Kichijōji Station and has carried us through the better residential quarters of the east, the Seikei area, the public service section, and the *danchi* district on the old Nakajima factory sites, continues to reveal the diversity of the city as we proceed. Turning southward outside the *danchi* entrance, we travel a broad avenue that leads eventually to Mitaka Station, two blocks in front of which sits the large Yokogawa Electric Works. A walk along the narrow streets that surround it reveals many small factories, producing sub-components for the precision equipment it manufactures, as well as many small rental flats, interspersed among large lots with stately mansions.

It is not unusual to uncover an expensive suburban home sitting next to cheap apartments on one side and a small workshop on the other, with perhaps a public bath behind and a golf driving range across the street. Land use patterns in Tokyo's suburbs differ markedly from those in America because the zoning laws that produce uniform residential streets in the United States are virtually

10. *Asahi shimbun,* November 26, 1975, p. 23.
11. *Asahi shimbun,* February 11, 1976, p. 17.

nonexistent in Japan. Consequently, the owner of a major corporation might well have for his neighbors several young factory workers, the residents of a bank-owned dormitory for unmarried clerks, a
liquor store operator, and a middle-aged schoolteacher.

This in fact nearly describes one street in Musashino, and it
highlights a comment alluded to earlier. Japanese suburbanites in-
vest little energy in forming homogeneous suburbs that attract only
certain socio-economic groups. Rather, to a large extent, the availability of land shapes neighborhoods. The teacher bought land in the
1950s when it was still cheap, and the liquor dealer inherited his.
The factory workers live in a building that provides a tidy income
for a retired farmer, while the company owner and the bank are the
only ones now able to afford land for new construction. In this way,
social heterogeneity—and social anonymity—define some suburban neighborhoods in western Toyko.

The bank-owned dormitory is one of many company housing
units that give Musashino a special character. Some are small and
inconspicuous, two-storied buildings with eight or ten apartments
stuffed between homes on a quiet side street. Others are large and
modestly ostentatious, like the dormitory for single men operated by
one of Japan's largest trading firms; it stands beside the Tamagawa
Canal, its idle tennis courts providing a genteel setting for the
three-storied brick structure that sweeps gracefully around its circu-
lar driveway. Although some company housing units in the city are
designed for families, a large number provide apartments for unmarried men and women who commute to their workplaces in large
firms outside the city. As a consequence, highly mobile twenty-
year-olds make up a relatively large share of the city's population, a
share larger than in the wards and in Fuchū. This has some bearing
on political participation and partisan preferences, as later comments will note.[12]

The road that has carried us past the singles dormitory for the
trading firm soon widens, when it passes between the Tamagawa
Canal and the high embankment across the street, behind which sits
the Sakai Water Filtration Plant. Although this public facility, imposed on the city in the late 1910s, does little to enhance the natural
beauty of the area, it is a quiet neighbor to the residential areas

12. 1970 National Census, pp. 6–9.

developing on its northern and eastern edges. The general quiet is often shattered, however, by huge trucks and speeding cars that travel this road as they move westward out of the city. They encourage the walker to hop onto the curb and follow a small footpath cut alongside the canal, where we begin to notice what appear to be cherry trees. Shortly after, we arrive at a busy crossroads called Sakurabashi, which calls to mind the strolls through Musashino (mentioned in chapter 2) taken by Kunikida Doppo.

Kunikida would neither recognize nor appreciate his old haunt. Exhaust fumes from the thousands of trucks and cars that ply this road daily have damaged nearly all the fragile cherry trees between Sakurabashi and Koganei. The small shop where he once lingered over a cup of tea before his canalside stroll has long since disappeared; a seven-story apartment building stands in its place. Only in the dead of night could one hope to walk along the canal and encounter no other people, for both sides are now lined with homes that crowd against the roadways. A stroll along the canal can still be a calming, pleasant experience, but recalling the setting Kunikida described seven decades before, one must acknowledge the natural expense of Tokyo's suburban development.

Another twenty minutes' walk brings us almost to the western edge of Musashino and its other major *danchi* development, Sakura Zutsumi. Housing almost twice as many residents as Midori Machi and covering a much larger area, Sakura Zutsumi forms a community physically isolated from the rest of the city, one to a large extent self-sufficient. Two elementary schools and a middle school stand within the *danchi* compound, and the city's only public high school is situated on its eastern boundary. A small shopping district, a post office, and a supermarket provide the other amenities families need, enabling them to live in large measure separated from the farmers whose land surrounds them.

In Sakura Zutsumi, too, one gets the feeling that promise has miscarried. The residents are obviously well off. Children have new balls, bikes, and trikes; mothers dress stylishly; fathers drive late-model cars. Yet, as in Midori Machi, they face blatant daily reminders of their relatively poor housing. These buildings also are decaying too fast. They afford little privacy inside, and only a sense of crowding outside, because families are jammed in the development at rates of forty thousand persons per square mile. Residents, who are college educated and avaricious readers, know the Japan Housing Corporation is now building far sturdier dwellings of greater size and convenience, and they lament their misfortune at having gotten in here when circumstances differed. They know they enjoy cheap housing as a result; most still pay only $10 to $40 per month rent. But they also see better opportunities closed out because of keen competition for public housing and its high cost (three to four times what they now pay), and they see the vision of their own home gradually disappearing. Although more and more are resigning themselves to their fate, their resignation only stimulates ambivalence, toward social conditions generally and toward political authorities in particular.[13]

The men who commute from Sakura Zutsumi generally hop a bus that carries them in about ten minutes to the shopping district near Musashi-Sakai Station. Older than the district near Kichijōji, since it was established ten years earlier, Musashi-Sakai still retains a far more rustic feeling. One large discount store opened recently, but most stores along the main business street leading to Sakurabashi are still family shops whose owners live in. The police protection league in Sakai is still active; criers still warn of fire in the dry fall season; and merchant associations still organize street dances during festivals. The city's few farmers, who still work land mostly in this area, find these activities congenial as well. Links to the past in this section of the city thus seem stronger than elsewhere, providing an undercurrent of continuity utterly missing in the shopping center at Kichijōji or in the *danchi* at Midori Machi and Sakura Zutsumi.

South of the Chūō Line lies the last segment of the city to be explored. Designated Kyōnan Ward, or South Sakai, it is perhaps the most diversified section of the entire city. It contains two large public institutions—an animal husbandry school and the Red Cross Hospital—as well as a nurses' college and several government offices. There are two prefectural housing developments in Kyōnan, several private corporation housing units, and some apartments for government workers. In addition to cheap, tiny rental apartments that sit along the tracks near the station, there are several spacious, expensive apartment buildings nestled in wooded settings farther south. Interspersed among them are many types of private housing

13. *Asahi shimbun,* March 30, 1976, p. 21.

as well as several small shopping districts, where merchants still dwell above their shops. Not only the most diversified section of the city, Kyōnan is also the most populous, and it is heavily contested by the city's council candidates.

Fuchū

Although it is more crowded and developed, the Kyōnan area of Musashino foretells what we are about to see as we depart Musashino for a short journey to Fuchū. Most people traveling to the city arrive by train, having gone directly from Shinjuku by the Keiō Line. Others take the Chūō Line to Musashi Sakai, where they transfer to the Seibu-Tamagawa Line that carries them to the eastern part of the city, or they travel farther west to Kokubunji, from which they can take a bus to the center of Fuchū. Since our location in southwestern Musashino puts us very close, however, we might imagine we are making the journey by bicycle, following a route that many American readers who have been to Tokyo will find familiar.

Leaving Musashino, we enter the city of Mitaka. As in most suburban areas situated at a distance from rail lines, we encounter an almost bewildering variety of both rural and urban artifacts: paddy fields and baseball fields, farm homes and rental apartments, market districts and shopping centers, feed dealers and auto factories. A fifteen-minute ride carries us to a major intersection where the road descends quite sharply as we leave the tableland of the Musashino area and enter the lower hill lands of the Tama River Valley. Passing the old International Christian University golf course and skirting the rear of a small enclave of foreign homes clustered near the American School in Japan, we soon cross a narrow arm of Chōfu that borders Mitaka and enter the city of Fuchū.

From the moment we begin our descent toward Fuchū, we note a difference in the topography and begin to sense a difference in the communities. There are few hills of any kind in Musashino, but here we encounter tree-covered knolls scattered across the terrain, sharp bluffs where the land drops off to form the river valley, and long, steep hills that make biking an effort. Far more of the land here also remains under cultivation, imparting a more agrarian image that is only reinforced by the clusters of farm dwellings that greet us at many bends in the road.

Immediately on entering Fuchū we encounter other sites that symbolize its diversity and signify its special character. To the left of the road that has brought us down the bluff from Mitaka, the first thing to catch our eye is a vast stretch of two-storied, American military housing, the deserted remains of Kantō Mura. Established in the early 1960s, when another site at Yoyogi was vacated for the Olympic Games, Kantō Mura was closed in 1975. Owned in part by the central government and in part by the prefecture, it now sits idle, barracks decaying, a modern school going unused, and playing fields growing thick with weeds. Five times the size of Hibiya Park in central Tokyo, Kantō Mura forms an extremely valuable site over which many different parties are likely to compete for years to come, while local citizens anxiously hope it will be converted to a public park.[14]

The eerie feeling prompted by this alien sight is repeated again just a few minutes farther along, when we confront a mostly abandoned, former American air base. Now used by a contingent of the Japan Air Self-defense Forces, this equally vast expanse of land—site of the army arsenal built in Fuchū in 1938—sits largely vacant and unused, a haunting reminder of the days of Occupation and a disquieting neighbor to residents of the new housing developments growing up around it.

Kantō Mura and the abandoned air base are just two of many government-owned sites in the city. The Tama Cemetery occupies a corner of northeastern Fuchū that is almost as large as Musashino's entire Kyōnan Ward. The Tokyo Horse Race Track covers an area almost as large south of the city center, near which also sits the Tamagawa Boat Race Track, a public facility operated by the city of Ōme. North of the downtown area are the Fuchū Prison, the Tokyo Agricultural and Technical College, six private schools and academies, four government research offices, and three national and prefectural hospitals. When one adds to the land covered by these institutions the streets, shrines, temples, and school yards of the city, the total reaches 45 percent of Fuchū's area, or nearly half the city, all of which remains off the tax rolls.

Recognizing the dilemmas posed by so much tax-free land, Fuchū's city fathers sought during the boom years of the 1960s to

14. *Asahi shimbun,* November 27, 1975, p. 20.

increase revenues by attracting industry. They first had to persuade prefectural and national authorities to approve plans permitting industrial development in Fuchū, a task at which they succeeded after considerable lobbying. They were then successful in attracting three industrial firms—two electrical manufacturers and a major brewery—as well as many small electrical sub-contractors. By contrast with Musashino, where residential and commercial expansion dominated postwar development, Fuchū intentionally fostered industrial development with a program of boosterism promoted by political leaders.

The most important firm to build a factory in Fuchū was the Nihon Electric Company (NEC), which began operations in 1964. Covering a large site in the center of the old Nishifu village area, the NEC factory employed in the 1970s more than six thousand workers, all of them members of a union affiliated with *Denki rōren* and *Chūritsu rōren,* the same unions with which their fellow workers up the street at Tōshiba were affiliated. In a somewhat capricious fashion, therefore, the course of Fuchū's industrial development brought to the city over twelve thousand electrical workers, tied to a federation that embraced only a tenth of the nation's organized workers but fully two-thirds of Fuchū's. This was a peculiarity that would have significant implications for local politics.[15]

Having mentally wandered from our course through the city, we should return to our initial position in the eastern part where we entered. Once the village of Tama, the area has now been subdivided and labeled with evocative Japanese terms, such as Asahi Ward, Momijigaoka, and Wakamatsu. This part of Fuchū was among the earliest to develop for residential purposes, when commuters began settling here in the late 1930s. Since express trains on the Keiō Line do not stop nearby, and since access to the general area calls for a transfer or two if one is coming from the central districts, this part of the city is less appealing than others and has attracted many low-income residents. Small rental apartments girdled with corrugated iron abound, and one finds very few middle-class homes, except in those neighborhoods that are obviously the remnants of Tama's old *buraku* (hamlet). Traveling through this area

15. Tōkyō to, Tachikawa rōsei jimusho, *Shōwa 50–nendo rōdō kumiai meibo* [1975 List of Labor Unions] (Tokyo, 1975), pp. 2 and 15–18.

before the 1976 Diet election, one saw dozens of full-color posters depicting Kōmeitō candidates who would be speaking at nearby lecture halls.

Crossing over a broad, concrete thoroughfare that bears the name National Highway Number 20: The Kōshū Road, we continue south a few minutes where we enter a narrow, quiet avenue. Now called the Old Kōshū Road, this is the route built by the Tokugawa house in the seventeenth century to link their capital with the castle towns in westerly provinces. Travelers, merchants, and probably a few revelers followed this road to Fuchū during its heyday as a post town.

As we approach the center of the city, heart of the former post town, we can almost imagine we are stepping into a forgotten past. The road is now hard surfaced, of course, and the occasional gas station is out of place, but many of the buildings are reminiscent of the open-fronted stores one would have found here in the 1890s or the 1920s. Mostly two-storied structures with living quarters above displaying the colorful bedding quilts on which the merchants sleep, many shops fully expose their wares to bypassers, with no glass fronts or sliding doors to prevent customers from handling a bolt of cloth or studying a sake label. Weather-beaten signs that stretch across the buildings above their entrances assert in peeling script that this shop offers ten generations of trusted service, or that one a century of honest performance. They continue along the Old Kōshū Road for four or five blocks, and riding past them, one feels almost as if he had been set down amidst the cluttered shops of a rural market town in 1913.

Doubling back for another look, we soon discover there is more to Fuchū's business district than its old post-town shops. Turning north across the street from the *torii* that protects the entrance to the Oh Kunitama Shrine, we enter a tree-lined boulevard called Keyaki Namiki, or the Zelkova Way. Initially laid out in the seventh century to connect the temple at Kokubunji with the government's administrative offices in Fuchū, this road is now the axis along which the city's new shopping district is developing. Work is still in progress, and it is obvious that some older shopkeepers in key locations are balking at the changes development imposes, but clearly a transformation has occurred.

Sheltered in the dark shade of the Zelkova, multi-storied buildings rise on both sides of the boulevard to provide a wide range of goods and services for the city's shoppers. At the end of the war, Fuchū had only one, small bank; now the nation's three largest banks all operate new branches on this street. Three large department stores sit within several blocks of each other, separated by a spate of fruit shops, clothing stores, ice cream parlors, insurance offices, book stands, and furniture stores. At the end of the street, where the Keiō Line still crosses at road level, a tastefully modern brick building houses several firms that cater to the thousands of commuters brought daily by bus and train to its area near Fuchū Station.

Despite similarities in physical appearance, Fuchū's major shopping area conveys a different tone than Musashino's. Blessed with a more pleasant natural setting, it still lacks the mood of affluence that surrounds commercial activity in Kichijōji. There one is constantly crossing paths with suburban matrons traveling in clutches of twos and threes, their Givenchy scarves blowing softly in the breeze as they adjust shopping bags brimming with boxes from Isetan or Tōkyū. In Fuchū, one is more likely to encounter young women, tugging at their ill-fitting discount woolens as they try to appease the screaming child in a stroller stuffed with the day's fresh vegetables. Musashino's decorous shoppers have incomes suited to the top-rank department stores, exclusive boutiques, and expensive import shops common there. But in Fuchū, the second-rank department stores and old-line merchants are catering to lower-income shoppers whose needs are more basic, and possibly less profitable, but not economically difficult, because these merchants pay only half as much to rent their land as do their counterparts in Kichijōji.

Paradoxically, for a city that appears far less affluent than Musashino, Fuchū has much better public facilities. South of the central shopping district, Fuchū's public library and the adjoining local museum nestle amidst tall trees near the shrine grounds. Designed in a modern style reminiscent of traditional structures, the library has open verandahs and numerous reading rooms that seem constantly crowded with school children, university students, and local citizens. The same busy air surrounds city hall, which sits just across the street to the west. Composed of two structures, a long, narrow, three-storied building in front backed by a six-storied unit that faces the library, city hall is a modern, spacious, light-filled building that must account in some part for the high morale and courteous service its officials offer.

Fuchū also possesses another type of public facility that one occasionally sees while riding through the city. We passed the first while traversing the old Tama area. It was a new, three-storied building done in white stucco, located in a calm, tree-lined setting off one of the main roads. In 1976 there were six others at various locations in the city, situated to provide access to a maximum number of residents. Sharing similar settings, appearance, and functions, these buildings, Fuchū's cultural centers (*bunka sentaa*), are the pride of Yabe Takaji's administration.

Established for the purpose of bringing city services to its residents, the cultural centers contain branch libraries, recreational facilities for children, public bathing facilities for the elderly, lecture halls, seminar rooms, public meeting places, and service desks for a small administrative contingent. While they are a symbol of the mayor's political concern for his constituents, they are also excellent babysitters for mothers with sudden errands, attractive gathering places for retirees frittering away the day, and essential meeting places for active suburbanites planning a camping trip for their *jichikai*. In a society where legal restraints and economic priorities usually prevented their appearance, Fuchū's cultural centers are small monuments to civic pride.

Proceeding westward from the city's central district, we soon enter the area of old Nishifu village. Its agrarian air still lingers, since most of the paddy and dryland fields that make up 15 percent of the city's area are in this section. Many of the old hamlets also remain, identified by their older housing, their jumbled settings, and the farm implements and pick-up trucks that sit nearby. Physically concentrated amidst the farmland on which their residents raise vegetables for the Tokyo market, these old hamlets still harbor the physical, economic, and social traits of rural Japan.[16]

They seem almost archaic and anomalous, however, in the setting

16. Evidence affirming the parochial nature of Fuchū's farm families and small shop owners appears in Ukai Nobushige and Kawano Shigeto, eds., *Ningen to toshi kankyō: Daitoshi shūhen bu* [Man and the Urban Environment: The Metropolitan Perimeter] (Tokyo, 1975), pp. 45–49, hereafter cited as the Fuchū Survey.

that grows to envelop them. In addition to its rural hamlets, the Nishifu area also possesses the city's two largest factories, the Tōshiba plant on its northeastern corner and the Nihon Electric plant centered in its southern half. Naturally, factory workers occupy a large share of the area's housing. Many Tōshiba employees reside in the company-owned housing development south of the factory, while engineers and technicians from Nihon Electric have built homes in the developing residential area near Nakagawara Station or have acquired apartments in the large Keiō Yotsuya Danchi on Nishifu's southern edge. Following a conventional pattern, the young newcomers who have moved in such numbers to the Nishifu area since the mid-1960s have settled in their own enclaves, separated from the hamlets where native farmers and merchants reside.

Fuchū's newcomers have found it easier to buy their own homes than recent arrivals in Musashino have. Of course, in order to take advantage of the city's lower land prices, they must accept longer commuting times and other inconveniences, but they are apparently willing to do so. We thus find that 27 percent of the newcomers to Fuchū between 1965 and 1970 became homeowners, while only half as many did in Musashino. That community's rising land prices were forcing more of its new arrivals into rental units, reducing its share of homeowners, and attracting more single people and newlyweds than married couples with families. The same tendencies were under way in Fuchū, also, but prices had not yet risen so high that most new entrants were prevented from buying homes. As a consequence, a larger share of Fuchū's residents (in 1970) were married homeowners than was the case in Musashino, disparities that may account in small part for different patterns of partisan preference in the two cities.[17]

Following the bicycle path that skirts the Tama River as we leave Fuchū, we look back on our trip to recall conflicting impressions. By contrast with Musashino, Fuchū seems more rustic, especially in those areas where its farm hamlets persist as viable economic and social units, and where the dowdy commercial sections survive along the Old Kōshū Road. While it has not yet achieved the stature of Kichijōji, Fuchū's central shopping district offers promising potential that will be tapped with further development. Already

17. 1970 National Census, pp. 595–596 and 103–104.

broad tracts of land are subdivided for construction nearby; even more land is available for development along the river, in Tama, and in Nishifu. Perhaps it is this sense of potential that makes it difficult to characterize the city. Or perhaps it is the diversity, which combines small farms and large factories, old shops and new *danchi* in a single municipal setting, that leaves one, as one departs Fuchū, with the image of a city raw, unfinished, and undefinable.

Some Comparisons

Our imaginary journeys through these two Tokyo suburbs have highlighted some aspects of diversity that are apparent to the naked eye. We have noted that both cities possess a broad range of dwellings, for everyone from the wealthiest corporation executive to the poorest day laborer. In Musashino, young, unmarried commuters living in company housing, middle-aged salary men with families in old *danchi* or rental units, and wealthy elder citizens owning homes form a large share of the local populace—and the city's electorate. In Fuchū, low-income families in small rental units, factory workers in company housing, and homeowners, including both young newcomers and old-line farmers and merchants, are three dominant groups in the city's population. To understand varying patterns of political behavior in these two cities, it is helpful to acknowledge the presence of these different social groups. But it would be even more helpful to know something about their social activities and perceptions.

Thanks to invaluable surveys conducted in the early 1970s, it is possible to penetrate the physical images and statistical features of these two cities and to develop a limited sense of the attitudes, perceptions, and behavior that distinguished their residents. Undertaken in Musashino at the instance of the city government and in Fuchū on scholarly initiative, the surveys on which the following comments rely employed a common questionnaire to elicit two types of information. One type dealt with attitudes toward community, civic participation, and the political process; another type, with social and political behavior. Political findings are treated in the second part of this chapter. In the remaining pages of this part of the chapter, we shall examine findings concerning social behavior, in order to illuminate some traits common to residents of Musashino and Fuchū, and in order also to highlight a few subtle differences that distinguish these two suburbs.[18]

The attitudes of residents toward their cities illustrate the depth of some common traits. When asked how they felt about living in Musashino and Fuchū, residents in both communities replied in eight of ten cases that they thought their city was a good place to live. Such a high level of satisfaction can be explained in several ways. It might, first of all, express a resident's true feelings and indicate that people were genuinely satisfied with their habitat. It might also be a sign of the diffidence that characterizes the modal Japanese personality, and indicate only that people who have been socialized to demonstrate satisfaction with their circumstances, whether they like them or not, were offering the proper response. Satisfaction might also be a testimony to the Japanese survey respondent's desire to please; they might have expressed frequent satisfaction because they thought the interviewer expected it. Or their responses might only indicate that, in order to cope with their fate, many suburban residents had rationalized satisfaction with their conditions. Most likely a blend of all these attitudes, this high level of satisfaction is nonetheless an optimistic undercurrent that ran strongly through both Musashino and Fuchū — at least in 1970, when, it should be noted, the country was nearing the peak of an extended period of prosperity.

Residents' attitudes toward neighbors mark another common undercurrent of social perception that obtained in both cities. Interviewers asked respondents which of four comments best described their feelings about contact with neighbors. The first two responses were approving. One conveyed the feeling that among people living in the same area, neighborly contact was natural and appropriate; the other, that if you did not have such contacts in times of trouble, it could be inconvenient. In both cities, nine in ten respondents chose one or two, 74 percent of Musashino's residents and 76 percent of Fuchū's opting for the first response. Again, despite the social diversity evident in both communities, respondents in a rep-

18. The surveys are reported in the work edited by Ukai and Kawano cited above, pp. 232–246, and in Musashino shi, kikaku bu, *Musashino shimin no jichi ishiki chōsa:* 1970 [A Survey of Political Attitudes among Musashino Citizens: 1970] (Musashino, 1970), especially pp. 72–102, hereafter cited as the Musashino Survey.

resentative survey sample revealed a high measure of affinity for a social aspiration more akin to the values of rural Japan than one might expect of contemporary suburbanites.

This assertion is underscored by responses to another question that put respondents on a more uncomfortable spot and betrayed a possible gap between social aspiration and actual fulfillment. Interviewers asked respondents to imagine an instance in which they were called on to help a neighbor at the physical task of cleaning out a dirty drain or exterminating rodents or insects. In Musashino, 36 percent said they would snap to the task, 39 percent conceded they would help if pressed, and 15 percent indicated that these were jobs for the city to handle. In Fuchū, the response rates were 39, 45, and 10 percent, respectively, indications of a slightly more neighborly atmosphere in that city. Since we recognize that cleaning drains and chasing rats are naturally offensive tasks, it is noteworthy that someone could count on his neighbor's purported help, though it was offered reluctantly in many cases, eight out of ten times. It is also noteworthy that more residents in Musashino than in Fuchū alleged that these were duties for their municipality. This suggests that a contractual attitude toward social relations was somewhat more widespread in the former than in the latter, a discovery in keeping with the more urban qualities of Musashino.

This distinction was reinforced by replies to another question dealing with *jichikai* and *chōnaikai*, which asked simply if respondents thought it was better having them than not. While 76 percent of the respondents in Fuchū approved of them, and only 7 percent felt them unnecessary (with 17 percent noncommittal), only 66 percent in Musashino approved of such bodies while 12 percent were opposed (and 22 percent noncommittal). These findings are somewhat surprising. They reveal that residents of Musashino, where, as chapter 4 indicated, neighborhood organizations were relatively weak, nonetheless harbored a pervasive feeling of approval toward them. Apparently, even many progressive suburbanites possessed a lingering affection for a social body strongly identified with prewar Japan. These findings are less surprising, however, for the distinctions they reveal between Fuchū, where support for neighborhood associations ran high, and Musashino, where opposition and indifference were more pronounced.

Not surprisingly, Musashino residents perceived the utility of neighborhood associations in a fashion different from Fuchū residents. In both cases, the largest group of respondents agreed that *chōnaikai* and *jichikai* should promote spiritual and social harmony; 40 percent affirmed this claim in Fuchū while 36 percent did so in Musashino. By contrast, 26 percent of Musashino's respondents felt that these bodies should function to articulate political demands, while only 22 percent in Fuchū felt that way. Remaining respondents in both cities felt that police protection, sanitation duties, and administrative liaison justified neighborhood associations. Although the margins are narrow, it is worthwhile to note that by embracing somewhat different conceptions of the utility of neighborhood associations, residents in Musashino and Fuchū were possibly inclined to employ them differently in the political process.

Indeed, evidence of the social activities undertaken by respondents suggests they probably did employ neighborhood associations differently in the two cities, for reasons of membership, if for no other. In Fuchū, 45 percent of the respondents declared activity in a *chōnaikai* and 36 percent in a *jichikai*, for a total of 81 percent, while in Musashino the figures were only 24 and 14 percent, for a total of 38 percent. Although 38 percent is a figure higher than might have been anticipated in light of the comments made in chapter 4, the sharp distinctions between Fuchū and Musashino remain. People organized neighborhood associations and participated on a broad scale in Fuchū, while only a minority of Musashino's residents were so involved. Important political implications rose from this distinction, as the second part of the chapter illustrates.

In both cities, involvement in other kinds of social activities was rather limited. Educational groups were the most active, with alumni organizations attracting the participation of 20 percent of the respondents in Fuchū and 25 percent in Musashino, and parent-teacher groups attracting about one in five respondents in both cities. Twelve percent of the respondents in Musashino and 14 percent in Fuchū claimed membership in a labor union. These figures mask the fact that most of Fuchū's members belonged to local unions aligned with one national federation whereas Musashino's union members belonged to many different unions with offices outside the city, circumstances that made it easier to marshal union support for political candidates in Fuchū than in Musashino. But we should also note that even after adding a spouse for each declared union member, prospective union voters constituted barely a fourth of the electorate in the two cities.

The surveys revealed one type of organization in which virtually no one participated—political parties. In Musashino, 2 percent of the respondents claimed activity in a political party, and in Fuchū, only 0.7 percent. Party activists are a small group in most societies, seldom surpassing a tenth of the population, but even by international standards, these are low rates of party activity. And they are not unique to these two suburbs, which reflected quite closely national rates of party membership.[19] This fact, however, is only one of many pieces that go to make up the confounding puzzle of contemporary Japanese political behavior, to which we can now turn for a fuller examination, having developed some sense of the subtly diverse patterns of social structure, perception, and behavior that characterized these two Tokyo suburbs and their residents.

A SEGMENTING POLITY

National Politics

Segmentation was the keynote of Japanese politics after 1960. The two parties that had dominated the scene in the late 1950s had to make way for four others by the late 1970s. These included the Democratic Socialist Party (DSP), formed in 1960 when right-wing dissidents broke off from the Japan Socialist Party; the Kōmeitō, or Clean Government Party (CGP), a political group drawing its strength from the Buddhist organization called Sōka Gakkai; the Japan Communist Party (JCP), which adopted a policy of responsible parliamentary government in the 1960s; and the New Liberal Club (NLC), a Liberal Democratic Party (LDP) splinter group created in time for the 1976 Lower House election.

Among these six, the LDP remained the party in power at the national level, relying on less than half the vote and a misapportioned legislature to retain control of both houses of the Diet. Its primary challenges came from a Marxist-oriented Japan Socialist Party, a tightly organized Japan Communist Party, and an energetic Kōmeitō. The small Democratic Socialist Party fought extinction by

19. See, for example, the findings from a major national survey conducted in 1966: Ikeuchi Hajime, *Shimin ishiki no kenkyū* [Studies of Civic Consciousness] (Tokyo, 1974), esp. pp. 439–465.

trying to walk a narrow line between inherent conservatism and aspiring progressivism, a difficult balancing act, which the New Liberal Club hoped to perform more adroitly.

Within Tokyo Metropolitan Prefecture, the LDP also remained the largest single party, despite its control of only a third of the seats and less than a third of the vote by the late 1970s.[20] The divisiveness of its opponents insured its continued preeminence, since none of them controlled a commensurate share of votes or seats. The results of the 1976 election left the Kōmeitō, the JSP, and the JCP in a close competition for a roughly equal share of votes and seats, with the DSP and the NLC following behind at some distance.

Tables 16 and 17 illustrate that partisan change in the ward area was a harbinger of change in the Santama region, where segmentation also characterized party trends.[21] As in the downtown wards, the LDP retained the largest single contingent of Diet members and supporters, followed in the late 1970s by the JSP, the Kōmeitō, the JCP, the New Liberals, and the DSP. These rankings represented the temporary culmination of trends that produced a steadily declining share of the vote for the Liberal Democrats and a rising share of the vote for opposition parties, especially those of the center.

The general tendency toward segmentation after 1960 was also reflected in both Musashino and Fuchū, as tables 18 and 19 indicate. In both communities, the LDP suffered a relative decline but still ranked first on many occasions. As in the district itself, parties of the left and center experienced substantial gains in the course of the period. There were some variations between the two cities. The many middle-aged, middle-level white-collar workers in Musashino supported in relatively large numbers candidates of the two Socialist parties. By contrast, the younger, somewhat poorer new suburbanites in Fuchū offered a slightly larger base of support for the Kōmeitō.

20. The basic reference for the following discussion of national politics in the Santama after 1960 is Shūgiin jimukyoku, *Shūgiin giin sōsenkyo ichiran* [Guide to Lower House General Elections], covering elections twenty-nine through thirty-four. All voting data cited are based on this source. Biographical data are drawn from standard references.

21. Since the Tokyo Seventh District, the Santama region, had become the largest constituency in the country by 1975, the election reform law of that year divided it into two districts, the Tokyo Seventh and the Eleventh. Covering the populous northeastern quarter of the Santama, the new Seventh District returned four members and included the city of Musashino. Also returning four members, the Eleventh District encompassed the southern and western portions of Kita Tama, including the city of Fuchū, as well as Minami and Nishi Tama.

TABLE 16. *Lower House Election Results, Santama District(s), 1960–1976 (vote, by party and in percentage)*

Year	JCP	JSP	DSP	CGP	NLC	LDP	Other	Total
1960	30,227 (6)	189,113 (37)	44,514 (9)			251,055 (49)	1,059 (0)	515,968 (101)
1963	49,692 (8)	243,960 (38)	52,161 (9)			248,796 (39)	41,199 (6)	635,808 (100)
1967	93,273 (10)	306,285 (34)	90,233 (10)	110,892 (12)		263,473 (29)	34,342 (4)	898,498 (99)
1969	154,836 (17)	205,825 (22)	119,995 (13)	142,898 (16)		295,066 (32)	635 (0)	919,255 (100)
1972	208,117 (18)	309,224 (26)	134,605 (11)	167,668 (14)		326,343 (28)	28,484 (2)	1,174,441 (99)
1976	203,541 (15)	270,399 (20)		226,244 (17)	145,119 (11)	377,736 (29)	99,195 (8)	1,322,234 (100)

SOURCE: Shūgiin jimukyoku, *Shūgiin giin sōsenkyo ichiran* [Guide to Lower House General Elections], nos. 29–34 (Tokyo, 1961–1977).

NOTE: Some columns do not add to 100 owing to rounding error.

TABLE 17. *Victorious Candidates for the Lower House, Santama District(s), 1960–1976*

Year	Victors				
1960	Yamahana (JSP)	Nakamura (JSP)	Hosoda (LDP)	Fukuda (LDP)	Tsugumo (LDP)
1963	Yamahana (JSP)	Nakamura (JSP)	Hasegawa (JSP)	Fukuda (LDP)	Koyama (LDP)
1967	Yamahana (JSP)	Hasegawa (JSP)	Ōno (CGP)	Fukuda (LDP)	Koyama (LDP)
1969	Dobashi (JCP)	Wada (DSP)	Ōno (CGP)	Fukuda (LDP)	Koyama (LDP)
1972	Dobashi (JCP)	Hasegawa (JSP)	Ōno (CGP)	Fukuda (LDP)	Koyama (LDP)
1976					
7th	Kudō (JCP)	Hasegawa (JSP)	Ōno (CGP)	Fukuda (LDP)	
11th	Yamahana[a] (JSP)		Haseo (CGP)	Itō (NLC)	Ishikawa (LDP)

SOURCE: Same as table 16.

NOTE: Victors are placed in this table as they would stand on a left-to-right ideological spectrum with their positions defined by their party and intraparty factional ties. The most progressive are in the far left column, and the most conservative, in the far right. Notice how victors from the older suburbs of the densely settled northeastern part of the Santama (District 7 in 1976) reflect the more progressive voting trends in that area, by contrast with the more conservative tendencies reflected by victors from the still agricultural 11th District of the south and west. Notice also that victors from right and center parties have always been a majority, except in 1963.

[a] Yamahana Sadao, son of Yamahana Hideo, who held a seat for the JSP in the old Seventh District for nineteen years before 1969.

TABLE 18. *Lower House Election Results, City of Musashino, 1960–1976 (vote, by party and in percentage)*

Year	JCP	JSP	DSP	CGP	LDP	Others	Total
1960	3,448 (8)	18,055 (42)	5,881 (13)		15,846 (37)	76 (0)	43,306 (100)
1963	4,386 (9)	20,883 (44)	5,958 (14)		15,635 (33)	498 (1)	47,360 (101)
1967	6,884 (11)	22,279 (37)	8,527 (14)	6,289 (10)	16,904 (28)	68 (0)	60,951 (100)
1969	9,345 (18)	12,701 (24)	9,103 (17)	6,624 (13)	14,576 (28)	32 (0)	52,381 (100)
1972	10,913 (18)	17,177 (29)	8,978 (15)	6,478 (11)	14,656 (25)	1,484 (2)	59,686 (100)
1976	9,248 (16)	12,253 (21)		7,430 (13)	16,168 (28)	12,713 (22)	57,812 (100)

SOURCE: Same as table 16.
NOTE: Some columns do not add to 100 owing to rounding error.

TABLE 19. *Lower House Election Results, City of Fuchū, 1960–1976 (vote, by party and in percentage)*

Year	JCP	JSP	DSP	CGP	NLC	LDP	Others	Total
1960	1,868 (6)	11,586 (40)	3,507 (12)			12,061 (42)	85 (0)	29,107 (100)
1963	3,298 (9)	14,233 (37)	3,523 (9)			10,190 (27)	7,048 (18)	38,292 (100)
1967	5,943 (11)	19,314 (35)	6,450 (12)	7,625 (14)		14,149 (26)	1,851 (3)	55,332 (101)
1969	10,623 (19)	12,131 (21)	7,530 (13)	9,453 (17)		17,279 (30)	42 (0)	57,058 (100)
1972	13,019 (18)	18,705 (26)	7,711 (11)	10,946 (15)		19,774 (27)	1,866 (3)	72,021 (100)
1976	11,961 (14)	16,283 (20)		14,850 (18)	18,588 (22)	21,115 (26)		82,797 (100)

SOURCE: Same as table 16.
NOTE: Some columns do not add to 100 owing to rounding error.

Because the concluding chapter examines changes in partisan alignments during the entire postwar period, it is possible here to focus attention sharply on recent developments, in order to illuminate some of the mechanisms that underlay this segmented polity. For our purposes, the 1976 Lower House election offers an excellent analytical opportunity. Because of the redistricting that occurred in 1975, it is possible to examine how the several parties active in the Santama dealt with the needs to recruit new candidates, to develop organizational skills, and to promote favorable images, three factors especially important in the politics of the 1970s. By comparing the 1976 election with that of 1972, it is also possible to examine how effective parties were in retaining the support of their voters, a critical task in such a volatile political environment.

The Liberal Democratic Party did reasonably well in the 1976 election. It increased its total vote in the Santama region by more than fifty thousand and took two of the eight seats contested. Knowing it had only enough supporters in the new Seventh District to return one candidate, the party endorsed Fukuda Tokuyasu alone. Although he was seventy-one years old, Fukuda managed not only to retain the votes that went to Koyama Shōji in 1972 but even to expand the party's vote by more than seventeen thousand. The additional support probably came from DSP adherents whose party ran no candidate. A former prefectural assemblyman and industrialist from Hachiōji with his *jiban* in the southern part of the Santama, Koyama ran in the new Eleventh District, where he captured over five thousand votes more in 1976 than in 1972. In both cases, the persistence of these LDP bases offers testimony to the loyalty of LDP voters, who appeared to back their party even in the absence of their favorite candidate.[22]

Aware of the still heavily conservative vote in the western and southern reaches of the Santama, the LDP endorsed a third candidate in 1976. With ties to the powerful faction of Fukuda Takeo (the man who would become prime minister after the election), Ishikawa Yōzō was a college-educated businessman of fifty-one who had resigned his post as mayor of Ōme City to run for election. Ishikawa

22. Surveys frequently confirm the unwavering loyalty of LDP supporters over time. See, for example, Asahi shimbun sha, yoron chōsa shitsu, ed., *Nihon jin no seiji ishiki: Asahi shimbun yoron chōsa no 30–nen* [Political Attitudes of the Japanese People: Thirty Years of the Asahi Shimbun Public Opinion Surveys] (Tokyo, 1976), pp. 16–17. Hereafter cited as the Asahi Survey.

attracted considerably more voters to the polls than LDP candidates had in 1972. He was able to capture 44 percent of the vote in the Nishi Tama area and 59 percent in the city of Ōme alone, thereby adding 25,000 votes to the LDP's 1972 total in that area. When combined with the votes that formerly went to Fukuda Tokuyasu, whose *jiban* within the new Eleventh District he inherited, Ishikawa captured nearly 120,000 ballots in all. While Koyama finished a weak sixth, Ishikawa finished third and won the LDP's only seat in the Eleventh District.

With his victory, Ishikawa redeemed the past for the LDP by recapturing the conservative voters of the Santama's western and southern reaches. Some had been straying from the party, for in 1972 the LDP attracted only 40 percent of the vote in the Nishi Tama area. In 1976, thanks to Ishikawa's strong showing, the party captured 50 percent. In one respect, Ishikawa's victory was an investment in the future for the LDP. If he could defend his base in coming elections against opposition party encroachment, or, what was far more likely, against intraparty encroachment, Ishikawa would have a decade or two of Diet service ahead of him before having to retire.

However, in 1976 the LDP rejected the future in another respect. The party had the opportunity to endorse Itō Kōzuke, a businessman in his thirties with a following among new suburbanites in the booming suburb of Machida. Competition among the party's factions prevented the LDP from endorsing Itō, who was tied to the discredited Prime Minister Miki Takeo. When his hopes for LDP support failed, Itō quickly joined forces with the New Liberal Club. Although he had won barely 20,000 votes in his first, 1972 campaign, Itō captured first place among all candidates in the new Eleventh District with more than 140,000 votes. Had Itō run on the LDP ticket with party endorsement, it is conceivable that the party could have captured at least two—and possibly three—seats in the district. But hamstrung by competition among party factions and tied to a policy that favored incumbents, the LDP opted for an older, experienced politician. Once again, it forswore the opportunity to penetrate the ranks of suburban newcomers.

With no DSP candidates running in either of the new districts, the JSP had over 400,000 prospective Socialist voters (if 1972 was any indication) from whom to draw support for two candidates. The incumbent Hasegawa Shōzō, a prefectural officer of the Japan

Teachers' Union *(Nikkyōso)*, ran in the Seventh, and Yamahana Sadao, the lawyer son of former Socialist Diet member Yamahana Hideo, in the Eleventh. The two drew over 270,000 votes and both won seats. However, by contrast with LDP candidates, who had been able to transfer one man's former *jiban* to another without loss, indeed with gains in most cases, the JSP had severe difficulty reorganizing its bases. In the Eleventh District, Yamahana captured more votes in every settlement than he had in his first campaign in 1972, but his totals fell below the combined JSP totals for that year in all but two cases. He simply did not lure all of Hasegawa's supporters into his camp. Nor could Hasegawa lure Yamahana's former supporters into his. He, too, fared better in every city in the Seventh District than he had in 1972, but his vote fell behind the combined JSP total for 1972 in every case.

The Socialist performance in 1976 underscored several serious problems that party faced after the 1960s. At the heart of the problem was divisive factionalism. At least three major sub-groups existed within the party, each with its own ideological bent, policy preferences, and party supporters. Such internal dissent prevented the party from pursuing a coherent, effective set of programs. This, in turn, undercut the tenuous loyalties felt by the party's supporters, weakened further its organizational capacities, and damaged its public image.

As the 1976 election suggests, the party found it difficult to transfer votes from one Socialist candidate to another. This was a recurring problem that had also damaged party fortunes as early as the 1960s. In his last campaign in 1967, Nakamura Takaichi attracted nearly 100,000 votes. In the following 1969 campaign, it appears that his former supporters may have divided their votes among five different candidates, most of them probably going to the DSP, the Kōmeitō, or the JCP.[23] Such diffusion of the Socialist vote was not unusual. Surveys in the period indicated that former JSP supporters accounted for a large share of new recruits to the Clean Government and Communist parties.[24] These observations all suggest that one-time Socialist voters were perhaps the least likely

23. This assertion is based on a comparison of candidates' *jiban* in the 1967 and 1969 elections, drawn from *Shūgiin giin sōsenkyo ichiran.*
24. See the Asahi Survey, pp. 16–17, for example.

to maintain a permanent attachment to their party, the most likely to be attracted by new parties and candidates, and the group that collectively accounted for most of the volatility in voting trends after 1960.

The party's organizational lassitude also plagued it in the 1970s. As chapters 3 and 4 revealed, the Socialists in the Santama had never devoted much energy as a party to the demanding task of establishing a strong organization. They preferred to rely on the good services of staff officers in labor unions and labor alliances. The party itself was content to rely on personal and idealistic appeals or to rest its fortune on the tides of social change. As long as the JSP did not face serious competition for the loyalties of incoming suburbanites, its approach was successful. But as the new parties that arose after 1960 began to appeal to this constituency, techniques of mobilization used by the Socialists proved inadequate to the competition.

The JSP paid the price for its lack of interest in organization with a poor public imagery. Opinion surveys depicted the party as a carping critic that was unreliable and ineffective.[25] Its isolation from power contributed to this imagery, by preventing it from being able to reward its voters with programs they wanted. The middle-aged white-collar workers mired in their crumbling *danchi* in Musashino were among those prone to the amorphous discontent that this imagery fostered. Its poor imagery was further compounded by the party's apparent unwillingness to undertake the kind of service activities that proved so beneficial to its leading opponents.

As parties for which organization was their greatest strength, the Kōmeitō and the JCP both did very well in 1976. The former ran a new candidate in the Eleventh District, and the latter a new one in the Seventh. Both men won easily. The Kōmeitō victor in the Eleventh inherited a *jiban* of nearly 80,000 votes won by Ōno Kiyoshi in 1972. He expanded it by more than 40,000 and captured his seat with nearly 120,000 votes. Ōno also won handily in the new Seventh District. The new Communist candidate in the Seventh District inherited a base of 114,000 votes won by Dobashi

25. Asahi Survey, pp. 215–221. See also Miyake Ichirō, et al., *Kotonaru reberu no senkyo ni okeru tōhyō kōdō no kenkyū* [Research on Electoral Behavior at All Levels] (Kyoto, 1967), pp. 81, 167, and 193. Hereafter cited as the Uji Survey.

Kazuyoshi in 1972. Although eight thousand voters slipped from his net, he still captured a seat with over 100,000 votes. Dobashi, however, lost his seat by having to run in the new Eleventh District.

By comparison with the Socialists, both the Kōmeitō and the Communists did a better job of recruiting candidates, organizing supporters, and promoting a favorable image. They preferred to nominate young men in their thirties and forties, usually white-collar workers of middling status with whom suburban voters could identify. Both parties also had strong organizations at the local level. Frequently staffed by city council members, each of whom had a specific geographic base within a city, these organizations strived to provide useful services. They helped fill out forms for municipal assistance, negotiated to get children into public nursery schools, intervened with the central government to secure pensions, and generally conducted a wide range of activities aimed at meeting the needs of lower-income voters, who often supported the two parties. At election time these organizations were mobilized to contact voters, and apparently did so effectively at rates two to three times greater than did the JSP.[26] Both parties also succeeded in establishing a favorable imagery for themselves, if not among all segments of Japanese society, at least among the ardent voters who provided the core of their loyal support.[27]

This examination of Diet politics in the Santama region after 1960 can be concluded by noting the status of each major party in the late 1970s. Still the largest party in the region, the LDP preserved its strength by relying on older voters in the rural areas of the Santama for the bulk of its support. Hampered in part by factional struggles and in part by its refusal to project a new image with younger candidates, the party essentially ignored the possibility of penetrating the ranks of young suburbanites in order to expand its support in the region. It preferred a reliable past to an uncertain future. The JSP was in serious straits by the 1970s, its base shrinking in virtually every election, its meager organizational apparatus weakening

26. For one assessment of mobilization activity, see the following report on the 1972 Lower House election in Tokyo: Tōkyō to senkyo kanri iinkai, ed., *Senkyo ni kansuru seron chōsa: Dai 33-kai Shūgiin giin senkyo* [Election Survey: The Thirty-third Lower House Election] (Tokyo, 1973), pp. 73–86.

27. These claims are affirmed by the Election Survey mentioned above, and by others undertaken by the Tokyo Election Management Commission, listed in the bibliography. See also the Asahi Survey, pp. 215–221.

further, and its voters becoming more disillusioned and less loyal. A small core of persistent supporters provided a foundation still adequate to keep the party in second place, though by a constantly narrowing margin. No longer a major factor in national politics, the DSP had temporarily abandoned the local scene and probably created a valuable opening for the New Liberal Club's Itō, who undoubtedly drew on former DSP supporters in building his base. The Kōmeitō and Communist parties enjoyed loyal, but small, bases of support in virtually every city of the district. Although the JCP may have reached the peak of its strength, the Kōmeitō continued to grow in those cities where newcomers attracted to it still entered in large numbers. Both parties, however, faced widespread suspicion and animosity that made dramatic growth in the future unlikely.

Prefectural Politics

In view of the electoral strength demonstrated in Diet contests after 1960 by opposition parties, one might expect a commensurate growth in their influence in prefectural elections as well. While some growth did occur, and while many opposition candidates were elected, the strength of the opposition parties at lower levels of the political system did not measure up to their showing in national elections. The reasons for this are complicated, and differ according to the type of election under consideration.[28]

Tokyo held four gubernatorial contests between 1963 and 1975, and two men served as governor in that period. Azuma Ryūtarō won a second term in 1963, and was succeeded in 1967 by Minobe Ryōkichi, who won his third term in 1975. Azuma was aligned with the conservative Liberal Decocratic Party, while Minobe captured great attention as the first Socialist governor of Tokyo. He usually ran on an opposition party fusion ticket, drawing support from the JSP, the JCP, and sometimes from the Kōmeitō. Table 20 illustrates how the major progressive candidate fared in the prefecture, the Santama, and Musashino and Fuchū after 1963.

The table highlights one noteworthy fact about Minobe's support in the Santama. Despite his relatively great popularity, he never captured as many votes in gubernatorial elections as all the opposi-

---

28. Voting results reported in this section of the chapter are based on the official records of prefectural assembly and gubernatorial contests available at the headquarters of the *Tokyo to senkyo kanri iinkai* (Tokyo Election Management Commission).

TABLE 20. *Vote for Major Progressive Candidate for Governor,*
Tokyo Metropolitan Prefecture, 1963–1975
(in percentage of total vote)

Year	Prefecture	Santama Area	Musashino	Fuchū
1963	44	43	50	42
1967	44	50	53	50
1971	64	68	69	66
1975	50	52	57	50

SOURCE: Official reports of the Tokyo Election Management Commission.

tion parties did in the nearest Diet election. Several reasons account
for this disparity. One has to do with his political allies. Although he
often won votes from purported DSP supporters, Minobe never ran
with the endorsement of the DSP, which in Tokyo was a small, weak
party closely identified with the LDP. This undercut his ability to
draw directly on all opposition supporters. Moreover, while he also
won votes from Kōmeitō adherents, he did not always win the
unequivocal endorsement of that party, which ran its own candidate
in 1967 and lent him qualified support on later occasions.[29]

A second reason for the disparity between Minobe's showing and
that of opposition candidates in Lower House contests has to do with
the format of gubernatorial contests. Although many candidates
often run, most campaigns become a two-way competition between
a major conservative and a leading progressive. Under such circumstances, the role of party endorsements is diminished. Candidates frequently offer programs that differ only in detail, and their
attachment to a specific party becomes far less important than other
factors.

Ultimately, and especially since Minobe's ascent to power, a
candidate's personality or public image becomes the salient consideration. Even before Minobe, Azuma Ryūtarō had developed a
highly favorable imagery in the eyes of Tokyo voters through his
association with the International Olympic Committee. Minobe
shaped his public image as the moderator of a popular television
show, to which his sunny disposition and eligibility as a bachelor

29. For an analysis of Minobe's victories in 1967 and 1971 based on survey data, see
Nishihira Shigeki, *Nihon no senkyo* [Japanese Elections] (Tokyo, 1972), pp. 214–229.

drew a large female following. He also called on an impressive family pedigree, a distinguished career, and personal friendships with leading intellectuals and politicians to radiate his personality across a broad spectrum of potential supporters.[30] After Minobe had been in office for eight years, his opponent in 1975 was able to turn some of the disadvantages of incumbency against him. Contrasting himself with the older, experienced politician that Minobe was, Ishihara Shintarō promoted himself as an energetic young man capable of giving the metropolis a new look and new vitality. Combining this image with the large following he had already won as a popular novelist and rising politician, Ishihara nearly unseated Minobe.

The importance of personal attributes thus tends to overshadow party affiliations, partisan alliances, and platforms in Tokyo's gubernatorial contests.[31] In an effort to build a constituency that draws supporters from all points on the political spectrum, gubernatorial candidates couch their appeals in a broad range of terms. Frequently, therefore, voters from one party find themselves supporting a gubernatorial candidate of another which they would not normally support. This leads to a marked disjunction between the partisan breakdowns that result in governor's contests and those that are revealed by survey research or in Lower House contests.

Prefectural assembly campaigns in Tokyo also produced outcomes in which partisan balances differed from those in Diet contests, as the materials in tables 21 and 22 suggest. These disparities are explained in large part by a markedly different factor: size of the constituency. Election districts for the prefectural assembly were of two types. Some were coterminous with city boundaries, as in Musashino, which had one assembly seat throughout this period, and in Fuchū, which had one assembly seat in every election except 1969. In that year Fuchū was part of a second type of district, what might be called a regional constituency. Such districts embraced

---

30. One incisive appraisal of Minobe's career appears in Alan G. Rix, "Tokyo's Governor Minobe and Progressive Local Politics in Japan," *Asian Survey*, 15, no. 6 (June 1975): 530–542.

31. A 1975 post-election survey by the Tokyo Election Management Commission revealed that 69 percent of the prefecture's voters (and 72 percent of those in the Santama) emphasized the individual over his party, and that younger voters were more apt to do so than older. See Tōkyō to senkyo kanri iinkai, *Senkyo ni kansuru seron chōsa: Shōwa 50-nen 4-gatsu 13-nichi shikkō Tōkyō to chiji senkyo* [Election Survey: The April 13, 1975, Tokyo Metropolitan Governor's Election] (Tokyo, 1975), pp. 50–51.

TABLE 21. *Election Results for the Tokyo Prefectural Assembly, Santama Region, 1963–1977 (vote, by party and in percentage)*

Year	JCP	JSP	DSP	CGP	LDP	Other	Total
1963		240,829 (44)			282,709 (51)	28,048 (5)	551,586 (100)
1965	65,080 (9)	266,853 (38)	18,448 (3)	34,009 (5)	204,783 (29)	107,012 (16)	696,185 (100)
1969	131,971 (14)	305,361 (34)	14,897 (2)	75,806 (8)	301,377 (33)	80,746 (9)	910,158 (100)
1973	255,629 (22)	321,709 (27)	6,372 (1)	91,711 (8)	433,374 (37)	63,555 (5)	1,172,350 (100)
1977[a]	201,078 (15)	277,012 (21)		112,559 (8)	534,290 (40)	200,412 (15)	1,325,351 (99)

SOURCE: Same as table 20, and *Mainichi shimbun*, July 12, 1977, pp. 16–17.

NOTE: Some columns do not add to 100 owing to rounding error.

[a] "Other" votes in 1977 included 82,810 (6 percent) for the New Liberal Club, 21,388 (2 percent) for the *Shakai shimin rengō* (a party established by the former leader of the JSP right wing, Eda Saburō), and 96,214 (7 percent) for unaffiliated candidates.

TABLE 22. *Seats by Party in Tokyo Prefectural Assembly, Santama Region, 1963–1977*

Year	JCP	JSP	DSP	CGP	LDP	Other	Total
1963	0	6	0	0	10	0	16
1965	0	9	0	1	6	0	16
1969	1	7	0	3	11	0	22
1973	1	5	0	3	13	0	22
1977	0	6	0	3	13	1[a]	23

SOURCE; Same as table 21.
[a]The other victor in 1977 was an unaffiliated representative from Musashino's southern neighbor, the city of Mitaka, who ran with backing from the DSP, the New Liberal Club, and the *Shimin shakai rengō*.

several cities, or in the west, several towns and villages, and possessed several seats. The size of a district thus shaped the electoral battlefield and determined the tactics and strategies that the parties employed.

Small districts encompassing a single city functioned as plurality systems, and like most plurality systems, they advantaged larger parties, the LDP and the JSP. Since these two parties shared between them a majority of supporters in most single-city districts, candidates from the LDP and the JSP usually struggled in a two-way contest for a city's prefectural assembly seat, unless factional strife produced multiple candidacies from one party. When that occurred, the other major party benefited enormously, because to split the LDP or the JSP constituency in one city was virtually to guarantee a plurality to the other party's candidate.

Since even under the best of circumstances, the JCP, the DSP, and the Kōmeitō each controlled less than a fifth of the vote in a given city, it was virtually impossible for them to win a seat in competition with the LDP and the JSP, which were each likely to control at the very least 20 percent of the vote, and usually more. The three smaller parties responded to this dilemma in two ways. The DSP and the Kōmeitō simply did not run candidates when they knew it would be impossible for them to win a seat. The Communists, by contrast, always ran candidates, even if they attracted only a small percentage of the vote. Costly as such efforts were, they kept the party apparatus tuned for other contests and they built widespread support for and identity with the party, as their 1973 vote implies. These efforts, however, resulted in very few victories, as table 22 indicates.

Large districts encompassing several municipalities and possessing several seats duplicated the conditions of a Diet contest and functioned as a modified form of proportional representation. The large districts, like systems of proportional representation, advantaged minor parties, which could combine small groups of loyal supporters in several cities to accumulate enough votes in the regional constituency to return one candidate. In this way the Kōmeitō and the JCP managed to win seats from the Santama in the prefectural assembly. The LDP and the JSP also eagerly contested regional constituencies because they offered an opportunity to return more than one of their candidates to office. Such eagerness could prove costly, however. If, for example, the LDP endorsed two candidates who evenly split its 38 percent of the vote, then it sacrificed its relative strength and allowed a minor party candidate from the Kōmeitō or the JCP to take office, even though his party controlled only 20 percent or less of the constituency's vote.

Constituency size thus explains in large part the disparities among parties, by contrast with their Diet performances, and it also explains why the LDP and the JSP often won more votes in assembly contests than in Diet campaigns. When the DSP and the Kōmeitō did not run their own candidates in a district, their ostensible supporters had to vote for candidates from three other parties. Since the DSP in Tokyo was closely identified with the LDP, many of its supporters seem to have cast ballots for LDP, not JSP, candidates.[32] The position of the Kōmeitō is more quizzical. Surveys illustrate that former JSP supporters made up part of the Kōmeitō constituency. But at the same time, many Kōmeitō supporters were of conservative persuasion and frequently cast their ballots for LDP candidates when they could not support a candidate from their own party. It seems very likely that Kōmeitō supporters in the Santama thus moved in two directions, some entering the JSP camp and others—probably more—entering the LDP camp.[33] Left adrift by

32. Some direct evidence from Fuchū is available to support this assertion. Cross-tabulations of several elections in the early 1970s indicated that many DSP voters would cast ballots for conservatives or abstain before voting for a JSP or a JCP candidate. Fuchū Survey, p. 227.

33. Ibid.

party strategies adopted in response to the demands of constituency size, small-party supporters contributed importantly to the distinctions that arose in the partisan vote between prefectural and national contests.

Another factor that may have had a small effect on partisan differences in the Santama between prefectural and national elections was the rate of turnout. The average turnout in four prefectural assembly elections after 1963 was 62 percent. In the five Diet elections held after 1963, it was 63 percent. Given such rates of turnout, a difference of 1 percent could have involved as few as 60,000 voters in 1963 but as many as 120,000 in 1973. These were more than enough votes to determine many contests because often only 20,000 ballots were needed to win an assembly seat. Since abstainers were likely to be young persons who would have supported progressive candidates, the relatively lower turnout in prefectural assembly contests may have produced a slight advantage for the LDP, enabling its candidates for the assembly to do better than its Diet candidates.[34]

Assembly contests in Musashino and Fuchū after 1960 provide concrete examples that illustrate these general trends. In Musashino, Jitsukawa Hiroshi retained his seat for the JSP in every election held through 1977. His share of the vote and the size of his electoral base declined through 1973, owing primarily to keener competition from the LDP and the JCP. But they both increased again in 1977, when he captured 51 percent of the vote in a two-way contest with a young LDP councilman from one of Musashino's old-line gentry families. Despite his declining position between 1963 and 1977, Jitsukawa always commanded votes in greater number and greater proportion than did his party cohorts in Diet contests. This attests to his continuing ability to attract voters from the moderate middle and the conservative right. It also reaffirms a claim made earlier: Musashino's progressive candidates always drew votes from people who considered themselves politically conservative and supported moderate or conservative parties.

While voters in Musashino returned Jitsukawa with comfortable

---

34. Virtually all the Tokyo Election Management Commission surveys reveal that older people are more likely to vote than younger. Since older voters are also more likely to support conservative candidates, the LDP generally benefits from low turnout rates, owing to the duty-bound loyalty of its relatively older supporters.

margins year after year, those in Fuchū witnessed spirited competition for its prefectural assembly seat. A by-election held in 1961, when the city's veteran LDP assemblyman resigned to run for the Diet, attracted only 44 percent of the city's voters. Banding together behind one of their long-time officials, union members at Tōshiba turned out in force to help provide 11,243 votes for Utsuki Zenjirō, a JSP candidate who easily defeated the LDP council member running against him. Alarmed by their defeat, conservatives drew together in the 1963 contest behind Kobayashi Moichirō, the former LDP mayor, who captured 53 percent of the vote while retrieving the city's assembly seat from Utsuki's hands. Chastened by the LDP scandal of 1965, Kobayashi stepped down after just two years in office. Unable to align behind a single candidate, conservatives backed two men who split 57 percent of the city's vote between them and allowed Miyashita Takehira, also a JSP-supported union official from Tōshiba, to capture a seat with just 33 percent of the vote, the remaining 10 percent going to a Communist candidate. Advantaged by heavy conservative abstention in 1961 and divisions among their major opponents in 1965, Fuchū's Socialist forces returned two of their candidates to office in the 1960s while attracting fewer than 14,000 votes on both occasions, in an electorate that surpassed 70,000.

Gerrymandering in 1969 placed Fuchū in a regional constituency and enabled Miyashita to retain his seat in the assembly, but it left no analysis of the Fuchū vote, whose continuing diversity was displayed once again in 1973, when four candidates ran in Fuchū's reestablished one-seat constituency. Retiring from the political scene, Miyashita made way for a middle-aged organizational official named Kainokuni. The Communists, who had built a Diet base of thirteen thousand voters in 1972, ran a young party official. And the city's conservatives, true to their nature and their history, failed to agree on a candidate. One faction promoted Ōmuro Masae. Owner of a prosperous *sakaya* (liquor store) on the Old Kōshū Road, Ōmuro was the son of a prewar councilman who had played a major role in mayoralty campaigns in 1947 and 1951. He was an heir to the hardline Seiyūkai tradition in Fuchū. His opponent was a company president associated with Yabe Takaji. He represented the more moderate Minseitō tradition.

Only six in ten of the city's voters troubled to cast ballots in the

1973 assembly contest, but 59 percent of those who did supported a conservative candidate. The moderate conservative did poorly, winning about 12,000 votes. The Communist candidate surpassed him with 16,000, as did the Socialist with 18,000. The winner, with nearly 24,000 votes in an eligible electorate that exceeded 112,000, was Ōmuro Masae, who assumed Fuchū's sole assembly seat in 1973 at the age of fifty-seven. In a city where five months earlier seven in ten voters had supported opposition parties, the active support of 24,000 voters—and the abstention of 42,000 others— returned to office a man representing the most conservative wing of the nation's conservative ruling party. Running four years later against young candidates from the New Liberal Club and the JSP, Ōmuro retained his seat by capturing 47 percent of the vote in the 1977 assembly election.

Municipal Politics: Voters and Councils

The conflicting tendencies noted in electoral behavior at the national and prefectural levels, especially in Fuchū, can only be explained—if at all—by resort to local circumstances, a task to which we now turn directly. Table 23 illustrates the results of city council elections held in Musashino after 1963, and table 24, the seats won by parties in those contests. In general, partisan divisions in city council elections closely reflected trends in national elections in the city, especially after 1967, by which time Socialists had secured a base for themselves at the municipal level. The major disparity between municipal and national elections is explained by the continuing support for nonaligned candidates (listed under "Other"), some of whom were conservatives and some, progressives. Running without a party label, they could draw support in a nonpartisan spirit from voters in their immediate neighborhood, whose interests they would be expected to represent.

The preceding chapter pointed to several reasons for the weak earlier performance of progressive parties in suburban council elections. These included the disinterest that Socialist parties showed in local politics, the difficulty of recruiting candidates for an underpaid job, the inattention of the media to local politics, and the apathy displayed by recent newcomers toward politics at the city level. To these might also be added the widespread notion that local politics should be nonpartisan. For all these reasons, conservative forces

TABLE 23. City Council Election Results, Musashino, 1963–1975
(vote, by party and in percentage)

Year	JCP	JSP	DSP	CGP	LDP	Other	Total
1963	3,562 (8)	9,551 (22)	2,599 (6)	3,607 (8)	16,076 (38)	7,250 (18)	42,645 (100)
1967	4,384 (9)	14,859 (32)	2,947 (6)	4,745 (10)	11,198 (24)	8,140 (18)	46,273 (99)
1971	7,994 (15)	15,600 (29)	3,312 (6)	4,748 (9)	10,315 (19)	11,343 (21)	53,312 (99)
1975	6,624 (13)	12,620 (25)	2,447 (5)	5,618 (11)	11,500 (23)	10,823 (22)	49,632 (99)

SOURCE: Official reports of the Musashino Election Management Commission.
NOTE: Some columns do not add to 100 owing to rounding error.

TABLE 24. *Seats by Party on Musashino City Council, 1963–1979*

Year	JCP	JSP	DSP	CGP	LDP	Others	Total
1963	0	9	2	3	0	22	36
1967	4	11	2	4	13	2	36
1971	6	12	2	3	6	7	36
1975	6	10	1	4	9	6	36

SOURCE: Same as table 23.

retained control over city councils in Musashino and Fuchū (as well as virtually every other community in Japan) through the 1950s.

In the 1960s, however, virtually all these conditions changed. The JSP adopted a far more serious attitude toward local politics, especially after the important symbolic victories of Governor Minobe in Tokyo and Mayor Asukata in Yokohama. In step with Japan's growing affluence, salaries for city council members rose. By the 1970s it was possible for someone to maintain a modest living standard on a council salary, a fact that enabled more people, especially young white-collar workers, to consider a council post. As the JSP, the Kōmeitō, and the Communists began expanding their strength in local assemblies, the media directed more attention to local politics, also. And, having grown older and better settled, migrants to the suburbs were likely to pay more attention to municipal affairs.[35] For these reasons, and for others as well, older suburbs, such as Musashino, began to witness spirited partisan battles in city council elections.

Municipal elections are perhaps a closer reflection of the social conditions of political behavior than any other. Candidates are not remote figures who spend their lives outside the city. They are neighbors, customers, colleagues, and friends, people whom one encounters frequently. Council members thus personify the social complexity of a city and its political subculture. Moreover, in promoting candidates for local office, political parties reveal their methods of operation and the social bases from which they draw their support. Finally, since most observers generally agree, and most surveys confirm, that Japanese voters tend to express greatest

35. For confirmation of this assertion, see the 1975 Election Survey by the *Tōkyō to senkyo kanri iinkai*, p. 15; the Uji Survey, pp. 336 and 805; and the Fuchū Survey, p. 222.

interest in local elections, we can assume that the results of council campaigns reflect the strongest feelings that Japanese voters harbor about the election process. Granted the importance of these points, the following sketches of local parties, council members, their attributes, and the attributes of their supporters are undertaken in order to highlight more sharply the distinctive features of Musashino's political subculture.[36]

By 1975 the Liberal Democratic Party in Musashino had suffered a marked decline in its fortunes since its foundation two decades earlier. Although it had an unusually large local membership, reported by one possibly optimistic leader at nearly six hundred, the party had been relegated to a minority status in virtually every election since the early 1960s. It still remained an active group, led by energetic individuals. In addition to their political activities, local LDP leaders also engaged in a wide range of other associations. Far more than other party members, they were involved in their communities. They served on chambers of commerce, traffic safety committees, sports clubs, neighborhood associations, and police protection groups, among others. Their intensive participation was attributable in part to the long history of their families in the community, because most of them were native born, some still landlords and others shopkeepers and businessmen. Their participation was also attributable to the leisure that accompanied their wealth, because the city's LDP council members in 1975 were unanimously members of the propertied class: all nine lived either in their own homes or above their shops. The party moreover drew far more votes from high income earners than other parties in the city, relying primarily on supporters from the older residential area near Kichijōji Station and from the farming and commercial districts in Nishikubo, Sekimae, and Sakai.

By contrast, the city's JSP council members drew important strength from the postwar residential areas, especially from the city's large public housing developments in Midori Machi and Sakura Zutsumi. The JSP in Musashino straddled the full range of the middle class, drawing its support from the middle- to lower-middle income groups that comprised most of the city's residents. JSP

36. The following analysis is based on biographical data and election returns made available by the Musashino Election Management Commission and on the findings of the 1970 Musashino Survey, especially pp. 114–128.

council members were representative of the party's local constituency. They included three homeowners and two shopkeepers, as well as five apartment dwellers, three from public housing tracts. The diversity suggested by their housing indicates the breadth of social groups encompassed by the Socialist party in Musashino (while it also intimates the party's general difficulty in serving a definable constituency), and it bespeaks two unusual features displayed by the city's Socialist organization.

In contrast with the pattern of JSP organization in most cities, Musashino's Socialists were not intimately associated with the union movement, for both developmental and personal reasons. Because the city's industrial development was arrested after the war, it had few local factories or large organizations to provide a foundation for a powerful union force in local politics. Moreover, none of Musashino's most prominent Socialist politicians were products of the labor union wing of the Socialist party. The Diet member Nakamura Takaichi had established his Socialist credentials by working with the prewar tenant movement. The prefectural assemblyman Jitsukawa Hiroshi worked with a highly personalized group of supporters, although he had a brief association immediately after the war with the teachers' union. And Mayor Gotō Kihachirō had built his personal following without relying on union support. The same was true to a large extent of the city's Socialist council members in 1975, among whom only three in ten were union members and only two, union officials.

The second distinctive feature of Musashino's Socialists was their reliance on personal organizations of support *(kōenkai)*. One of the three union members on council, for example, also belonged to his local parent-teacher association and was active in a number of sports groups in his area of the city. These gave him contacts with a broad range of fellow citizens and probably assisted in his election. Six of the nine remaining Socialist candidates also belonged to parent-teacher groups. These groups did not openly endorse candidates, but they provided an organizational setting in which good will and common interests fostered support for a council candidate who could exploit such ties at election time. In sharp contrast with the national party, whose Diet candidates eschewed *kōenkai* as feudal bodies tainted by conservatism, Socialist candidates for council in Musashino relied for their success on personally organized *kōenkai*, usually based on their area of residence and an affiliation with a school group.

The Communists in Musashino bore traits commonly associated with their party. Their members were highly committed, their supporters came predominantly from lower-income groups, and their organization was well run. All six of the Communist council members after 1975 were party officials. Some were also members of labor unions and parent-teacher associations, but their party activities seemed to consume their lives. When not working as full-time council members, it was their responsibility to staff six party offices. These were located in carefully chosen sites to offer maximum geographic exposure to the party, whose council members came one from each major area of the city, where they lived in small rental units, three of them public.

Communists in Musashino demonstrated their organizational prowess both in providing services to their constituents and in managing their electoral constituency. The party was able in 1975 to capture 16 percent of the city's council seats while winning only 13 percent of the vote, by carefully marshalling support for each candidate. Only 217 votes separated the party's first-place finisher, who won 1,064 votes, from its only losing candidate, who took 847 and missed a seat by 40 votes. By contrast, the Socialist candidates who organized their support on an individual basis attracted a low of 714 and a high of 1,319 votes. With its support confined primarily to a limited segment of the city's lower-ranking socio-economic group, the JCP in Musashino exploited its base to maximum advantage in city council elections by relying on the commitment of its followers and the effectiveness of its organization.

The Kōmeitō might have done the same, but chose not to. Careful management of their 5,618 supporters in 1975 would have enabled them to win five seats comfortably, and possibly six, rather than the four they took. Instead, the party chose to build strong support for its small contingent of victors, all of whom finished in the top ten. Least likely of all party candidates to be joiners, the Kōmeitō council members were absorbed in two undertakings, their party and their religious group. Their supporters included some middle-income shop owners and professionals, but a majority were lower-income residents in clerical and technical jobs or in the retail and service trades. As was the case elsewhere in Japan, the Kōmeitō in Musashino represented the interests of a mobile and socially isolated group drawn from the lower reaches of urban society. Perhaps they saw a large plurality for their candidates as a psychic reward that salved a sense of deprivation.

One should be cautious in offering this portrait, based as it is on one survey and information concerning council members, as a full and accurate depiction of Musashino's political sociology. Nonetheless, these findings do resonate with others noted earlier and lend credence to a general image of the city's polity and society. The LDP appeared to be a small and declining group, drawing leadership from old-line families in agriculture and commerce and support from farmers, shopkeepers, and upper-level white-collar workers. Idealistic, broadly based, tolerant, and even practical (all in marked contrast to their national counterparts), Musashino's Socialists drew support from the middle-level white-collar workers who dominated the city's population. The Kōmeitō and JCP were small parties that occupied separate, but similar, corners of local society. They cultivated support from voters committed to them, most likely for religious or ideological reasons, which themselves were underlain by signs of social, economic, and psychological deprivation. To a large extent, Japan's fragmented political parties catered to the divisions in a highly variegated society, even in a wealthy, white-collar suburb like Musashino.

Returning to Fuchū for the last time to examine municipal politics after 1960, we encounter the most inconsistent electoral tendencies yet, as tables 25 and 26 illustrate. Every major party attracted significantly less support in municipal contests than did its candidates in national elections, owing, of course, to the large vote that unaffiliated ("Other") candidates won. As a result, opposition parties seldom held more than a third of the city's council seats, even as late as 1975, while unaligned members generally regarded as conservatives occupied a majority.

To understand the persisting conservative subculture in Fuchū, we can forego an analysis of each local party and turn instead to five other phenomena. Each has a bearing on partisan alignments in the city, but they all have a significance as much sociological as political. The five are the community's level of development, the organi-

TABLE 25. *City Council Election Results, Fuchū, 1963–1975*
(vote, by party and in percentage)

Year	JCP	JSP	DSP	CGP	LDP	Other	Total
1963	2,233 (5)	2,783 (7)		3,367 (8)	1,565 (4)	31,189 (76)	41,137 (100)
1967	3,960 (7)	5,718 (11)	1,809 (3)	5,532 (10)	2,459 (5)	33,918 (64)	53,396 (100)
1971	8,337 (12)	7,491 (11)	1,666 (2)	7,754 (11)	4,056 (6)	39,523 (57)	68,827 (99)
1975	7,595 (10)	11,237 (15)	2,323 (3)	10,588 (14)	6,225 (8)	36,218 (49)	74,186 (99)

SOURCE: Official reports of the Fuchū Election Management Commission.
NOTE: Some columns do not add to 100 owing to rounding error.

TABLE 26. *Seats by Party on the Fuchū City Council, 1963–1979*

Year	JCP	JSP	DSP	CGP	LDP	Others	Total
1963	2	1	0	2	1	24	30
1967	3	3	1	4	2	17	30
1971	4	2	1	4	2	17	30
1975	1	6	0	5	3	15	30

SOURCE: Same as table 25.

zational features of the local JSP, the character of the city's major labor unions, the persistence of neighborhood associations, and Fuchū's process of growth.

If events in Musashino and Fuchū are any guide to general trends, opposition parties that participate successfully in municipal politics arise well after a suburb's development. Both individual and contextual reasons account for this. People disposed to vote for opposition parties can do so easily in national contests, where party platforms, imagery, and candidates are familiar, even to newcomers in a community. But younger people moving in for the first time are preoccupied for a year or so with the practical difficulties that attend resettlement, and they are unfamiliar with the candidates and problems that dominate local politics in their suburb. Moreover, they are poorly integrated into the local community, in part because the kind of dualistic society illustrated in chapter 3 still persists in contemporary suburbs, and in part also because full participation in such local institutions as parent-teacher groups, neighborhood associations, and *kōenkai* requires time. Frequently, therefore, four to five years can pass before most new arrivals vote regularly.[37] When thousands of newcomers are moving into a community annually, and when such newcomers constitute half or more of the local populace, opposition parties find many of their potential supporters, in effect, sitting on the sidelines.

To incorporate them successfully into participation at the local level requires organization. In Musashino, Socialists initiated this effort in the 1950s, when they began building their *kōenkai,* and they won rewards for their efforts in the 1960s and after. In Fuchū,

37. The Fuchū Survey certainly confirms this observation: see table 6–14, p. 222. Also, Musashino Survey, p. 114.

JSP activists who were not tied to the union movement only began to establish *kōenkai* for council candidates in the late 1960s. One, for example, was a young white-collar worker living in a new development north of the town center, where his activities in the local parent-teacher association and *jichikai* gave him a base of contacts and support. Another was a young housewife who had formerly worked at the party's national headquarters. She, too, built a *kōenkai* by relying on school groups in her new residential neighborhood. In both cities, therefore, JSP support in municipal elections depended heavily on the personal initiative and organizational efforts of young, middle-class newcomers who were not aligned with labor unions. Such efforts often followed the initial surge of suburban growth by a decade or more.

Despite the presence in Fuchū of more than ten thousand workers affiliated with a Socialist-inclined union, this was of little benefit to the JSP in municipal elections, partly for structural and partly for ideological reasons. Council constituencies numbered between 1,500 and 2,500 voters. A large union thus could not throw all its weight behind one candidate, because in concentrating his support it would undercut other Socialist candidates. The union might have endorsed a slate of candidates, as an alternative, hoping that its members would split their vote among several men and return a small contingent of Socialist members loyal to the union cause. This did not happen in Fuchū, however, owing to the moderate nature of the major unions at Tōshiba and Nihon Electric. Rather than endorsing individuals or a slate, the unions as collective entities stayed aloof from council campaigns.

However, union members still played a role in council elections, both as voters and as candidates. Union candidates were often white-collar personnel, and they nearly always ran unaffiliated (*mushozoku*), which in Fuchū was tantamount to running as a conservative. In this way they could attract support from the shopkeepers and farmers in their home neighborhood at the same time they drew votes from fellow union members who realized they were company workers. Under these circumstances, union members as voters had several options. They could support their fellow union member and company worker out of loyalty to the union or the firm or both; they could support another Socialist candidate out of ideological loyalty to the party's cause; or they could support a known conservative from their neighborhood out of loyalty to their residential group. In exercising these various options, workers from Tōshiba and NEC sharply reduced the collective influence of their unions in electoral politics.

A fourth explanation for persisting conservative support rests with the community's social ethos, which is best described by analyzing its neighborhood associations. The most important function of such groups from a political perspective was to create a climate of social harmony characterized by informality, reciprocity, and a sense of common purpose. Neighborhood associations reduced the anonymity of urban living, preserved the psychological mood of rural Japan, and conditioned people to value their sense of social obligation. The mood created by these associations was in the end more important than any overt political actions they might have taken.

This might seem surprising, because it is often alleged that *chōnaikai* can serve as bodies to collectively promote (*suisen*) candidates to local office. Such promotion is possible in old farm villages or in long-settled urban areas, where residents share homogeneous social traits and have lived in the same area for generations. Collective promotion of a candidate for local office is more difficult in an expanding suburb, however, because people are more mobile and diverse. Individual associations, even in old rural neighborhoods or downtown districts, are likely to encompass members of all ages and all political persuasions. In the interest of retaining the *social* participation of everyone in the *chōnaikai*, sensible association leaders do not impose uniform *political* demands on their members. To do so would only breed resentment and possibly create a backlash that would destroy their intentions.[38]

Nonetheless, the mood created by neighborhood associations can be conducive to political ends. For example, a *chōnaikai* president might go out of his way to help a young housewife organize her *ikebana* (flower-arrangement) group. When he runs for city council as an unaligned conservative, she may well feel a debt of obligation to him and discharge it by casting a conservative ballot, even though she thinks of herself as an ardent Socialist. Or, the young union

38. Bradley Richardson has discovered the same to be true of *chōnaikai* in the Yokohama area. See his "Japanese Local Politics: Support Mobilization and Leadership Styles," *Asian Survey*, 7 (1967): 860–875.

official, who received funds from his neighborhood *jichikai* to buy uniforms for the Little League team he manages, might feel deeply indebted to the neighbor who interceded for him. When that man runs for council as an unaffiliated candidate, the young union official, ostensibly a Socialist, might well vote for him. Such examples are legion. Many could be cited to illustrate how neighborhood associations, often led by older men with conservative social values, can envelop people in a constraining web of obligation. Emphasizing reciprocity and social responsibility, such associations muffle the significance of issues in political contests and smother—often intentionally—the signs of partisan difference. In this fashion Fuchū's neighborhood associations nourished the continuity of a social ethos supporting the city's conservatively tinged political subculture.

Finally, the social processes underlying Fuchū's suburban development also sustained its conservative character. Musashino had from the beginning of its suburban growth in the 1930s attracted many newcomers from the ward area in Tokyo and from other cities around the country. However, owing to its role as an industrial city, Fuchū attracted through the late 1950s many newcomers from other communities in the Santama as well as many young men directly from rural areas. These people tended to be more parochial than their cosmopolitan counterparts in Musashino; they were less frequently college educated, less likely to have been exposed to urban mores, and more likely to harbor conservative social and political attitudes.[39] They cushioned the social and political shocks that sometimes accompanied large waves of suburban newcomers, and they underwrote the persistence of conservative modes of social relationship and political activity through the early 1960s, when out-migrants from the wards began entering in large numbers. Contrary to normal expectations, therefore, Fuchū's development after the war as a mixed industrial-residential suburb facilitated the continuity of its conservative subculture.[40]

39. Fuchū Survey, pp. 45–49. Also, 1970 National Census, pp. 160, 164, and 490–491.
40. When Miyake and associates conducted their survey in 1961–62, the city of Uji was much like Fuchū in the late 1950s. With a population nearing fifty thousand, Uji was undergoing the first phase of suburban growth. Miyake hypothesized that newcomers from large cities would be progressives, and those from rural villages, conservatives, but, in his words, they "could not achieve that result" with their cross-tabulations (p. 809). Since he does not present direct evidence to support this finding, one can only speculate what he meant. His own disclaimers indicate that in all probability the rural newcomers were fre-

Municipal Politics: Mayors and Policies

Yabe Takaji, mayor of Fuchū after 1962 and a candidate of the LDP, benefited greatly from this conservative ethos. When he first ran for office, Yabe captured 56 percent of the votes in a three-way contest between himself, a Tōshiba employee and long-time city council member, and the chairman of the city's JSP branch. In subsequent elections, the JSP acting alone or in coalition with the JCP promoted Yabe's opponents, but to little avail. In three straight contests, Yabe won handily by capturing two-thirds or more of the ballots, in a city where LDP Diet candidates had not taken even one-third since 1960.[41]

The strength of Yabe's support derived from many sources. He often benefited, in a way LDP candidates in Diet contests could not, from the endorsements of the DSP and the Kōmeitō, and from the votes of their supporters. Depending on their rates of turnout and the loyalty of their support, voters from those two parties could have accounted for 10 to 25 percent of the city's electorate. Yabe also benefited from the weak candidates who ran against him. In 1974, for example, the progressive was an outsider whose only former contact with Fuchū was a brief stint as a teacher at the agricultural college. Moreover, he confessed openly at the end of the campaign that he was only running to build political capital for the forthcoming Upper House election, an act that endorsed his image as a carpetbagger. And Yabe inevitably won advantages when the JCP took the leading role in his opponent's campaign, as it did in 1970 and 1974. Finding such endorsements anathema, the moderate unions at Tōshiba and NEC refused to support the progressive cause, and it is apparent that many of their members drifted into Yabe's camp.

More than party activity and weak opponents accounted for Yabe's abundant support, however. Most local observers credit

---

quently progressives, and not that urban newcomers were conservatives. One must note, however, that his entire sample was skewed toward progressives, that the total population for the test of this particular hypothesis was only 116 (at the most), and that the sample's rural in-migrants numbered only 26. In view of these problems, we can hardly call his observations conclusive. By contrast, the Fuchū Survey, testing an in-migrant sample numbering 602, reveals that early postwar newcomers were more likely to be conservative supporters in 1970 than were more recent newcomers who arrived in the late 1960s; see table 6–14, p. 222.

41. These remarks are based on the official election returns published by the Fuchū Election Management Commission.

much of his support to Yabe himself, and well they might. He is the kind of figure who electrifies a room by his presence. Short, trim, and bounding with energy, he seems to be dealing mentally with two future tasks at the same time he earnestly converses on the issue at hand. The fawning attention common among younger subordinates is tempered in his case by a mixture of reserve and awe, signs of respect for someone who conceives more new ideas at age seventy than they do at thirty. His conversation is filled with abstract platitudes about community welfare and social harmony that he obviously believes in deeply, when it is not sprinkled with incisive accounts of the city's administrative achievements supported by copious reference to statistical details. Yabe exudes an air of integrity, of efficiency, and of plain dedication to the welfare of his citizenry, in which he takes great and obvious pride. If voting returns are any indication, he has obviously communicated these traits to the city's residents with some success.

Yabe also possessed other unique personal attributes that made him a potent vote-getter in Fuchū. He called, for example, on the memory of his father's reputation in Fuchū's political history. That reputation appealed both to moderates in the conservative camp, who remembered his service as a Minseitō politician, and to progressives, for whom Yabe Jingo was the first man in the Santama to run as a proletarian candidate for the Diet. Yabe could also call on his long experience as a local administrator, beginning as a lowly clerk in 1930 and continuing without interruption until 1962, by which time he had served eleven years as assistant mayor. During those years, he had worked under both reformist and somewhat reactionary conservatives. Such experience enabled him to win the support, albeit begrudging, of both factions in Fuchū's divided conservative camp. Yabe thus saw himself, as apparently others did, too, as a logical synthesis of the city's two conservative factions, representing the idealism of his father's Minseitō tradition, on the one hand, and the pragmatism of the Seiyūkai tradition, on the other. Like few others in Fuchū, Yabe Takaji could rein in the city's fractious conservatives at the same time he embraced support from beyond LDP ranks, among Kōmeitō, DSP, and JSP voters alike.[42]

42. I am indebted to conversations with Professor Satō Atsushi of Seikei University, who has often served as a consultant to the Fuchū City government, for some of the observations noted here, as well as to Yabe Takaji himself, in an interview conducted on February 13, 1976, at city hall in Fuchū, and to a number of voters and officials in the city.

In a city where opposition parties enjoyed considerable strength, Yabe Takaji stayed in office by drawing support from outside his own party at the same time he preserved its unity. Gotō Kihachirō, his progressive counterpart in Musashino after 1963, did precisely the same thing.[43] Successful three times as a JSP council member, Gotō first ran for mayor in 1963, when he defeated the four-term incumbent, Arai Genkichi of the LDP. Arai won 44 percent of the vote while Gotō captured 56, virtually the same share the Socialist parties won in that year's Diet contest. So weakened in 1967 it could not even run a candidate, the LDP allowed Gotō a second term uncontested. The LDP did run a candidate in 1971. He attracted only 22 percent of the vote while Gotō walked off with 78 percent, a share even greater than that won by all four opposition parties in the next year's Diet election. Dismayed by this sorry showing, the LDP again sat out the 1975 election, when Gotō returned uncontested to a fourth term in office.

Gotō's secure hold on the mayoralty in Musashino attests to the firm foundation of support which that city's voters offered opposition parties after the 1960s. But it attests also to his ability to win support from conventionally conservative voters, especially in his 1963 contest with Arai. Informed local observers all agree that support from family, relatives, boyhood chums, schoolmates, shopkeepers, and farmers in the Sakai area, where his family had lived for generations, was the key to his victory over Arai. This has given rise to the popular local claim that Gotō is really not a member of the *Shakai-tō* (the Socialist party) but of the *Sakai-tō* (or the party of the Sakai area of Musashino). His powerful showing in the 1971 contest also indicated that he did indeed receive votes from the conservative camp.

Like Yabe Takaji, Gotō possessed a number of special qualities that made him attractive to local voters. He was a hometown boy, his father a local farmer who fell on hard times after the war. After completing eight years of elementary education in Musashino schools and a middle-school education at Tachikawa, Gotō had embarked on further studies, but before he could complete them, the war intervened. He chose to enter the elite suicide squads and was

43. The following sketch of Gotō is based on an interview conducted at the mayor's office in Musashino on May 14, 1976, on materials provided by the Musashino Election Management Commission, and on interviews with a number of local officials and scholars, noted in the bibliography.

awaiting assignment when the war ended, leaving him—like many members of his age group—socially and emotionally adrift, ill prepared to deal with an unpredictable new society.[44] He returned home and devoted great energy to invigorating the local shrine group and participating in traditional festivals. At the same time, he began to help with the editing of a union magazine. By 1947 he had become active in Socialist politics in his area of Musashino, the western settlement of Sakai. Soon after, he attached himself to the city's right-wing Socialist leader, Nakamura Takaichi, and entered electoral politics seriously. He won a council seat in 1951, and he made his reputation by working assiduously for his constituents, attending to their smallest demands while familiarizing himself with local affairs by riding an old bicycle everywhere. His essentially conservative personal background, his attentiveness to his constituents, and his accommodating political style were rewarded by victory in the 1963 mayoralty race.

In many respects, Gotō resembled Musashino's other major Socialist figures, Nakamura and Jitsukawa. Like them, he was able to convey an understanding of both conservative and progressive constituents, and reach accommodation with both parties. Like them, also, he relied on some voters who in other campaigns undoubtedly supported conservatives. And even in the city council, he relied primarily on a coalition of moderate members to carry through his programs. Resisting alliance with the sizeable Communist contingent (see table 24), he relied instead on DSP, Kōmeitō, and unaffiliated members to form a majority with his Socialist colleagues, most of whom, like Gotō, Jitsukawa, and Nakamura, were associated with the moderate right wing of the Socialist party. Gotō's progressive local administration thus sustained its policies on the basis of a slightly left-of-center coalition of Socialist, centrist, and unaligned council members.

In explaining the success of these two men and their long incumbencies, reference has been made to their personal traits, to the political subcultures in their respective communities, and to the personal and political groups they mobilized. Little has been said about their policies and the way they influenced support for Gotō and Yabe, but this topic must now be addressed. It is not possible to

44. For a sensitive account of the problems that men of Gotō's age and background have faced in postwar Japan, see David W. Plath, "Bourbon in the Tea: Dilemmas of an Aging Senzenha," Japan Interpreter, 11, no. 3 (Winter 1977): 362–383.

measure precisely how their policies affected their political support, because surveys of this phenomenon are unavailable. We must simply assume that policies may have played some role in their ability to retain office, while leaving aside the exact role. We can, however, assess the achievements for which they were best known in their communities, for the light this casts on their ability to attract votes from certain groups. We can also examine policies they implemented in order to evaluate the conservative or progressive nature of their achievements in office. The product of these comparisons is a set of paradoxical findings that help resolve some of the inconsistencies noted above.

Gotō's two most publicly conspicuous achievements in Musashino were his leadership in developing the shopping district north of Kichijōji Station and his success at retaining the old Green Park area for public uses.[45] The latter achievement owed something to his role as a Socialist politician in a prefecture where the governor, Minobe Ryōkichi, was also a Socialist. Finding access easier and persuasion less necessary, Gotō was able to win a political victory in a controversy (described briefly in chapter 4) that had simmered in the community for more than two decades. His success may have rested on his political ties, but the victory was one that a broad spectrum of local society could savor, for by the 1970s Japanese voters of all partisan casts were anxiously demanding more parks and recreation areas.

Former mayor Arai Genkichi had originally initiated the plans for construction of a new shopping area north of Kichijōji Station, but he had been unable to bring them to fruition during his administration. On assuming office, Gotō quickly moved to reactivate them. He negotiated personally with representatives of the Isetan Department Store, whom he persuaded to lease a multi-story building the city constructed at its own expense. Isetan's entry into Musashino's affluent consumer market sparked further developments that lured new Tōkyū and Kintetsu department stores soon after, as well as many smaller establishments. One of Gotō's main achievements, therefore, catered to commercial interests, conventionally conservative, and was aimed ultimately at fostering the economic expansion

45. Gotō also attracted considerable attention from the media in the 1970s when he tried to establish local laws to guarantee "rights to sunlight" (*nisshō ken*), aimed at protecting residents against having their homes cast in permanent shadows by new high-rise buildings. Having led to controversy and litigation, his actions on this count were innovative as policies but as yet unrealized as political achievements.

of the community. Although markedly different from the policies his party was advocating at the time, Gotō's efforts allayed conservative fears of a Socialist mayor and made his administration acceptable to a crucial segment of the city's voters.

In Fuchū, Yabe Takaji's most publicly conspicuous achievements were his cultural centers (*bunka sentaa*) mentioned earlier in the chapter. A special source of revenue made these centers possible and also made Fuchū one of the nation's wealthiest cities. The revenues stemmed from a law passed in 1951, when many municipalities were in severe financial straits and the nation's machine industries were suffering acute depression. That legislation sought to stimulate machine production by creating boat race tracks and other racing enterprises, the revenues from whose gambling concessions would go to support poor cities and towns. In the 1970s, Fuchū still derived from such sources revenues that amounted to nearly a fourth of the city's annual income.[46] Blessed with this financial margin, Yabe employed it to build public facilities that appealed to a wide range of the city's population, everyone from children using their libraries, through adults employing their meeting rooms, to elder citizens enjoying their steam baths. A unique testimony to Yabe's ingenuity as an administrator—and politician—the *bunka sentaa* of Fuchū were a manifest symbol of civic concern conveying a sense of pride and identity to the diverse array of newcomers settling in the variegated suburb.

While they engaged in promoting projects with public impact, Gotō and Yabe also pursued the obscure tasks involved in daily administration. The decisions they made in allocating municipal revenues and creating new policies provide some measure of the conservative, or the progressive, quality of their administrations. The last pages of this section present a brief comparison of aspects of their administrative activities, focusing on people-oriented, or social, services. This comparison is designed to determine which administration appeared to serve best the goals articulated in the mid-1970s by opposition parties.

We can begin with a brief survey of general activities associated with social programs. Final budgets for fiscal year 1973-74 revealed that Musashino allocated 17 percent of its expenditures to ''social

46. I am indebted to Mr. Katagiri Tatsuo, Director, Municipal Affairs Research Institute, for ferreting out this information.

welfare," and Fuchū, 24 percent. Musashino allocated another 22 percent of its budget to fund education, while Fuchū allocated 30 percent. This enabled Fuchū to operate thirteen public nursery schools, designed primarily to serve the working mother, while Musashino operated six. By contrast, Fuchū made do with a slightly higher student-teacher ratio in its elementary and secondary schools. Neither city was active in providing municipal housing. Musashino operated 154 units, which were only 0.29 percent of the total units in the city, and Fuchū, 421, or 0.76 percent of the total. Largely under Yabe's personal inspiration, Fuchū devoted substantial resources to its libraries, allocating twice as much money for library support as Musashino. In response, Fuchū's citizenry borrowed over fifty thousand volumes in 1974 while Musashino's borrowed less than five thousand. Blessed with more open space than Musashino, Fuchū had forty different public park areas, providing 3.24 square meters for each citizen. Seven sites in Musashino provided 1.28 square meters for each of its citizens. Fuchū also provided fourteen public facilities (the *bunka sentaa*, gyms, wedding halls, and civic auditoriums) for its residents, while Musashino provided six. Everyone in both cities was served by public water facilities, although in 1974 only 37 percent of Fuchū's residents and 59 percent of Musashino's enjoyed sewer facilities. With regard to these general activities, Fuchū seemed to be more attentive to the social needs of its citizenry than Musashino on virtually every count.[47]

Both cities also administered extensive programs of social welfare for babies, children, students, the elderly, and the handicapped. A detailed comparison of the services available to these groups in Musashino and Fuchū, based on the municipal handbook distributed to all households in both cities, reveals that Fuchū slightly outperformed Musashino in three of these categories, fell behind in one, and tied in the other. Since a full list comparing all services and provisions would involve us in a tedious undertaking, let us look at only one representative comparison, services provided to the elderly.[48]

47. These comparisons are based on data found in Zenkoku shichō kai, ed., *1975 Nihon toshi nenkan* [1975 Municipal Year Book of Japan] (Tokyo, 1975), and Tōkyō to, *Tōkyō to tōkei nenkan* [Tokyo Metropolitan Prefecture Statistical Yearbook] (Tokyo, 1976).

48. As sources where the citizenry would be most likely to encounter information about these services, the following comparisons are based on Musashino shi, *Watashi no benri chō: '75* [My City Handbook for 1975] (Musashino, 1975), and Fuchū shi, *Watashi no benri chō: '75* [My City Handbook for 1975] (Fuchū, 1975).

Fuchū provided the following for its residents over sixty-five. It offered low-interest loans to those who wished to remodel their homes. It provided monthly subsidies and rental beds for the bed-ridden and incontinent, as well as free diaper service for the latter. It also provided free phone service, as well as a free interphone system that enabled older persons to keep in contact with emergency agencies. The city provided annual financial assistance to old folks' clubs, amounting to ¥180,000 per club (about $600 in 1974), plus ¥400 per member. The city offered a payment of ¥8,000 annually to everyone reaching the age of sixty-five, and ¥3,000 annually to everyone in the city over the age of seventy. It also gave gifts to couples celebrating a golden anniversary and birthday presents to all over sixty-five. While some of these undertakings were obvious giveaways conceived to retain the support of elderly voters, many others were sincere, thoughtful services calculated to meet the real needs of older people.

In Mushashino elderly citizens enjoyed the following services. If they met a means test, people over sixty-five who belonged to the national health system could apply for subsidies to pay nurses. Residents over seventy were eligible for an annual grant of ¥12,000 (about $40), again if they met a means test. The city provided the same monthly assistance to those bedridden over the age of sixty-five that Fuchū did, but it made no provisions for the incontinent. Musashino gave ¥2,000 annually to those over sixty-five who wished to visit an inn. (Fuchū, by contrast, owned and operated its own seaside villa where city residents could visit at a nominal sum, resulting in a lower overall cost than that incurred by Musashino's residents traveling to a private inn.) Musashino gave those over seventy the same ¥3,000 annually that Fuchū did, and it provided free bus passes for all residents over seventy. Musashino offered a series of administrative services for its elderly. It helped them win admission to nursing homes, find jobs, and arrange for participation in voluntary activities. The city also had a "greening brigade" comprised of elderly persons who traveled about the city planting flowers and trees between 9 A.M. and 2 P.M., for which activity the city paid them ¥1,300 ($4.33) per day.

These detailed comparisons reveal how difficult it is to measure policies in the two cities, and how subjective conclusions might become. Nonetheless, with respect to its elderly, as with its young and handicapped, Fuchū seemed to offer slightly more generous benefits with fewer conditions attached than did Musashino. This was largely a tribute to Yabe's personal concern and his policy-making ingenuity. He employed the same ingenuity in serving working mothers, newborns, and young children. Gotō, by contrast, did a better job in providing assistance to children of school and college age. Having been unable to complete the college training he had begun, Gotō seemed to value education and hard work in preference to gratuitous service. On the whole, when these detailed programs are considered beside the general provision of welfare in the two cities, it appears that the conservative Yabe in Fuchū implemented policies more in keeping with progressive ideals than his Socialist counterpart in Musashino.[49]

How these different policy positions influenced voters in Musashino and Fuchū we do not know. Many surveys in Japan and elsewhere indicate that few voters cast ballots knowing—or even caring—precisely where a candidate or party stands on specific issues.[50] We should not be sanguine, therefore, in thinking that conservatives in Musashino recognized the restraint of their progressive mayor, or that Socialists in Fuchū acknowledged the innovativeness of their conservative mayor. Nonetheless, there is reason to think that some voters did appreciate the policies their mayors implemented, because enough informed observers and political activists in 1975 and 1976 remarked on Gotō's conservatism and Yabe's progressivism to confirm public awareness at least of their most conspicuous achievements. We cannot define what portion of a voter's decision was determined by his perception of a man's policies, but we can suggest that such perceptions—along with a complex set of other considerations—probably did play some role in determining whether an elderly conservative in Musashino voted for Gotō, or a young Socialist in Fuchū voted for Yabe.

The findings drawn from these comparisons are important not

49. A broader analysis of some of the topics addressed here, one that concludes with a different thrust, is Terry Edward MacDougall, "Japanese Urban Local Politics: Toward a Viable Progressive Political Opposition," in Lewis Austin, ed., *Japan: The Paradox of Progress* (New Haven and London, 1976), pp. 31–56.

50. One of the few works in English that comments on the relationship between issues and partisan change in Japan is Bradley M. Richardson, "Stability and Change in Japanese Voting Behavior, 1958–1972," *Journal of Asian Studies*, 36, no. 4 (August 1977): 675–693. See especially pages 682–683, where Richardson draws a cautious correlation between declining confidence in the LDP and rising support for the CGP and JCP.

only for an understanding of Japanese electoral behavior. They also have significant implications for our understanding of partisan change in contemporary Japan. If it is indeed true that an LDP mayor in a conservative suburb implements policies discernibly more progressive than his Socialist counterpart in an opposition suburb, then it is necessary to revise conventional views of partisan competition in Japan.

This chapter has sought primarily to describe and analyze the complex, sometimes even contradictory, political changes that occurred in suburban Santama after 1960. In pursuit of this purpose, it has employed a somewhat unconventional approach to voting studies, by relying heavily on evidence of actual political behavior reflected in voting returns that define partisan change and determine who holds office. The chapter has also examined the relationship between fluid social groups that compose communities and the aggregate consequences of their political action.

The approach in this chapter thus departs in two obvious ways from conventional survey research on voting behavior. Ordinarily, such research focuses on individuals rather than on groups, and it examines either socio-economic attributes or political attitudes or both. Although individual data can be aggregated to illuminate the behavior of certain groups bearing common socio-economic characteristics, information concerning the individual remains the ultimate point of reference. Employing data gathered from respondents to questionnaires, the survey method also examines imputed—rather than actual—behavior. It relies primarily on information reported by voters themselves rather than on concrete evidence (such as voting returns) of what they did.

Each of these approaches enjoys strengths and suffers weaknesses. The conventional method has the virtue of being more scientific, because those who employ it are better able to control variables in order to test hypotheses. Its greatest weakness is its inability to appreciate adequately the rich variety of influences that operate on voters, because of their complex social relationships, changes in their age and status, and the changing community setting in which they live. The less conventional method employed here suffers the weakness of being relatively "unscientific," and relying in part on subjective observations and intuitive reasoning, the method courts the danger of the ecological fallacy. But even one of the forerunners of a scientific politics, V. O. Key, sanctioned the necessity of such an approach when he noted that "vast areas of politics must be treated, if they are treated at all, by intuition, impression, sagacity, insight—all processes that are of the utmost importance but which yield results not readily verifiable."[51]

A brief comparison of the two techniques might illustrate their relative merits. Because researchers who employ the survey method seek primarily to predict voting behavior, they try to identify those traits in an individual that determine his voting preferences. Had someone conducted a survey in the city of Musashino in the early 1970s, he would have produced findings to indicate how persons of a given age and sex, with certain educational attainments, pursuing a particular occupation, and possessing a certain income might have voted, in an abstract sense. Correlating the attributes of many individuals with their voting preferences, this researcher might be quite successful in predicting the general outcome of most elections.

If he discovered what most other students of voting behavior in Japan discovered in the 1970s, he would have produced the following profile of one hypothetical voter. According to his socio-economic attributes, this voter is a fifty-year-old male. He possesses an eighth-grade education and operates his own small shop, where he earns an income slightly better than most of his countrymen. This person is quite likely to reply to his interviewer that he supports the Liberal Democratic Party. Finding that many like him are LDP supporters, the researcher would conclude by predicting that people from this segment of Japanese society, bearing these traits, would vote conservatively in most cases, and he would be right—usually.

However, let us inject life into this figure abstracted from a random sample and give him flesh and blood in a real social setting. Let us imagine that our fifty-year-old shop owner operates a small hardware store in the Sakai section of Musashino, one he inherited from his father, heir to a long-resident family named Gotō. Let us assume, moreover, that our shop owner finished his training at a local elementary school in 1937, and that he is something of a joiner. He still retains ties to his old schoolmates, for example, by attending

51. V. O. Key, Jr., *A Primer of Statistics for Political Scientists* (New York, 1966; originally, 1954), p. 155.

class reunions, and he is active among his fellow merchants in Sakai as an officer in the merchant association (*shōtenkai*).

It is perfectly conceivable that our shopkeeper might have voted in elections during the early 1970s as follows. In Diet contests, he cast his ballot loyally for Fukuda Tokuyasu of the LDP, not only because the president of his merchants' association was the head of Fukuda's *kōenkai* branch in Sakai, but also because he felt special satisfaction in supporting a Diet member who had graduated from Tokyo University, served in the Ministry of Foreign Affairs, and assisted Prime Minister Yoshida Shigeru. In gubernatorial contests, he voted for Minobe Ryōkichi, not his conservative opponents, primarily because Minobe's family (which had once lived in Musashino) used to buy goods on occasion from his father. He was proud to support the son of that distinguished family. Since he had maintained ties to fellow classmates who all studied under Jitsukawa Hiroshi, our shopkeeper always felt obliged to support his former *sensei* when he ran for the prefectural assembly. Gotō Kihachirō was a distant relative, so Gotō the hardware dealer supported him as mayor, although he also voted for the president of his merchants' association, a personal friend and colleague, who held one of the LDP seats on city council.

If we asked this shopkeeper which party he supported, he would say forthrightly the LDP. If we evaluated his political attitudes, we would probably find most of them quite conservative. Yet, a detailed examination of his actual voting behavior in the life setting provided by western Musashino discloses that in three of five cases he was likely to vote for acknowledged Socialists. This is just one example of the many cross-pressures that work on Japanese voters and determine their choices. The same pressures also play on individuals at the other end of the political spectrum.

Another hypothetical voter abstracted from surveys could be described as follows. He is a younger man, forty years of age. He belongs to a union at the factory where he works. Although he has only nine years of schooling, he earns a comfortable income only slightly lower than our hardware dealer's. By all rights, this man is a Socialist supporter; his age, sex, education, occupation, and organizational ties all tell us so.

Let us, however, set this young man down in Fuchū, where he arrived in 1955 to take a job in the Tōshiba factory. Raised in a small

farm village in Kyūshū, he had wanted to be a novelist while growing up, but his family's financial straits forced him to take a job
early. He had given up his ideals and dedicated himself whole-
heartedly to his work at Tōshiba, where he had risen to become an
officer in the union. He and his wife have recently purchased a new
home in the Yotsuya area of old Nishifu village, where many of their
neighbors are farmers. They have two boys now, aged ten and
twelve, both as energetic as their father.

This man made the following political choices in Fuchū during
the early 1970s. Having always supported Nakamura Takaichi, a
right-wing Socialist, he faced great difficulty in transferring his
support to one of the other Socialists from the district. Nakamura
had close ties to his union and was a moderate. The others,
Hasegawa and Yamahana, were associated with the left wing of the
party, whose views he did not appreciate. Nonetheless, when his
union decided to endorse Yamahana's candidacy, he cast his ballot
reluctantly for him. In the preceding gubernatorial election, he had
voted for Ishihara, despite Minobe's Socialist endorsement, because
he liked his youthful, energetic style and felt Tokyo needed a
change. Although he was not pleased about Miyashita Takehira's
successor, he nonetheless supported him because he won the union's
endorsement. Learning that Yabe's opponent for mayor had long-
standing ties to the Communists, our Socialist union member felt
serious misgivings. As he thought about the cultural centers that
Yabe had built, he decided Yabe was not so bad, even though he was
an LDP politician. After all, it was nice to have the boys playing
there after school and not crashing around their small apartment
while he recovered from work and his wife cooked supper, probably
using a little meat she had bought from the corner shop. Run by the
father of a conservative council member, the shop offered discounts
to anyone who joined his son's *kōenkai*. After equivocating for
some time, our factory worker had finally followed his wife into this
organization, because the council member had used his influence to
get a small park for their area and to improve some of its muddy
streets.

Just as the hardware dealer presented himself as a loyal conservative, this factory worker would have claimed with equal sincerity
that he was a Socialist. Like the hardware dealer, he was subject to a
variety of different pressures. Some stemmed from his union affilia-

tion and resulted in less than happy choices. Others stemmed from ideological positions. While he accepted the goals of the union movement so ardently supported by postwar Socialists, he could not accept the extreme ideas of Marx or what he felt were the radical policies of the Communists. This deterred him from supporting left-wing Socialists in some cases, and it made supporting a conservative like Yabe more palatable. Anxious to avoid what he perceived to be impending isolation in his new neighborhood, he decided to support a conservative council member. Such support offered an entree into local society, and it might provide tangible benefits for his sub-community, where city services still fell short of legitimate needs.

These two hypothetical voters might strike the reader as extreme examples, and they are. The hardware dealer and the factory worker are moved by attitudes, experiences, and relationships that are unique to them. But equally contradictory pressures operate on virtually every Japanese voter, repeating in different social contexts the dilemmas these two men face as they try to make their voting choices, decisions so complex they make generalization exceedingly difficult.

One final example of how unique attitudes, experiences, and relationships complicate generalization is provided by an anecdote about an elderly voter.[52] Throughout the campaign, this older woman passed daily by the small office young Socialist workers used as their headquarters. Although they noticed her wanderings, they ignored her and made no attempt to solicit her vote; they imagined that—like other elderly women—she was a staunch conservative. However, on the day after the campaign, she stuck her head in the door while passing by to tell the dejected Socialists she had voted for their defeated candidate. She explained that they deserved her support because, like good boys and girls, they breakfasted frugally on a hot cup of bean curd soup!

In closing the chapter with these remarks, it has not been my purpose to denigrate voting studies based on survey research, or to argue that explanation of Japanese voting behavior is impossible. It is certainly difficult, and to achieve that end voter surveys are an

52. A young official from the Fuchū Labor Alliance recounted this story in an interview on February 16, 1976.

essential tool, but they are not sufficient. In order to interpret Japanese voting behavior it is necessary to supplement conventional methods with others that sensitively examine phenomena that have come to be overlooked, such as candidates, their personalities, their organizational affiliations, the developmental level of regions and communities, and the distinctive political subcultures that survive in many parts of Japan—as well as the amorphous collage of traits and attitudes that bear on individual voters. Having done all this, we may not be able to predict voting results more successfully than before, but we hope we will have understood more about the complex pressures—emanating from individual, group, and community relationships—that motivate and shape Japanese electoral behavior.

Finally, if it is indeed true that Japanese voters often cast their ballots for a politician because he is a distant kin, because he comes from their neighborhood, or because his supporters eat the proper breakfast, then relationships among the voting choice, partisan change, and party policies become even more difficult to fathom. This study suggests that—paradoxically—one suburban mayor aligned with conservative parties was responsible for policies substantively more progressive than another mayor aligned with opposition parties. The diverse criteria that voters apply when they cast their ballots seem to offer local executives this kind of latitude in implementing their programs. The result is a weak correlation between partisanship and policies, if we may generalize boldly from our two cases.[53]

We might therefore conclude that the content of municipal policies in Japan will display great diversity over the coming decade. Such policies may well be more a product of the personal concerns of local executives and the developmental state of their communities than a reflection of a party program or, as in the past, of central government directives. If this speculation is correct, then even dramatic partisan shifts in particular campaigns might lead to little or no alteration in the substance of policies, especially at the local level, but possibly also at the national, as comments in the concluding chapter suggest.

53. A fuller, more systematic treatment of this claim appears in the chapter by Ronald Aqua in Kurt Steiner, Ellis Krauss, and Scott Flanagan, eds., *Political Opposition and Local Politics in Japan: Electoral Trends, Citizens' Movements and Progressive Administrations* (forthcoming).

six

CONCLUSION

The American political scientist Robert A. Dahl has called politics "a side-show in the great circus of life. Even when citizens use their resources to gain influence, ordinarily they do not seek to influence politicians but family members, friends, associates, employees, customers, business firms and other persons engaged in non-governmental activities."[1] A student of Japanese political behavior has also remarked recently on "the peripheral nature of politics for most people" while noting that "politics may be . . . a minor component of people's lives."[2] If politics are indeed this unimportant, then we must acknowledge that electoral behavior—merely one sporadic diversion in the political side-show—is a relatively modest part of the human undertaking.

However unimportant they might seem in the general scheme of things, politics and electoral behavior remain fascinating, intractable subjects for study. The voting choice culminates in the deceptively simple flick of a switch or the jotting down of a name, but it is preceded by a set of conscious and unconscious, formal and informal actions whose understanding challenges the ingenuity of the best researchers. It sometimes seems that their prolific output has only heightened the inexplicability of voting behavior. One analyst perhaps anticipated their dilemma over four decades ago when he noted that "the study of politics can lead to no once-for-all accomplishment, no gratifying certainty; it can give some measure of

1. Robert A. Dahl, *Who Governs?* (New Haven, 1961), p. 305.
2. Bradley Richardson, reviewing a book by Joseph Massey, in *Journal of Japanese Studies,* 3, no. 2 (Summer 1977): 450.

orientation for the incessant reappraisal of the shifting lines of communal insecurity.''[3]

These words remind us how risky it is to offer any interpretation of political change. It is perhaps even more risky to draw broad conclusions from a case-study of two communities. But one can be too tentative and apologetic. Although this study deals with only two among more than two hundred suburbs in contemporary Japan, it seems warranted to use its findings as a point of departure from which to discuss issues bearing on national politics. After all, political and social changes in Musashino and Fuchū have conformed broadly to those in other suburbs; they clearly distinguish the two from small rural villages, on the one hand, and large metropolitan centers, on the other. Moreover, subsequent remarks make clear that partisan change in the Santama has also conformed closely to trends in other suburban areas. Until studies of more suburbs are available, therefore, we can hope the conclusions drawn from this study will, to use Lasswell's words, "give some measure of orientation" for our own "reappraisal of the shifting lines of communal insecurity" in contemporary Japan.

Each chapter has dealt in differing degree with four aspects of electoral politics: participation, mobilization of voters, the role of voluntary organizations, and the recruitment of leaders. It will be helpful to summarize briefly the findings concerning these topics, before considering partisan change and its implications.

Political participation can assume many forms, but this study has focused almost exclusively on two of its aspects: the laws that determine voting eligibility and the rates of turnout that result.[4] From the purely legal perspective, Japan has broadly expanded eligibility since its first national election in 1890, when barely one percent of the nation's populace was able to cast a ballot. Extending the suffrage to all males over twenty-five in 1925, then to all men and women over twenty in 1946, Japan increased the size of its electorate so that it included nearly two-thirds of the citizenry by the 1970s. Moreover, following a half-century during which it had im-

3. Harold D. Lasswell, *Politics: Who Gets What, When, How?* (New York, 1958; orig. 1936), p. 178.
4. For one recent, complex typology of participation see Sidney Verba and Norman H. Nie, *Participation in America* (New York, 1972).

posed rather severe residential requirements on its voters, the country after 1950 greatly relaxed such laws, making it possible for all but the most recently mobile residents to participate in both national and local elections.

Citizens in the Santama responded to the voting opportunity in different ways before the Pacific War and after.[5] In the six Lower House elections held between 1928 and 1942, 83 percent of eligible voters turned out on average. While 84 percent of Fuchū's voters cast ballots during this period, only 73 percent of Musashino's did. The twelve postwar elections between 1947 and 1976 attracted an average turnout of 67 percent in the district at large, 68 percent in Fuchū, and 61 percent in Musashino. Unfortunately, materials are not available to permit prewar and postwar comparisons of turnout rates for prefectural and local contests. Postwar returns do illustrate that 72 percent of Fuchū's voters turned out on average for city council elections between 1955 and 1975, while only 57 percent did so in Musashino.[6] In general, therefore, discernibly lower rates of turnout distinguish postwar from prewar elections.

High voting rates in the prewar period are conventionally explained by reference to the strong sense of duty felt by Japan's voters. Schooled to support the state and practiced at deferring to their social superiors. most prewar voters appeared loyally at the polls in order to fulfill their roles as political subjects. These habits of mind still persist among some Japanese voters, especially among those born before the mid-1930s, and they explain in part why older people are still more likely to vote than younger persons in their twenties and thirties.

One might argue that the lower rates of turnout in the postwar period are proof of a citizenry with a weaker sense of its subject orientation and its political duty, and some evidence affirms this.[7] It is quite common for as many as one in five abstainers to express

5. Turnout rates in Diet elections are based on data from Shūgiin jimukyoku, *Shūgiin giin sōsenkyo ichiran* [Guide to Lower House General Elections], nos. 16–34 (Tokyo, 1928–1977). Those for municipal elections are taken from official returns available at the election commissions in Musashino and Fuchū.

6. Different levels of political interest and involvement as well as different patterns of political orientation account for disparities between turnout rates in Musashino and Fuchū. But such disparities are also explained in part by the high rates of population turnover in Musashino, where as many as three or four in every ten residents move annually, by contrast with notably lower rates in Fuchū. Such high rates of mobility promote disinterest, restrict eligibility, complicate registration, and increase the likelihood of administrative error.

7. These remarks on participation in the Santama are based on Musashino shi, kikaku bu, *Musashino shimin no jichi ishiki chōsa: 1970* [A Survey of Attitudes toward Local Govern-

cynical attitudes about politics and voting as the reason for not casting a ballot, while another one in five often reveals political disinterest as the reason for abstention. It seems, therefore, that part of the declining turnout that characterizes postwar voting in Tokyo and its suburbs is attributable to a diminishing sense of political duty, complemented by a growing sense of individual autonomy, rising cynicism, and some measure of political apathy.

However, the majority of abstainers fail to vote, owing not to psychological but to practical causes. While findings differ from election to election, they often indicate that people cite the following reasons for abstaining. At any election some 10 to 20 percent of the abstainers are unable to reach the polls because they are sick or bedridden. Another 10 percent indicate they are ineligible because they did not receive the proper voting card, neglected to register, or moved too recently prior to an election. Another portion of abstainers, often as many as 20 percent, cite temporary absence as a reason for not voting. The final 20 percent indicate they are simply too busy to vote. This explanation is especially understandable in the case of suburban commuters. Because the polls open at seven in the morning and close at six in the evening, most commuters must either reach work late or leave work early if they wish to vote. This difficulty undoubtedly contributes to the unusually low rates of turnout that characterize voting in Musashino, where two in every three employed residents commute to work.

Taking note of findings like these, some observers have concluded that white-collar workers living in the suburbs do not participate very actively in politics.[8] Closer observation proves this conclusion hasty and oversimplified, however, as several types of evidence indicate. In Musashino, for example, white-collar workers were heavily concentrated in the two *danchi* in Midori Machi and Sakura Zutsumi. Nonetheless, precinct returns for the period 1953 through 1969 indicate that voters in those two areas turned out at rates that exceeded the citywide average on every occasion.[9] A survey following the 1975 Tokyo gubernatorial election found that some types of white-collar workers were more likely

ment among Musashino City Residents] (Musashino, 1970), pp. 103–110; on the Fuchū Survey (see n. 16, chap. 5, above); and on the five surveys by the *Tōkyō to senkyo kanri iinkai* cited in the bibliography.

8. See, for example, Ezra F. Vogel, *Japan's New Middle Class* (Berkeley, 1967), p. 98, and Nobutaka Ike, *Japanese Politics* (New York, 1972), p. 101.

9. Musashino Survey, p. 24.

to vote than farmers, who usually turn out very loyally.[10] Finally, a survey of over one thousand white-collar workers in Tokyo conducted in 1965 revealed that 80 percent or more of the respondents claimed to vote in Diet elections.[11] Some allowance must be made for the two latter sources of evidence because survey respondents tend to exaggerate their actual voting habits when confronted with a face-to-face question. Nonetheless, the evidence from Musashino offers persuasive proof that some white-collar suburbanites did indeed turn out at fairly high rates for elections of all types.

If high rates of abstention do characterize white-collar suburbanites, they are attributable not simply to their occupational status but to their age and residential mobility. Election reports from Fuchū, for example, illustrate that young people in their twenties abstained at rates much higher than those of people in their thirties, forties, and fifties.[12] Survey data also confirm that 40 percent of those in their twenties were likely to abstain in the 1970s, while only 10 to 20 percent of those over thirty confessed to abstention.[13] Moreover, as was mentioned earlier, longer residence in a community sharply increased the likelihood that a citizen would vote.[14] Generally, therefore, married white-collar workers in their thirties and above who had lived for many years in a suburb were likely to vote at rates that exceeded the suburban average. Young, unmarried, white-collar workers who had not yet settled in a permanent residence were likely, on the contrary, to turn out at very low rates in all types of elections, and especially in local elections. The very low voting rates in Musashino's municipal campaigns can therefore be partly explained by its disproportionate share of young, unmarried suburbanites.

Lower rates of political participation in Tokyo's postwar suburbs were not simply the result of a declining sense of duty. Certainly, the strong sense of duty that characterized voting in the prewar period had diminished, to be replaced by feelings of apathy and cynicism

10. Tōkyō to senkyo kanri iinkai, *Senkyo ni kansuru seron-chōsa: Shōwa 50-nen 4-gatsu 13-nichi shikkō Tōkyō to chiji senkyo* [Election Survey: The April 13, 1975 Tokyo Metropolitan Prefecture Gubernatorial Election] (Tokyo, 1975), p. 38. Hereafter, 1975 Election Survey.

11. Watanuki Jōji, *Nihon no seiji shakai* [Japan's Political Sociology] (Tokyo, 1967), pp. 162–177.

12. Fuchū senkyo kanri iinkai, *Fuchū shichō senkyo no kiroku* [Returns of the 1974 Fuchū Mayoralty Election] (Fuchū, 1974), pp. 32–36.

13. 1975 Election Survey, p. 38.

14. Ibid.

on the part of some voters. But most abstainers were the victims of practical difficulties imposed by the social and economic realities of a dynamic society. Commuting patterns, working demands, life-cycle imperatives, and residential changes appear on the surface to explain why most voters abstained, thus suggesting that socio-economic causes contributed as much to low turnout rates as did marked changes in political attitudes.

Social and economic changes have also played a crucial role in determining how political parties have mobilized their supporters. In some respects, such changes have facilitated the growth of na-scent parties; in other respects, they have damaged the position of entrenched interests. And in every respect, social and economic changes have obliged political parties to adapt and innovate as they seek to mobilize the vote.

Socialist parties benefited more than any others from social change in Tokyo's western suburbs. From the advent of suburban development in the 1920s through the early phases of its maturity in the 1960s, Socialists found themselves the unwitting benefactors of an influx of new voters disposed to cast their ballots for the opposi-tion. Inclined by virtue of their age, their education, their migratory experience, their social status, their occupations, and their organiza-tional ties to be Socialist supporters, these new suburbanites nourished a nascent Socialist movement in the 1930s and early 1940s, propelled its electoral fortunes in the late 1940s, and brought it to a temporary crest of power in the 1950s and 1960s. Without a rigorous organizational apparatus and in the absence of strong party discipline, Socialist parties—and the Japan Socialist Party in particular—were able to enhance their strength in the Santama and some of its cities by relying, almost passively, on the salutary politi-cal consequences of suburban development.

In time, the organizational lassitude of the JSP and its indiffer-ence to the demands of its supporters proved costly. Although the party realized during the 1960s that progressive local executives offered an excellent opportunity with which to demonstrate its abilities and refute its critics, its efforts may have come too late. Unable to respond effectively to the needs and often unarticulated concerns of its natural political constituency, it frittered away its promise, promoted the growth of political cynicism, and undercut its attraction not only to new voters but to older supporters as well.

Nourished too long with only the thin fare of idealism and rhetoric, once-loyal Socialist supporters began to drift away from the party under the influences set in motion by the segmenting polity of the 1960s.

Two parties profited from the Socialist backlash, the Kōmeitō and the Japan Communist Party. In the course of a few short years, both built strong bases of support in national and local elections. By the mid-1970s, their representatives in some legislative bodies (especially the Lower House and municipal assemblies) stood on an almost equal footing with Socialist delegates. It is no coincidence that these parties enjoyed two strengths the Socialists did not have. As the second part of chapter 5 illustrates, they commanded effective organizations and they offered valued services.

The Liberal Democratic Party also excelled at these tasks. Relying in large measure on lingering attachments to individual candidates and the persistence of a subject orientation toward politics, this party was able to retain its dominant position in Santama politics through the 1950s, and even through the 1970s in some cities. Enjoying both the advantages of uninterrupted power on the local scene and affiliation with national leadership, the LDP and its activists in the Santama were able to provide constituents with tangible services, the spoils of office, and a strong sense of identity with a party that could get things done. By combining this practical ability with support derived from voters habitually loyal to it, the LDP was able to retain power and to increase its absolute strength, although it suffered a drastic decline in its relative position.

Its relative decline was not the function of a weak organization.[15] In those areas of the Santama where conservatives had historically enjoyed loyal support, and among those groups in suburban cities that had always been supportive of conservative politicians, the LDP was extremely effective in mobilizing its vote. Decline was attributable to the party's unwillingness, or possibly its inability, to

15. It is important to correct what is a general misperception of LDP organizational strength in the suburbs, suggested, for example, in Frank Langdon, *Politics in Japan* (Boston, 1967), p. 131. He notes that young conservatives can encounter difficulty in establishing bases "in the burgeoning new urban districts in the suburbs of large cities *where traditional organization* is weak and the population fluid." (My italics.) Among the members of its historical constituency, "traditional organization" is strong, at least as far as organizational strength among Japanese parties is concerned. LDP organization is weak *among newcomers,* because owing to inability, indifference, or both, the party has failed to penetrate the ranks of young, new suburbanites, who, when utterly ignored, gravitate toward the opposition.

penetrate effectively the ranks of newcomers to the area who were not previously a part of its supporting network. The failure of conservative parties to embrace newcomers to the region was not damaging during the 1930s and 1940s. But by the 1950s, when newcomers dominated the local populace, indifference toward their recruitment spelled inevitable decline, owing to the political consequences of suburban development and social change. Even in the 1970s, when the simple act of endorsing Itō Kōzuke as an LDP candidate offered an opportunity to establish support within a different segment of suburban society, the party retreated to the rural hinterlands, preferring to tap the assured strength of its historical base rather than attempt the challenge of mobilizing new supporters.

Social change obliged even the conservative parties to adapt their mobilization techniques, leading them to establish new kinds of organizations that would preserve their electoral strength in a changing society. In the rural villages of the Santama district, such adaptation was less essential. There conservative politicians could rely on networks of political activists who marshalled support by organizing voters in territorial units, farm villages where families had lived in close interdependence for generations. In such areas the party continued to employ techniques the Santama *sōshi* had first devised nearly a century before. In the rapidly changing urban areas of the region, however, conservative politicians established personal support organizations *(kōenkai)* that sought to draw together people who shared the perceptions, aspirations, and social attachments that identified loyal conservatives. Neighborhoods having grown too diverse socially to permit organizing them in their entirety, conservatives attached themselves to or drew support from such organizations as merchants' associations *(shōtenkai)*, traditional sports, dance, and recreation clubs, chambers of commerce, fire squads, and police protection leagues, the kinds of bodies in which they could hope to find the older voters who shared their political outlook.

In municipal elections conservative politicians were also able to exploit the supportive features of another type of voluntary organization, the neighborhood association *(chōnaikai* or *jichikai)*, as chapters 4 and 5 illustrate. Like the rural hamlet, *chōnaikai* aided conservative electoral purposes because they brought together people living in close proximity who shared the cultural values, educational backgrounds, occupational callings, and political attitudes that identified conservative supporters. The *chōnaikai* magnified their influence under certain circumstances, moreover, by enveloping others in the web of obligation and duty that characterized the associations' undertakings. In this fashion, younger citizens who were inclined to vote for opposition parties found themselves, sometimes intentionally, sometimes inadvertently, lending support to conservative candidates and causes.

One organization that arose after the Pacific War remained a vehicle of support for opposition parties. Labor unions in Japan emerged under the impetus of Socialist leadership, and they never lost their identity with the Socialist cause. Although Socialists never succeeded in winning the unanimous loyalty of all union voters, union organizations usually offered their nominal support to candidates of the opposition, in particular those of the JSP, the DSP, and the JCP.

The political effectiveness of union strength varied dramatically, however, depending primarily on the type of election and the economic structure of a community. In the suburbs of the Santama, union strength was confined largely to those communities, such as Fuchū, which had large concentrations of organized, resident workers, and to elections in which large groups of union members could be drawn together in support of single candidates, such as Lower House elections and regional constituencies in prefectural assembly contests. But even where union strength was concentrated, as it was in Fuchū, it offered no assurance of electoral support for the opposition. Although labor unions were closely identified with progressive political forces in this part of Japan as elsewhere, union groups acting collectively and union members acting individually provided electoral support for candidates of many partisan persuasions.

One reason why labor unions have not served either in the Santama or elsewhere in Japan as an impregnable source of opposition strength since the 1950s is that rising affluence has promoted political moderation in working ranks. Studies of workers in Japan's auto industry, for example, have shown that they moderated their political allegiances significantly in step with their growing affluence.[16]

16. Gary D. Allinson, *Japanese Urbanism: Industry and Politics in Kariya, 1872–1972* (Berkeley, 1975), esp. chaps. 5–8; and, by the same author, "The Moderation of Organized Labor in Postwar Japan," *Journal of Japanese Studies*, I, no. 2 (Spring 1975): 409–436.

The same appears to have occurred in Fuchū, especially at the Tōshiba factory, where a worker's nominal base pay increased fifteen times over in the two decades between 1956 and 1975, producing a rise in real income that can only be called phenomenal.[17] Although further evidence would be helpful, we may reasonably conclude that the improved economic position of workers in a community like Fuchū contributed to their electoral support of an LDP mayor and unaligned council members, as well as moderate Socialists.[18]

The partisan tendencies of Fuchū's organized workers highlight a fundamental problem that confronted Japan's progressive parties after the early 1960s: How could a party premised on inequity survive when the policies of an established regime were reducing inequity for the party's key constituents? The Japan Socialist Party failed to grasp this problem and to conceive programs to resolve it. On one hand, the growing affluence of organized workers brought them closer to management's views on economic questions, and often on political issues as well. On the other hand, the inability of the JSP to address its programs toward the increasingly affluent industrial worker and his white-collar counterpart either allowed natural constituents to drift away, or, in some cases, may actually have driven supporters away. As a result, despite inconsistent and ambivalent behavior, some organized blue- and white-collar workers after the mid-1960s rejected radical alternatives in order to support either moderate parties of the center or the established party of the right. And some, those who despaired completely of the possibility for reform, simply stopped voting.

The citizens' movements that have attracted so much attention recently in Japanese politics are notably absent from the foregoing discussion of suburban Tokyo. They have not been discussed because neither in Musashino nor in Fuchū did persisting organizations growing out of citizen protests serve as enduring actors in

17. These figures are based on data provided by an official of the Tōshiba Fuchū Labor Union.

18. The disparate partisan identities of workers in the Tōshiba enterprise are documented in a rare survey commissioned by its union: Tōshiba rōdō kumiai, *Tōshiba kumiaiin no ishiki: Sono jittai to kōzō bunseki* [The Attitudes of Tōshiba Union Members: Empirical and Structural Analysis] (Kawasaki, Kanagawa, 1973). This study also affirms that a large share of Tōshiba workers, about 40 percent, were homeowners with savings, a fact all the more remarkable when it is realized that 53 percent of the respondents were under age twenty-nine.

electoral campaigns. This is attributable in large part to the sharply focused interests of such groups, to the requirements for internal unity that prevent their participating in partisan politics, and to the short-lived, terminal nature of the movements themselves.[19]

Although citizens' movements have not had widespread influence on electoral politics, in some communities men who developed reputations as leaders of such movements have gone on to enjoy successful political careers.[20] Identity with such a movement is often an effective means of eliciting support from voters who would like a change, in the same way that promotion of a young, new candidate can lead to a change in party fortune. Indeed, after the mid-1960s, those parties able to promote younger men for national office in the Santama districts were nearly always rewarded, especially the Kōmeitō, the JCP, and the New Liberal Club.

By contrast, the LDP and the JSP were seriously hampered by their attachment to what has been called the "incumbent first" principle.[21] Obliged by party rules to endorse incumbents, irrespective of their age, the LDP found it difficult to promote the new candidates it apparently needed in the Santama to attract votes from the younger suburbanites who dominated the populace. The JSP, also, was hampered on occasion by its allegiance to incumbents, especially in the case of Nakamura Takaichi in the early 1960s. The retirement of Yamahana Hideo and the succession of his son, on the other hand, permitted the continuity of a base associated with a particular candidate while transferring its leadership to the hands of a younger man. In general, however, the preference for incumbents restricted parties in their choice of candidates and inhibited their ability to promote men with attributes that suburbanites seemed to prize.

Other practices imposed different kinds of constraints on the parties. The LDP and its conservative predecessors in the Santama always preferred two types of individuals for national office: either

---

19. Two illuminating articles in English that deal with citizens' movements are Margaret McKean, "Citizens' Movements in Urban and Rural Japan," in James W. White and Frank Munger, eds., *Social Change and Community Politics in Urban Japan* (Chapel Hill, 1976), pp. 61–100, and Donald R. Thurston, "Aftermath in Minamata," *Japan Interpreter*, 9, no. 1 (Spring 1974): 25–42.

20. See the chapter on Mishima by Jack G. Lewis in Kurt Steiner, Ellis Krauss, and Scott Flanagan, eds., *Political Opposition and Local Politics in Japan* (forthcoming).

21. Gerald L. Curtis, *Election Campaigning Japanese Style* (New York, 1971), esp. pp. 22–32.

experienced local politicians (usually large landlords or wealthy businessmen) or prominent men with national or international, and often bureaucratic, experience. In selecting Diet candidates, the JSP seldom strayed from the principle of choosing men from labor union backgrounds. The popular impression that these two parties represented rather narrow interests was probably confirmed after the 1960s by the type of candidates the Kōmeitō, the Communists, and the New Liberals put forward. Often upwardly mobile members of the middle class, they appealed to that broad segment of voters who found it difficult to identify personally either with the LDP candidate and his privileged background or the JSP candidate and his union career. Increasing segmentation of parties, which brought with it increased opportunity for political candidacy among men of middling status, therefore served to highlight the political shortcomings of recruitment policies the LDP and JSP had long pursued.

These remarks are less applicable, however, to candidate recruitment at local levels. If we may use mayoralty candidates in Musashino and Fuchū as an illustration, they signify that candidates for municipal office were perhaps most advantaged by a strong local identity. Those lacking such an identity, with its attendant foundation of local support, such as Moriya Senzō in Fuchū, found reelection difficult if not impossible. Those possessing such an identity—such as Arai Genkichi (scion of a prominent gentry family), Gotō Kihachirō (descendant of an old-line farm family), and Yabe Takaji (son of a prominent local politician)—usually enjoyed lengthy terms of service. As discussions in chapters 4 and 5 illustrate, these men relied on far more than native birth to build their electoral constituencies. But this does not deny that local origin was an almost indispensable attribute for successful municipal politicians, even in suburban communities where newcomers predominated.

The suburbs examined in this book witnessed a broad range of changes in electoral behavior, especially after the Pacific War. Rates of political participation declined, owing both to changes in attitudes among voters and to the practical demands of suburban living. Parties were obliged to adopt new techniques of mobilization, and did so in varying fashion with mixed success. Some voluntary organizations (such as *kōenkai* and *chōnaikai*) served to bolster the political standing of entrenched, conservative interests, while others (labor unions) benefited opposition parties, though in less than uniform fashion. Finally, the recruitment of new political candidates and the failure to recruit new candidates both had direct influence on partisan changes in the Santama.

To assess the significance of these changes, concluding remarks in this chapter will focus primarily on party performance in Lower House elections, the most important battleground on which parties wage their contest for power. The trends of partisan change in Musashino and Fuchū justify this approach. We have noted marked disparities in partisan strength at the municipal level in the two communities, but these peculiarities are explained at some length in chapter 5. The disparities narrow at the prefectural level, and they virtually disappear in national contests, where partisan tendencies in both cities adhered closely enough to district-wide trends to permit the drawing of conclusions on the basis of Diet returns for the Santama region as a whole.

Partisan trends in all of Japan's suburban districts provide a second justification for this approach. A comparison of table 27 with tables 16 and 17 reveals striking similarities in party strength between the two districts of the Santama and all sixteen of Japan's suburban constituencies. Indeed, in three cases parties won exactly the same share of the vote in the Santama that they captured in all suburban constituencies, and in two other cases there were differences of only one and four percentage points. The major disparities arose because no DSP candidates ran in the Santama districts in 1976 and because unendorsed candidates took a relatively large

TABLE 27. *Lower House Election Results, All Suburban Districts, 1976 (number and percentage of seats won, and percentage of vote, by party)*

	JCP	JSP	DSP	CGP	NLC	LDP	Other	Total
No. of seats won	4	15	5	12	8	16	0	60
% of seats won	7	25	8	20	13	27	0	100
% of votes[a]	15	20	8	17	12	25	2	99

SOURCE: *Asahi shimbun,* December 7, 1976, p. 8.

NOTE: Returns for the following sixteen districts are included in the totals above: Chiba 1 and 4; Tokyo 7 and 11; Saitama 1 and 5; Kanagawa 1, 2, 3, 4, and 5; Osaka 3, 4, 5, and 7; and Hyogo 2.

[a]This column does not add to 100 owing to rounding error.

share of the total vote. Given such similarities, we may claim with some assurance that conclusions based on evidence from national elections in the Santama district are, in a broad sense, applicable to most of suburban Japan in the late 1970s.

Suburban trends on the national level deserve a moment's attention. The long-term trends that produced the partisan divisions of 1976 closely paralleled those in the Santama. The LDP, for example, saw its share of all suburban voters slip from 53 percent in 1958 to 32 percent in 1972, before reaching a historic low of 25 percent in 1976. Likewise, the JSP reached a peak of strength in other suburban districts during the early 1960s, only to see its share of the vote decline to 22 percent in 1972, before reaching a new low of 20 percent in 1976. And the Communists, too, duplicated the pattern of their Santama performance in all suburbs, by expanding from only 4 percent in 1958 to 18 percent in 1972, before dropping to 15 percent in 1976. The three parties of the center displayed mixed performances in all suburban districts, just as they did in the Santama, with the Kōmeitō the only one to show steady gains.[22]

Several features of table 27 warrant special comment. Although the JCP won 15 percent of the suburban votes in 1976, it took only 7 percent of the suburban seats, two in the Tokyo area and two more in Osaka. This discrepancy is explained by the party's election strategies. The JCP ran candidates in every district, whether or not they had a chance of winning. Many failed by wide margins to capture a seat, but their combined vote gave the party a respectable share of the total. The JSP also ran candidates in every district, but—contrary to past practice—the party rigorously limited candidates to one per district, a tactic that paid off with victories in all but one constituency. The DSP contested eight districts, winning in five, three of which were in Tokyo's southwestern suburbs and two in Osaka suburbs. The CGP contested fifteen districts and won in twelve.

The New Liberal Club put on the most startling performance in Japan's suburban districts. The party ran eight candidates in the suburbs and all eight won. Five came from the suburban crescent lying southwest of Tokyo in Kanagawa Prefecture, where the leader

22. These findings are based on election returns published in the *Shūgiin giin sōsenkyo ichiran,* and they treat the following districts before 1975: Chiba 1, Tokyo 7, Saitama 1, Kanagawa 1–3, Osaka 3–5, and Hyogo 2.

of the party, Kōno Yōhei (and his father before him), had his electoral base. The victories of these new conservatives came in some measure at the expense of the JSP and, of course, at the expense of the party's progenitor, the LDP. Its share of the suburban vote dropped from 32 percent to 25 percent, and its share of suburban seats fell from 34 percent to 27 percent, between 1972 and 1976.

As this study has demonstrated, opposition parties enjoyed considerable strength in suburban Japan by the late 1970s. Table 28 illustrates that the LDP, which drew 42 percent of the national vote, attracted only 25 percent in the suburbs. By contrast, all opposition parties except the JSP did better in suburban districts than in the nation as a whole. The Communists, the Kōmeitō, and even the DSP all fared better in suburban districts than nationally, and the NLC won fully three times more votes in the suburbs than it won nationwide.

We can attempt to summarize changing patterns of partisan allegiance in Japan's suburbs over the past three decades by looking first at table 29, which presents the results of twelve postwar elections according to three categories, the left (the JCP and the JSP), the center (including the Kōmeitō, the DSP, and the New Liberal Club), and the right (the LDP). The percentage of votes won by unaligned or unendorsed candidates appears in the fourth column under "Others." Let us examine the electoral achievements of these three partisan elements in turn, after considering for a moment recent trends among unaligned candidates.

Trends of change in column four of table 29 suggest that a special contemporary phenomenon may have been at work in the electoral politics of suburban Tokyo. Unaligned candidates won 1 percent of the vote in 1969, doubled that share in 1972, and quadrupled their showing in 1976. This could indicate the growth of an independent

TABLE 28. *Lower House Election Results, Nationwide and Suburban Districts, 1976 (percentage of vote, by party)*

	JCP	JSP	DSP	CGP	NLC	LDP	Other	Total
All Districts	10	21	6	11	4	42	6	100
Suburban Districts[a]	15	20	8	17	12	25	2	99

SOURCE: *Asahi shimbun*, December 7, 1976, p. 8.
[a]This column does not add to 100 owing to rounding error.

TABLE 29. *Lower House Election Results, Santama District(s),*
1947–1976 (percentage of vote by partisan category)

Year	JSP+JCP	CGP+DSP+NLC	LDP	Others	Total
1947	46		51	3	100
1949	25		60	15	100
1952	31		63	6	100
1953	33		61	6	100
1955	34		59	6	99
1958	41		53	5	99
1960	43	9	49	0	101
1963	46	8	39	6	99
1967	45	22	29	4	100
1969	39	29	32	0	100
1972	44	26	28	2	100
1976	35	28	29	8	100

SOURCE: Shūgiin jimukyoku, *Shūgiin giin sōsenkyo ichiran* [Guide to Lower House General Elections], nos. 23–34 (Tokyo, 1948–1977).
NOTE: Some columns do not add to 100 owing to rounding error.

constituency disillusioned with the established parties and anxious to form a new, nonpartisan role for unaligned candidates. Certainly Japan, like the United States, was experiencing a marked increase in the number of voters who reported no identity with any party and who preferred to think of themselves as independents.[23] Moreover, the cynicism provoked by the Lockheed scandal in Japan may have increased rejection of established parties in the same way the Vietnam war and the Watergate incident did in the United States.[24]

Such speculation must be dismissed, however, because the Santama district offered little proof for such assertions. The growth in unaligned votes was the product of new candidates who always create differences in the "Other" column until a figure establishes himself or until he retires in despair. In 1972, most of the unaligned votes went to Itō Kōzuke. Running for the first time as an unendorsed conservative, he attracted only a small share of the vote in an effort obviously aimed at building a constituency that would enable

23. Gary D. Allinson, "Japan's Independent Voters: Dilemma or Opportunity?" *Japan Interpreter,* 11, no. 1 (Spring 1976): 36–55.
24. Norman H. Nie, Sidney Verba, and John R. Petrocik, *The Changing American Voter* (Cambridge, Mass., 1976), esp. pp. 345–356.

him to succeed one of the older LDP figures from the district. In 1976, two candidates attracted virtually all the "Other" votes. One was a young man associated with the feminist Ichikawa Fusae. He ran as an "unaligned progressive" (*kakushin mushozoku*) and may have attracted some votes from independents eager for an unaligned candidate, although it must also be noted that the reorganization of Socialist *jiban* in 1976 left an opening for a new progressive candidate, but little hope of victory. The other unaligned candidate in 1976 was the designated successor to Koyama Shōji. He was a middle-aged conservative endorsed by the major-domo of the LDP, Shiina Etsusaburō. In short, the unaligned votes in 1976 should probably be distributed equally to the left and the right. Only in the most limited sense did they represent support for genuine independents.

Turning now to examine the electoral achievements of the three partisan elements, we find those of the left—the JCP and the JSP—revealed in table 29, which illustrates a discernible pattern. Disregarding the possibly spurious achievement of the left in 1947, when (as chapter 4 explained) one unusual candidate skewed actual support for the Socialists, we find that electoral support for the left climbed steadily after 1949 until it reached a peak in the early 1960s. Thereafter, support for leftist parties faltered, shifting perceptibly with each election in a generally downward direction. The dramatic decline in 1976, from 44 to 35 percent, may have been a temporary phenomenon attributable to the special problem of creating new *jiban* in new districts. But, in the face of these figures, it would be difficult to deny that the parties of the far left suffered electoral decline after the late 1960s.

In pace with the faltering fortunes of the left, the parties of the center expanded their support significantly. By the late 1960s, they were attracting nearly three in every ten suburban voters, apparently at the expense, after 1969, of the left opposition parties. Sudden shifts of fortune were common among the parties of the center. Having commanded all the centrist votes in 1960, the DSP won none at all in 1976, when it was unable to run a candidate in either Santama district. By contrast, the Kōmeitō established a substantial base immediately upon entering the district in 1967 and expanded it steadily thereafter. And the New Liberal Club was unexpectedly successful in its initial effort in 1976, its candidate capturing 11

TABLE 30. *Partisan Vote in Lower House Elections, Santama District(s), 1960–1976*

Year	JSP+JCP	CGP+DSP+NLC	LDP	Others	Total
1960	219,340	44,514	251,055	1,059	515,968
1963	293,652	52,161	248,796	41,199	635,808
1967	399,558	201,125	263,473	34,342	898,498
1969	360,661	262,893	295,066	635	919,255
1972	517,341	302,273	326,343	28,484	1,174,441
1976	473,940	371,363	377,736	99,195	1,322,234

SOURCE: Same as table 16.

percent of the Santama's total vote. Such evidence suggests that suburban voters, apparently repelled by the practices of the older parties, were readily attracted to new parties.

These findings might suggest that partisan change in the Santama was leading, not to the growth of a strong left-wing opposition focused on the progressive parties, but rather to the emergence of a potentially strong group of centrist parties. A glance at the second column of table 30 might confirm such a claim, illustrating as it does that centrist parties expanded their electoral support in every election after 1960. Further affirming that partisan change was producing a strong center are the faltering performances of the leftist parties, illustrated in the first column of table 30, and the apparent stasis of the LDP, illustrated in the third column of table 29.[25]

It would be imprudent to conclude, however, that these tendencies were leading to a centrist coalition that could eventually command a majority of suburban voters, because the parties of the center were united neither programmatically nor organizationally. Each was a relatively small party that drew support from distinct segments of the electorate, and each had peculiar historical, organizational, and reputational attributes that complicated their consolidation, or even their coalition, as a unified centrist body. The Kōmeitō, for example, drew support from the lower socio-economic ranks of urban society, possessed a close relationship with the Sōka Gakkai, and enjoyed a strong organizational apparatus that relied

25. I wish to thank Terry MacDougall for first calling my attention to the consistent expansion of the center, and to relieve him of all responsibility for the manner in which I have interpreted the phenomenon.

heavily on symbiotic relations with its religious society, an attachment that impeded its ability to represent the interests of a general public. The DSP had virtually no organization, was linked historically to the Socialist movement, and relied on highly educated white-collar workers and intellectuals for both leadership and support, while retaining its ties to one segment of the labor movement. And the New Liberal Club, still in its infancy, was as yet little more than an LDP splinter group eager to exploit the dilemmas confronting the majority party in order to enhance the power of its own leaders. Under such circumstances, these three parties hardly formed the material from which to construct a new centrist party.

One can deny with some assurance that a strong centrist party was emerging, but one should not deny that there were strong aspirations among Tokyo's suburbanites for centrist politics. Indeed, the best support for this assertion rests on the analysis in chapter 5 of the policies that Yabe and Gotō pursued. If those policies are any guide at all, they suggest that successful politicians in contemporary suburbs implemented programs that appealed to a broad spectrum of voters situated in the political middle, a position so common it hardly deserves mention. But in the Japanese context, this observation assumes some significance.[26]

The symbols and rhetoric of postwar Japanese politics have led us to believe that there have been essentially two alternatives in the political arena. Voters, activists, and analysts alike have grown accustomed to a polarized competition between the conservative LDP on one side and its progressive opponents on the other. The policies of Yabe and Gotō, their successful incumbencies, the results of city council elections, the outcome of prefectural assembly contests, and partisan performances in Diet contests all contradict this imagery. They suggest strongly that, however segmented the Japanese polity might have appeared, most voters have actually supported conservative and moderate candidates. If we assume that in 1976 the LDP, the NLC, the CGP, and the DSP put forward such candidates, then about two in every three suburban voters expressed a preference for parties of the right and center.

26. Progressive mayors who pursue an obsessive interest in a few ideological issues while appearing to neglect the mundane aspects of administration suffer quick defeat, as the progressive mayor of Tachikawa City learned to his regret in 1975. See the *Asahi shimbun* for August 3, 20, and 30, and September 2, 1975.

Better, then, to replace the old image with a new one. The LDP and its opponents were not really shouting at one another across an abyss separating two clearly defined camps. They all stood together on a common battleground, sparring among themselves. Outside opponents directed their wrath essentially at the established LDP insiders, but they also dissipated much energy in struggling among themselves. The Japanese electorate stood by in witness of this chaotic struggle, unable to express unified demands that would bring the segmented conflict to a halt.[27]

While contention prevailed, the LDP continued to exercise control at most levels of Japan's political system, retaining in the 1976 Diet contest roughly the same suburban strength it had preserved since the late 1960s. In their virtually unchallenged heyday before the Pacific War, parties of the right in the Santama could expect to win at least three in every four of the district's votes, even under the worst circumstances. Socialist expansion began in the 1930s to undercut their dominance, and by the early 1950s had produced a declining share of the vote for conservative candidates in every election. Between 1952 and 1976, conservatives saw their commanding position deteriorate steadily, as their share of the vote declined from more than 60 percent to less than 30 percent, a demise that convinced many of the impending defeat of conservative power.

But to conclude from these figures that the LDP is near extinction and that its obituary can be read at any moment would be premature. Considerable evidence illustrates the persistence of both conservative electoral support and LDP power in the Santama, not to mention other suburban areas in Japan. One piece of evidence appears in table 30, where column three indicates that the LDP increased its absolute vote in every Lower House election after 1963. It still retained in 1976 a fourth of the Diet seats from the Santama area. The LDP also returned thirteen of the Santama's twenty-two representatives to the prefectural assembly, and council members sympathetic to the LDP still were a majority in the district, even though

27. Nobutaka Ike has noted that "when we look at the leadership strata, the Liberal Democratic party is far to the right and the Socialist party is far to the left, whereas when we look at the membership, there is no sharp division, but an overlap in the middle." *Japanese Politics* (New York, 1972), p. 38. The findings from this study seem to confirm the latter claim while casting some doubt on the former. If Gotō and Yabe are at all indicative, it appears that leaders, also, when obliged to implement policies, find themselves overlapping in the middle.

a third of the mayoralty posts in the district's cities had slipped from LDP control. And, despite its declining electoral position, there were indications that the LDP still enjoyed more support than it actually received. For example, a national survey by the *Asahi shimbun* in 1976 found that only 27 percent of respondents hoped the LDP would increase its vote in the next election, but 38 percent wanted the LDP to continue as the ruling party![28]

This combination of ambiguity and ambivalence characterizes the conclusions to which this study leads. It is undeniably true that the LDP and its candidates suffered a widespread loss in support among Santama voters, especially after the early 1960s. Opposition parties sent six of the Santama's eight representatives to the Diet, their supporters always cast a majority of ballots for the opposition candidate for governor, and their local politicians had achieved what for the Santama area was an unprecedented intrusion on conservative power in city assemblies and mayors' offices. But, the LDP could still balance off these losses with continued electoral gains in Diet contests, a majority of the Santama's prefectural assembly seats, and a preponderance of control at the local level, not to mention, of course, its continuing (albeit precarious) control of the national legislature.

Moreover, the LDP in the Santama could offer evidence of dramatic successes in the face of sweeping social changes that advantaged the opposition parties, successes that affirmed its continuing viability. This study has described one success, the administration of Yabe Takaji in Fuchū. Granted the special abilities and attributes that Yabe brought to office, it is necessary to affirm how effective he was in retaining support for the conservative cause. His support, moreover, appears to have aided conservatives in city council, prefectural assembly, and gubernatorial elections as well. Yabe seems to demonstrate, rather conclusively, that the LDP can expect to derive firm, continuing support from the electorate, *if* it (1) presents attractive candidates, (2) pursues innovative policies, and (3) appears to serve the interests of a broader constituency. The prospects of its attaining these goals are perhaps brighter at the local level, where factional strife seems to be less incapacitating, than at

28. Reported in *Asahi shimbun*, April 2, 1976, p. 6. Another 41 percent of the respondents wanted the opposition to rule, while 21 percent were undecided.

the national level, where the power of entrenched interests and deference to age both restrict opportunity for innovation.

By the late 1970s the prospect of a coalition government in Japan was becoming a certainty. But if we can take as a guide the behavior of suburban voters, who represented at least a third of the nation's populace, the likelihood of political instability was diluted by the persisting strength of moderate, if not conservative, partisan sentiment. Suburban voters appeared to be shunning the parties of the left in favor of the centrist parties that often complemented, rather than confronted, the entrenched conservatives.

Despite the fractious nature of Japan's partisan battle, therefore, suburbanites of the Santama could probably look forward during the near future to a national government with a partisan character that accorded with their political aspirations, however ambiguous these were. In casting their votes during the 1970s, suburbanites emphasized subjective assessments of their needs, perceptions of their own status in a diverse society, obligations to groups and individuals, the images of parties and candidates, and the capabilities of parties, in no easily definable order of importance. For many years they had thought, out of some sense of resignation, the political left offered the best hope of satisfying their expectations, but their hopes withered in the face of Socialist ineffectiveness. Despite contradictory and ambivalent behavior, with their electoral choices in the late 1970s suburban voters appeared willing to condone moderately conservative rule by the political right and center, in the substantiable hope that it might embody progressive policies.

BIBLIOGRAPHY

JAPANESE SOURCES

Akamatsu Kōichi. "Chiiki minshuka undō no ichidanmen: Toka Kunitachi chō ni okeru jichitai minshuka undō [One Phase in the Movement for Local Democracy: The Movement for Municipal Democracy in Kunitachi Town]." *Shisō*, 446 (August 1961): 58–74.

Asahi shimbun.

Asahi shimbun sha. *Fusen sōsenkyo taikan* [General Survey of the Universal Suffrage General Election]. Osaka and Tokyo, 1928.

Asahi shimbun sha, shakai bu. *Chūō sen: Tōkyō no dōmyaku imamukashi* [The Chūō Line: Now and Then on the Tokyo Main Line]. Tokyo, 1975.

Asahi shimbun sha, yoron chōsa shitsu, ed. *Nihonjin no seiji ishiki: Asahi shimbun yoron chōsa no 30-nen* [Political Attitudes of the Japanese People: Thirty Years of the Asahi Shimbun Public Opinion Surveys]. Tokyo, 1976.

Fuchū shi. *Fuchū no fūdo shi* [A Local Gazeteer of Fuchū]. Fuchū, 1972.

――――. *Mukashi no Fuchū shashin shū* [A Photo Collection of Old Fuchū]. Fuchu, 1975.

――――. *Watashi no benri chō: '75* [My City Handbook for 1975]. Fuchū, 1975.

Fuchū shi senkyo kanri iinkai. *Senkyo kanri 15-nen no ayumi* [Fifteen Years of Electoral Management]. Fuchū, 1969.

――――. *Fuchū shichō senkyo to Fuchū shigikai giin hōken senkyo no kiroku* [Records of the Fuchū Mayoralty Contest and Fuchū City Council By-election]. Fuchū, 1970.

――――. *Tōitsu chihō senkyo no kiroku* [Records of the Unified Local Election; 1971]. Fuchū, 1971.

――――. *Fuchū shichō senkyo no kiroku* [Record of the 1974 Fuchū Mayoralty Contest]. Fuchū, 1974.

Fuchū shi shi hensan iinkai, comp. *Fuchū shi shi* [The History of Fuchū City]. 2 vols. Fuchū, 1968–1974.

――――. *Fuchū shi shi kindai hen shiryō shū: Fuchū shi no kindai gyōsei shiryō shū* [Materials Collection for the Fuchū City History: Fuchū City Modern Period Administrative Materials Collection]. 5 volumes. Fuchū, 1970–1972.

Fuchū shigikai, ed. *Fuchū shigikai shi* [A History of the Fuchū City Council]. Fuchū, 1975.

Fuchū shiyakusho. *Tama shi shūi ki* [Gleanings from the History of the Tama Region]. Fuchū, 1972.

Fujiwara Kōtatsu. *Gendai Nihon no seiji ishiki* [Political Attitudes in Contemporary Japan]. Tokyo, 1958.

Hachiōji shi shi hensan iinkai, comp. *Hachiōji shi shi* [The History of Hachiōji City]. 3 vols. Hachiōji, 1963–1968.

Hashimoto Akikazu. *Shiji seitō nashi: Kuzureyuku seitō shinwa* [Independents: The Myth of the Crumbling Parties]. Tokyo, 1975.

Hatakeyama Takeshi. *Habatsu no uchimaku: Nihon no seiji kōzō* [Inside the Factions: Japan's Political Structure]. Tokyo, 1975.

Hattori Shūichi. "Seiji ishiki to senkyo kōdō no jittai: Gifu ken Kamioka machi ni okeru chōsa [Actual Conditions of Political Consciousness and Voting Behavior: A Survey of Kamioka Town, Gifu Prefecture]." *Senkyo chōsa kenkyū kiyō*, no. 2 (1973). Tokyo, 1974.

Horie Taishō, comp. *Machida kindai hyakunen shi* [A History of the Last 100 Years in Machida]. Machida, Tokyo, 1975.

Ikeuchi Hajime, ed. *Shimin ishiki no kenkyū* [Studies of Civic Consciousness]. Tokyo, 1974.

Irokawa Daikichi. *Shimpen Meiji seishin shi* [Revised Edition: A History of the Spirit of Meiji]. Tokyo, 1973.

———. "Santama no hyakunen: Jiyūminken undō [A Century of Santama History: The People's Rights Movement]." *Asahi shimbun*, December 30, 1975, p. 13.

Irokawa Daikichi and Murano Ren'ichi, comps. *Murano Tsuneemon den* [A Biography of Murano Tsuneemon]. 2 vols. Tokyo, 1969–1971.

Katsumura Shigeru, ed. *Gendai Nihon no kyōdōtai: Chiiki shakai* [Communities in Contemporary Japan: Local Society]. Tokyo, 1973.

Kawai Takao. "Gendai Nihon no kaikyū kōzō no henka to white-collar zō [The White-collar Strata and Changes in Social Class Structure in Contemporary Japan]." *Hōgaku kenkyū*, 46, no. 9 (September 1973): 31–85.

Kawasaki Hideji. *Waseda no seijika tachi* [The Politicians of Waseda]. Tokyo, 1976.

Kimbara Samon. *Taishōki no seitō to kokumin* [Taishō Political Parties and the People]. Tokyo, 1973.

Kitaoka Kazuyoshi. "Hirakata shichō shikkyaku jiken no zenbō [A Full Portrait of the Fall of the Hirakata Mayor]." *Chūō kōron* (December 1975), pp. 182–196.

Kokumin seikatsu sentaa, ed. *Toshi no seikatsu kankyō: Sono jittai to ishiki* [The Urban Living Environment: Reality and Consciousness]. Tokyo, 1975.

Kokusai kirisuto kyō daigaku, shakai kagaku kenkyūjo, ed. *Chiiki shakai to toshika* [Urbanization and the Local Community]. *Kokusai kirisuto kyō daigaku gakuhō, 2-A: Shakai kagaku kenkyū*, no. 8. Tokyo, 1962.

———. *Kinkō toshi no henbō katei: Mitaka shi sōgō chōsa hōkoku* [The Process of Change in a Suburban City: Report on the Comprehensive Survey of Mitaka City]. *Kokusai kirisuto kyō daigaku gakuhō* II-A (June 1964).

Kōmei senkyo renmei, ed. *Shūgiin giin senkyo no jisseki* [Results of General Elections for the Lower House]. Tokyo, 1968.

Kōsei-minshuteki na kakushin Habikino shisei o susumeru kai, ed. *Chihō jichi to minshushugi no toride: Habikino kakushin shisei* [Fortress of Local Government and Democracy: The Progressive Administration of Habikino]. Kyoto, 1975.

Kunikida Doppo. *Musashino* [Musashino]. Originally, 1901. Tokyo, 1975.

Kuroda Kaname. *Shūsengo no Fuchū chō to watakushi* [Fuchū and I in the Postwar Era]. Fuchū, 1972.

Kyōto daigaku, bungaku bu, chirigaku kyōshitsu. *Daitoshi kinkō no henbō: Ōsaka fu, Kadoma shi ni okeru toshika to kōgyōka ni tsuite* [Change in a Metropolitan Suburb: On the Urbanization and Industrialization of Kadoma City, Osaka Prefecture]. Kyoto, 1965.

Matsuoka Kyōichi. *Santama kindai hyakunen shi nempyō* [A Chronology of a Century of Santama History]. Rev. ed. Tachikawa, Tokyo, 1974.

Miyake Ichirō, et al. *Kotonaru reberu no senkyo ni okeru tōhyō kōdō no kenkyū* [Research on Electoral Behavior at All Levels]. Kyoto, 1967.

Musashino machi. *Musashino chō shi* [The History of Musashino Town]. Musashino, 1932.

————. *Shōwa 14-nen Musashino chōsei yōran* [The 1939 Musashino Town Handbook]. Musashino, 1939.

————. *Chōsei gairan* [An Outline of Town Conditions]. Musashino, 1942.

Musashino shi. *Musashino shisei yōran: 1962* [1962 Guide to Conditions in Musashino City]. Musashino, 1962.

————. *Musashino shigikai hō* [Reports of the Musashino City Council]. 2 vols. Musashino, 1966–1975.

————. *Watashi no benri chō: '75* [My City Handbook for 1975]. Musashino, 1975.

————. *1975 Shisei tōkei* [1975 Municipal Statistics]. Musashino, 1976.

Musashino shi, kikaku bu. *Musashino shimin no jichi ishiki chōsa: 1970* [A Survey of Political Attitudes among Musashino Citizens: 1970]. Musashino, 1970.

Musashino shi senkyo kanri iinkai. *Musashino shimin no seikatsu to sansei taido* [Social and Political Attitudes of Musashino Citizens]. Musashino, 1956.

Musashino shi shi hensan iinkai, comp. *Musashino shi shi* [The History of Musashino City]. Musashino, 1970.

Musashino shiyakusho, sōmu ka. *1949 Musashino shisei yōran* [The 1949 Guide to Conditions in Musashino City]. Musashino, 1949.

Naikaku tōkei kyoku. *Taishō 9-nen Kokusei chōsa hōkoku: Tōkyō fu* [1920 National Census Reports: Tokyo Metropolitan Prefecture]. Tokyo, 1925.

————. *Shōwa 5-nen Kokusei chōsa hōkoku: Tōkyō fu.* Tokyo, 1934.

Nakamura Kikuo. "Seiji ishiki to senkyo kōdō no jittai: Sono tōzaikan no hikaku [Actual Conditions of Political Consciousness and Voting Behavior: Comparisons between the Kantō and Kansai Regions]." *Senkyo chōsa kenkyū kiyō,* no. 1 (1973). Tokyo, 1973.

Nakamura Takaichi. *Santama shakai undō shi* [A History of the Santama Social Movement]. Tokyo, 1966.

Nihon jihō sha, comp. *Yasui Seiichirō den* [A Biography of Yasui Seiichirō]. Tokyo, 1967.

Nihonjin kenkyū kai, ed. *Nihonjin kenkyū: Shiji seitō betsu Nihonjin shūdan* [Research on the Japanese People: Support for Political Parties among Japanese Groups]. Tokyo, 1975.

————. *Nihonjin kenkyū: Onna ga kangaete iru koto* [Research on the Japanese People: What Women Are Thinking]. Tokyo, 1975.

Nishihira Shigeki. *Nihon no senkyo* [Japanese Elections]. Tokyo, 1972.

Odauchi Michitoshi. *Teito to kinkō* [The Imperial Capital and Its Suburbs]. 1918, reprint. Tokyo, 1974.

————. "Dai Tōkyō no kinkō toshi Musashino no seikaku [The Character of the Tokyo Suburb of Musashino]." *Shintoshi*, 6, no. 7 (July 1952): 1–6; and 6, no. 9 (September 1952): 2–7.

Ōme shi shi hensan jikkō iinkai, comp. *Jōhon shishi: Ōme* [The Published City History: Ōme]. Ōme, 1966.

Ōshio Shunsuke. "Chiiki shakai to shite no danchi no seikaku [The Character of *danchi* as Communities]." *Toshi mondai kenkyū*, 12, no. 9 (September 1960): 17–31.

Rōyama Masamichi, ed. *Seiji ishiki no kaibō* [An Analysis of Political Consciousness]. Tokyo, 1949.

Rōyama Masamichi, et al., eds. *Sōsenkyo no jittai* [A Case Study of a General Election]. Tokyo, 1955.

Santama taikan hensan kai, ed. *Santama taikan: 1955* [The Santama Panorama: 1955]. Tokyo, 1954.

Satō Atsushi. *Tenkanki no chihō jichi* [Local Autonomy at the Turning Point]. Tokyo, 1976.

Seikei daigaku, Seikei gakkai. *Musashino shi* [Musashino City]. 3 vols. Musashino, 1953–1957.

Shūgiin jimukyoku. *Shūgiin giin sōsenkyo ichiran* [Guide to Lower House General Elections]. 31 volumes, to date. Tokyo, 1904–.

Soma Masao. *Nihon no sōsenkyo: 1969 nen* [The 1969 Japanese General Election]. Tokyo, 1970.

————, ed. *Kokumin no sentaku* [The People Choose]. Tokyo, 1973.

Sōrifu tōkei kyoku. *1940 Kokusei chōsa hōkoku* [1940 National Census Reports]. 2 vols. Tokyo, 1965.

————. *1950 Kokusei chōsa hōkoku: Tōkyō to* [1950 National Census Reports: Tokyo Metropolitan Prefecture]. Tokyo, 1953.

————. *1955 Kokusei chōsa hōkoku: Tōkyō to*. Tokyo, 1959.

————. *1960 Kokusei chōsa hōkoku: Tōkyō to*. Tokyo, 1964.

————. *1970 Kokusei chōsa hōkoku: Tōkyō to*. Tokyo, 1972.

————. *1975 Kokusei chōsa: Zenkoku todōfuken shichōson betsu jinkō gaisū* [1975 Population Census of Japan: Preliminary Count of Population]. Tokyo, 1975.

Suzuki Hitoshi. *Kinkō toshi: Aru chihō toshi no sengo shakai shi* [Suburban City: The Postwar Social History of a Regional City]. Tokyo, 1973.

Suzuki Sunao. "Koshiminteki kakushin senryaku wa kanō ka [Is a Progressive

Strategy for the Common Citizen Possible]?'' *Shimin*, no. 7 (March 1972), pp. 68–76.

Suzuki Takeo, ed. *Santama rōdō undō shi* [A History of the Santama Labor Movement]. Tokyo, 1976.

Taiyō shimpō sha. *Musashino chō shi* [A History of the Town of Musashino]. Tokyo, 1930.

Takahashi Genichirō. *Musashino rekishi chiri* [A Historical Geography of Musashino]. 9 vols. Tokyo, 1927–1932.

Tama chūō shinyō kinko, Tama bunka shiryō shitsu. *Tama no ayumi* [Tama's History]. 2 volumes, to date. Tachikawa, 1975–.

Tōkyō fu. *Tōkyō fu tōkei sho* [Tokyo Metropolitan Prefecture Statistical Handbook]. 56 vols. Tokyo, 1886–1942.

Tōkyō fu, gakumu bu, shakai ka. *Tōkyō fu gogun ni okeru kaoku chintai jijō chōsa* [A Survey of Housing Rental Conditions in the Five Counties of Tokyo Metropolitan Prefecture]. Tokyo, 1932.

Tōkyō fu, sōmu bu, chōsa ka. *Tōkyō fu shichōsonzei yōran* [Outline of Conditions in Tokyo Metropolitan Prefecture's Cities, Towns, and Villages]. Tokyo, 1940.

Tōkyō hyakunen shi henshū iinkai. *Tōkei kara mita sengo Tōkyō no ayumi* [A Statistical Perspective on Postwar Tokyo]. Tokyo, 1971.

Tōkyō shisei chōsa kai, ed. *Tōkyō ni okeru chiiki shakai soshiki* [Local Social Organizations in Tokyo]. Tokyo, 1971.

Tōkyō shiyakusho. *Tōkyō shiiki kakuchō shi* [A History of the Expansion of Tokyo City]. Tokyo, 1934.

Tōkyō shōkō kaigi sho. *Henbō suru Tōkyō 30-kilometer ken toshi* [Changing Cities within 30 Kilometers of Tokyo]. Tokyo, 1973.

Tōkyō to. *Tōkyō tōkei sho* [Tokyo Metropolitan Prefecture Statistical Annual]. 4 vols. Tokyo, 1950–1953.

———. *Eisei toshi jittai chōsa sho* [Report on Survey of Satellite Cities]. Tokyo, 1952.

———. *Tōkyō to senzai shi* [A History of War Damage in Tokyo]. Tokyo, 1963.

———. *Tōkyō to tōkei nenkan* [Tokyo Metropolitan Prefecture Statistical Yearbook]. 24 vols., to date. Tokyo, 1954–.

———. *Tōkyō to kushichōsonzei yōran: 1960* [1960 Survey of Conditions in Tokyo's Wards, Cities, Towns, and Villages]. Tokyo, 1960.

Tōkyō to jichi shinkōkai. *Tōkyō to chōkai binran: 1962* [1962 Guide to chōkai in Tokyo]. Tokyo, 1962.

Tōkyō to senkyo kanri iinkai. *Chihō senkyo no kiroku* [Records of Local Elections]. 11 volumes, to date. Tokyo, 1947–.

———. *Senkyo ni kansuru seron chōsa* [Election Opinion Surveys]. 5 vols., to date. Tokyo, 1971–.

Tōkyō to shichōkai. *Yakushin suru Tama* [The Rapidly Developing Tama Region]. Mitaka, 1968.

Tōkyō to, sōmukyoku. *Santama chiiki ni okeru jūmin no seikatsu ken ni kansuru chōsa* [Survey of the Activity Sphere of Santama Region Residents]. 2 vols. Tokyo, 1974–75.

Tōkyō to, sōmukyoku, gyōsei bu. *Chōkai jichikai no jittai chōsa hōkokusho* [Report on a Survey of Neighborhood and Self-governing Associations]. Tokyo, 1956.

Tōkyō to, Tachikawa rōsei jimusho. *Shōwa 50-nendo rōdō kumiai meibo* [1975 List of Labor Unions]. Tokyo, 1975.

Torigoe Hiroyuki. "Buraku dantai no tenkai katei: Tōkyō to, Fuchū shi, Yotsuya chiku no jirei o tsūjite [The Development Process in a Hamlet Organization: The Case of Yotsuya District in Fuchū City, Tokyo]." *Shakaigaku hyōron*, 23, no. 3 (December 1972): 51–70.

Tosei chōsa kai, ed. *Daitoshi ni okeru chiiki seiji no kōzō* [The Structure of Local Politics in a Metropolis]. Tokyo, 1960.

Tōshiba Fuchū rōdō kumiai. *Kumiai undō shi* [A History of the Union]. Fuchū, 1955.

――――. *Kumiai tōitsu jūshūnen kinen shi* [The Tenth Anniversary History of the Unified Union]. Fuchū, 1961.

Tōshiba rōdō kumiai. *Tōshiba kumiaiin no ishiki: Sono jittai to kōzō bunseki* [The Attitudes of Tōshiba Union Members: Empirical and Structural Analysis]. Kawasaki, Kanagawa, 1973.

Ukai Nobushige and Kawano Shigeto, eds. *Ningen to toshi kankyō: Daitoshi shūhen bu* [Man and the Urban Environment: The Metropolitan Perimeter]. Tokyo, 1975.

Watanabe Kinjō. *Santama seisen shiryō* [Materials on the Santama Political Wars]. Tachikawa, 1924.

Watanabe Seiichi. *Nyū taun: Ningen toshi o dō kizuku* [New Towns: How to Build a Humane City]. Tokyo, 1973.

Watanabe Shō. "Ishizaka Masataka no shōgai: Gōnō no seitai [The Life of Ishizaka Masataka: Conditions of a Wealthy Farmer]." *Tama bunka*, no. 21 (September 1969), pp. 21–45.

Watanuki Jōji. *Nihon no seiji shakai* [Japan's Political Sociology]. Tokyo, 1967.

――――. "Seiji ishiki to senkyo kōdō no jittai: Daitoshi yūkensha no datsu seitōka gensō ni tsuite no chōsa: Tōkyō Setagaya ku no baai [Actual Conditions of Political Consciousness and Electoral Behavior: A Survey of the Phenomenon of Throwing Off One's Party among Voters in a Large City, The Case of Setagaya Ward in Tokyo]." *Senkyo chōsa kenkyū kiyō*, no. 3 (1972). Tokyo, 1973.

Yajima Miyoshi. *Musashino no shūraku* [Rural Settlements of the Musashino Upland]. Tokyo, 1954.

Yamaga Seiji. "Dai toshi kinkō no toshika: Tōkyō nishi kō o rei to shite [The Urbanization of Metropolitan Suburbs: Western Tokyo as a Case]." *Chigaku zasshi*, 719 (1960): 187–199.

――――. *Tōkyō daitoshi ken no kenkyū* [Studies of the Tokyo Metropolitan Region]. Tokyo, 1967.

Yamazaki Tokihiko. "Seiji ishiki to senkyo kōdō no jittai: Kinkō toshi ni okeru seinenzō no seiji ishiki [Actual Conditions of Political Consciousness and Voting Behavior: The Political Consciousness of Young Men in a Suburban City]." *Senkyo chōsa kenkyū kiyō*, no. 3 (1969). Tokyo, 1970.

Yanai Michio and Iida Yoshiaki. *Gendai no senkyo* [Contemporary Elections]. Tokyo, 1975.

Yokoyama Kendō, ed. *Takagi Seinen jijōden* [An Autobiography of Takagi Seinen]. Tokyo, 1932.

Yokoyama Noboru. *Satsue Musashino meguri* [An Illustrated Tour of Musashino]. Tokyo, 1922.

Yoron kagaku kyōkai. *Daitoshi shūhen ni okeru jichi ishiki no jittai chōsa hōkokusho* [Report on a Survey of Political Attitudes in the Metropolitan Periphery]. Tokyo, 1969.

Zenkoku shichō kai, ed. *1975 Nihon toshi nenkan* [1975 Japan Municipal Yearbook]. Tokyo, 1975.

INTERVIEWS

Andō Seiichi. Vice-chairman of a *chōnaikai* in Izumisano City, Osaka. March 24, 1976.

Arai Genkichi. Mayor of Musashino, 1947–1963. March 17, 1976.

Arai Mikio. Political Correspondent, Japan Broadcasting Company (NHK). May 13, 1976.

Gotō Kihachirō. Mayor of Musashino City, 1963–. May 14, 1976.

Higuchi Takeshi. Director, Musashino Election Management Commission. March 6, 1976.

Horiuchi Katsuhiro. Vice-director, Office of the Fuchū Regional Labor Alliance. February 16, 1976.

Jitsukawa Hiroshi. Musashino Prefectural Assemblyman, 1951–. April 25, 1976.

Katagiri Tatsuo. Director, Municipal Affairs Research Institute. May 10, 1976.

Kondo Katsuhiro. Secretary of the Tōshiba Labor Union in Fuchū. February 16, 1976.

Koyanagi Hiroshi. Director, Fuchū Election Management Commission. February 2, 1976.

Maruyama Hiroshi. Secretary, Fuchū Branch of the Japan Socialist Party. February 16, 1976.

Mitarai Tateki. Secretary, Tachikawa Labor Affairs Office. February 9, 1976.

Nakamura Takaichi. Socialist Diet Member, 1937–1942, 1946–1947, and 1952–1967. April 16, 1976.

Narita Tadayoshi. Supervisor, Tokyo Metropolitan Prefecture Election Management Commission. March 5, 1976.

Nishinoya Tadao. Secretary, Musashino Election Management Commission. February 26, 1976.

Nonaka Takashi. Manager, Office of the Progressive Mayors' Association. May 10, 1976.

Sakamoto Sadao. Mayor of Mitaka City, May 15, 1976.

Shimizu Yūzō. Secretary, Mitaka Labor Affairs Office. January 28, 1976.

Suzuki Takeo. Director of the Business Office of the Santama Labor Alliance, Tachikawa. February 9, 1976.

Takano Shōsei. Vice-President, Fuchū Liaison Council of Neighborhood Associations. March 12, 1976.

Takeshita Yuzuru. Research Associate, Tokyo Institute of Municipal Research. April 27, 1976.
Takeuchi Satoru. Director, Civic Action Group in Tama New Town, Tokyo. May 7, 1976.
Tanshō Yoshihiko. Political Consultant in Mitaka City. April 25, 1976.
Yabe Takaji. Mayor of Fuchū, 1962–. February 13, 1976.
Yamahana Hideo. JSP Diet Member, 1947–1949 and 1952–1969. February 10, 1976.
Yamanouchi Nobuo. Director of Research Department, Yokogawa Denki Labor Union (Musashino). April 15, 1976.
Yoshida Hirotaka. Counselor, Japan Housing Corporation. May 7, 1976.
Yoshimura Tōkichi. Chairman, Santama Region Confederation of Japan Labor Unions (*Dōmei*). February 16, 1976.

ENGLISH SOURCES

Akita, George. *Foundations of Constitutional Government in Modern Japan, 1868–1900*. Cambridge, Mass., 1967.
Allinson, Gary D. "The Moderation of Organized Labor in Postwar Japan." *Journal of Japanese Studies*, 1, no. 2 (Spring 1975): 409–436.
———. *Japanese Urbanism: Industry and Politics in Kariya, 1872–1972*. Berkeley, 1975.
———. "Japan's Independent Voters: Dilemma or Opportunity?" *Japan Interpreter*, 11, no. 1 (Spring 1976): 36–55.
———. "Opposition in the Suburbs." In Scott Flanagan, Ellis Krauss, and Kurt Steiner, eds., *Political Opposition and Local Politics in Japan: Electoral Trends, Citizens' Movements, and Progressive Administrations*. Forthcoming.
———. "Japanese Cities in the Industrial Era." *Journal of Urban History*, 4, no. 4 (August, 1978).
August, Robert A. "Urbanization and Political Change in Tokyo, Japan: 1890–1932." Ph.D. dissertation, University of Pittsburgh, 1975.
Banton, Michael, ed. *Political Systems and the Distribution of Power*. London, 1965.
Beasley, William, ed. *Modern Japan: Aspects of History, Literature, and Society*. Berkeley and London, 1975.
Beckmann, George M., and Okubo, Genji. *The Japanese Communist Party, 1922–1945*. Stanford, 1969.
Bell, C. G. "A New Suburban Politics." *Social Forces*, 47, no. 3 (March 1969): 280–288.
Berger, Gordon M. *Parties out of Power in Japan, 1931–1941*. Princeton, 1977.
Butler, David, and Stokes, Donald. *Political Change in Britain*. New York, 1971.
Campbell, Angus, et al. *The American Voter: An Abridgement*. New York, 1964.
Chudacoff, Howard. *Mobile Americans: Residential Mobility in Omaha, 1880–1920*. New York, 1972.
Clark, S. D. *The Suburban Society*. Toronto, Ont., 1966.
Cole, Allen B. *Japanese Society and Politics*. Boston, 1956.

Cole, Allen B., et al. *Socialist Parties in Postwar Japan*. New Haven, 1966.

Collison, P. *The Cutteslowe Walls: A Study in Social Class*. London, 1963.

Colton, Kenneth E. "Prewar Political Influences in Postwar Conservative Parties." *American Political Science Review*, 42 (1948): 940–957.

Curtis, Gerald L. *Election Campaigning Japanese Style*. New York, 1971.

Dahl, Robert A. *Who Governs?* New Haven, 1961.

——. *Regimes and Oppositions*. New Haven and London, 1973.

Dahl, Robert A., ed. *Political Oppositions in Western Democracies*. New Haven, 1966.

Dahl, Robert A., and Tufte, Edward R. *Size and Democracy*. Stanford, 1973.

Dixon, Karl. "The Growth of a 'Popular' Japanese Communist Party." *Pacific Affairs*, 45 (Fall 1972).

Dobriner, William, ed. *The Suburban Community*. New York, 1958.

——. *Class in Suburbia*. Englewood Cliffs, N.J., 1963.

Dogan, Mattei, and Rokkan, Stein, eds. *Quantitative Ecological Analysis in the Social Sciences*. Cambridge, Mass., 1969.

Dore, Ronald P. *City Life in Japan*. Berkeley, 1963.

Dowse, Robert E., and Hughes, John A. *Political Sociology*. London, 1972.

Duus, Peter. *Party Rivalry and Political Change in Taishō Japan*. Cambridge, Mass., 1968.

Edelman, Murray. *The Symbolic Uses of Politics*. Urbana, Ill., 1964.

Eulau, Heinz, and Prewitt, Kenneth. *Labyrinths of Democracy*. Indianapolis, Ind., 1973.

Fagen, Richard R., and Tuohy, William S. *Politics and Privilege in a Mexican City*. Stanford, 1972.

Farley, Reynolds. "Suburban Persistence." *American Sociological Review*, 29, no. 1 (February 1964): 38–47.

Flanagan, Scott C. "Voting Behavior in Japan." *Comparative Political Studies*, 1, no. 3 (October 1968): 406–423.

Fukui, Haruhiro. *Party in Power*. Berkeley, 1970.

Gale, Roger W. "The 1976 Election and the LDP: Edge of a Precipice?" *Japan Interpreter*, 11, no. 4 (Spring 1977): 433–447.

Gans, Herbert. *The Levittowners: Ways of Life and Politics in a New Suburban Community*. New York, 1967.

Glaab, Charles N. "Metropolis and Suburb: The Changing American City." In John Braeman, et al., eds. *Change and Continuity in Twentieth-century America: The 1920s*. Columbus, 1968.

Goldstein, Sidney. "Some Economic Consequences of Suburbanization in the Copenhagen Metropolitan Area." *American Journal of Sociology*, 68, no. 5 (March 1963): 551–564.

Goldthorpe, John H., et al. *The Affluent Worker: Political Attitudes and Behaviour*. Cambridge, 1967.

Greenstein, Fred, and Wolfinger, Raymond. "The Suburb and Shifting Party Loyalties." *Public Opinion Quarterly*, 22, no. 4 (1958): 473–482.

Guest, Avery. "Population Suburbanization in American Metropolitan Areas." *Geographical Analysis*, 7 (1975): 267–283.

Halebsky, Sandor, ed. *The Sociology of the City*. New York, 1973.

Harris, Chauncy. "Suburbs." *American Journal of Sociology*, 49, no. 1 (July 1943): 1–13.

Hirsch, Herbert. "Suburban Voting and National Trends: A Research Note." *Western Political Quarterly*, 21 (September 1968): 508–514.

Ike, Nobutaka. *Japanese Politics: Patron-Client Democracy*. New York, 1972.

Irokawa Daikichi. "The Survival Struggle of the Japanese Community." *Japan Interpreter*, 9, no. 4 (Spring 1975): 465–494.

Jackson, J. A., ed. *Migration*. Cambridge, 1969.

Janosik, G. Edward. "The New Suburbia: Political Significance." *Current History*, 31, no. 180 (August 1956): 91–95.

Jessop, Bob. *Traditionalism, Conservatism, and British Political Culture*. London, 1974.

Johnson, Chalmers. *Conspiracy at Matsukawa*. Berkeley, Los Angeles, and London, 1972.

Kasperson, Roger E. "On Suburbia and Voting Behavior." *Annals of the American Association of Geographers*, 59, no. 2 (June 1969): 405–411.

Kawai, Kazuo. *Japan's American Interlude*. Chicago, 1960.

Key, V. O. *A Primer of Statistics for Political Scientists*. Originally 1954. New York, 1966.

Kim, Young C. "Political Recruitment: The Case of Japanese Prefectural Assemblymen." *American Political Science Review*, 61, no. 4 (December 1967): 1036–1052.

Kramer, John, ed. *North American Suburbs: Politics, Diversity, and Change*. Berkeley, 1972.

Krauss, Ellis S. *Japanese Radicals Revisited: Student Protest in Japan*. Berkeley, 1974.

Kubota, Akira, and Ward, Robert E. "Family Influences and Political Socialization in Japan." *Comparative Political Studies*, 3, no. 2 (July 1970): 140–175.

Kuroda, Yasumasa. *Reed Town, Japan: A Study in Community Power Structure and Political Change*. Honolulu, 1974.

Kyogoku, Jun'ichi, and Ike, Nobutaka. *Urban-Rural Differences in Voting Behavior in Postwar Japan*. Stanford, 1959.

Langdon, Frank. *Politics in Japan*. Boston, 1967.

Langer, Paul F. *Communism in Japan: A Case of Political Neutralization*. Stanford, 1972.

Lasswell, Harold D. *Politics: Who Gets What, When, How?* Originally, 1936. New York, 1958.

Lee, Tosh. "Tokyo Metropolitan Assembly Election: 1973." *Asian Survey*, 14, no. 5 (May 1974): 478–488.

Lewin, Leif; Jansson, Bo; and Sörbom, Dag. *The Swedish Electorate, 1887–1968*. Stockholm, Sweden, 1972.

Liebman, C. S. "Functional Differentiation and Political Characteristics of Suburbs." *American Journal of Sociology*, 66 (March 1961): 485–490.

Lifton, Robert J. *History and Human Survival*. New York, 1971.

Lijphart, Arend. *The Politics of Accommodation: Pluralism and Democracy in the Netherlands.* Berkeley, 1975. Rev. ed.

Lipset, S. M., and Rokkan, Stein, eds. *Party Systems and Voter Alignments: Cross-National Perspectives.* New York, 1967.

MacDougall, Terry Edward. "Japanese Urban Local Politics: Toward a Viable Progressive Political Opposition." In Lewis Austin, ed. *Japan: The Paradox of Progress.* New Haven and London, 1976. Pp. 31–56.

McClain, James L. "Local Politics and National Integration: The Fukui Prefectural Assembly in the 1880s." *Monumenta Nipponica,* 31, no. 1 (Spring 1976): 51–75.

Manis, J. G., and Stone, L. C. "Suburban Residence and Political Behavior." *Public Opinion Quarterly,* 22, no. 4 (1958): 483–489.

Maruyama, Masao. *Thought and Behavior in Modern Japanese Politics.* London, 1963.

Mason, R. H. P. *Japan's First General Election, 1890.* Cambridge, 1969.

Masotti, Louis, ed. "The Suburban Seventies." *The Annals of the American Academy of Political and Social Sciences,* vol. 422 (November 1975).

Masotti, Louis, and Dennis, Deborah, eds. *Suburbs, Suburbia, and Suburbanization: A Bibliography.* 2nd edition. Evanston, Ill., 1973.

Masotti, Louis H., and Hadden, Jeffry K. *The Urbanization of the Suburbs.* Beverly Hills, Calif., 1973.

Massey, Joseph A. *Youth and Politics in Japan.* Lexington, Mass., 1976.

Masumi, Junnosuke. "A Profile of the Japanese Conservative Party." *Asian Survey,* 3 (1963): 390–401.

Mayer, Lawrence C. *Comparative Political Inquiry: A Methodological Survey.* Homewood, Ill., 1972.

Merton, Robert K. *On Theoretical Sociology: Five Essays, Old and New.* New York, 1967.

Milbrath, Lester W. *Political Participation: How and Why Do People Get Involved in Politics?* Chicago, 1965.

Mills, C. Wright. *The Sociological Imagination.* New York, 1959.

Milnor, A. J. *Elections and Political Stability.* Boston, 1969.

Najita, Tetsuo. *Hara Kei in the Politics of Compromise, 1905–1915.* Cambridge, Mass., 1967.

———. "Inukai Tsuyoshi: Some Dilemmas in Party Development in Pre World War II Japan." *American Historical Review,* 74, no. 2 (December 1968): 492–510.

Nie, Norman H.; Verba, Sidney; and Petrocik, John R. *The Changing American Voter.* Cambridge, Mass., 1976.

Peattie, Lisa Redfield. *The View from the Barrio.* Ann Arbor, Mich., 1968.

Plath, David W. "Bourbon in the Tea: Dilemmas of an Aging *Senzenha.*" *Japan Interpreter,* 11, no. 3 (Winter 1977): 362–383.

Ranney, Austin, ed. *Essays on the Behavioral Study of Politics.* Urbana, Ill., 1962.

Richardson, Bradley M. "Japanese Local Politics: Support Mobilization and Leadership Styles." *Asian Survey,* 7 (1967): 860–875.

———. "Urbanization and Political Participation: The Case of Japan." *American Political Science Review*, 67, no. 2 (June 1973): 433–452.

———. *The Political Culture of Japan*. Berkeley, 1974.

———. "Party Loyalties and Party Saliency in Japan." *Comparative Political Studies*, 8, no. 1 (April 1975): 32–57.

———."Stability and Change in Japanese Voting Behavior, 1958–1972." *Journal of Asian Studies*, 36, no. 4 (August 1977): 675–693.

Rix, Alan. "Political Change in Tokyo and the 1973 Metropolitan Assembly Elections." *Pacific Affairs*, 47, no. 1 (Spring 1974): 20–36.

———. "Tokyo's Governor Minobe and Progressive Local Politics in Japan." *Asian Survey*, 15, no. 1 (June 1975): 530–542.

Rose, Richard, ed. *Electoral Behavior: A Comparative Handbook*. New York, 1974.

Scalapino, Robert A. *Democracy and the Party Movement in Prewar Japan: The Failure of the First Attempt*. Berkeley and Los Angeles, 1962.

———. *The Japanese Communist Movement, 1920–1966*. Berkeley, 1967.

———. "Elections and Political Modernization in Prewar Japan." In Robert E. Ward, ed., *Political Development in Modern Japan*. Princeton, N.J., 1968. Pp. 249–292.

Schnore, Leo F. "The Growth of Metropolitan Suburbs." *American Sociological Review*, 22 (April 1957): 165–173.

———. "Socio-economic Status of Cities and Suburbs." *American Sociological Review*, 28 (February 1963): 76–85.

Schnore, Leo F., ed. *The New Urban History: Quantitative Explorations by American Historians*. Princeton, N.J., 1975.

Seeley, John R.; Sim, R. Alexander; and Loosley, Elizabeth W. *Crestwood Heights: A Study of the Culture of Suburban Life*. New York, 1956.

Southall, Aidan, ed. *Urban Anthropology: Cross-cultural Studies of Urbanization*. New York, 1973.

Steiner, Kurt. *Local Government in Japan*. Stanford, 1965.

Steiner, Kurt; Krauss, Ellis; and Flanagan, Scott, eds., *Political Opposition and Local Politics in Japan: Electoral Trends, Citizens' Movements and Progressive Administrations*. Forthcoming.

Swartz, Marc J.; Turner, Victor W.; and Tuden, Arthur, eds. *Political Anthropology*. Chicago, 1966.

Taeuber, Irene. *The Population of Japan*. Princeton, N.J., 1958.

Tallman, Irving, and Morgner, Ramona. "Life-style Differences among Urban and Suburban Blue-collar Families." *Social Forces*, 48, no. 3 (March 1970): 334–348.

Thayer, Nathaniel. *How the Conservatives Rule Japan*. Princeton, N.J., 1969.

Thernstrom, Stephan, and Sennett, Richard, eds. *Nineteenth-Century Cities: Essays in the New Urban History*. New Haven, 1969.

Thorns, David. *Suburbia*. London, 1972.

Thurston, Donald R. "Aftermath in Minamata." *Japan Interpreter*, 9, no. 1 (Spring 1974): 25–42.

———. *Teachers and Politics in Japan*. Princeton, N.J., 1973.

Tilly, Charles, ed. *An Urban World*. Boston, 1974.

Totten, George O. *The Social Democratic Movement in Prewar Japan*. New Haven, 1966.

Tsurutani, Taketsugu. "A New Era of Japanese Politics: Tokyo's Gubernatorial Election." *Asian Survey*, 12 (May 1972).

———. *Political Change in Japan: Response to Postindustrial Challenge*. New York, 1977.

United States, Strategic Bombing Survey. The Effects of Air Attack on Japanese Urban Economy. March, 1947.

———. Nakajima Aircraft Company Ltd. Report no. 2. June 1947.

Verba, Sidney, and Nie, Norman H. *Participation in America*. New York, 1972.

Vogel, Ezra F. *Japan's New Middle Class: The Salary Man and His Family in a Tokyo Suburb*. Berkeley, 1963.

Ward, Robert E., ed. *Political Development in Modern Japan*. Princeton, N.J., 1968.

Watanuki, Joji. "Patterns of Politics in Contemporary Japan." In S. M. Lipset and Stein Rokkan, eds., *Party Systems and Voter Alignments*. New York, 1967. Pp. 447–466.

White, James. *The Sokagakkai and Mass Society*. Stanford, 1970.

———. "Political Implications of Cityward Migration: Japan as an Exploratory Test Case." *Sage Professional Paper in Comparative Politics*, 01–038. Beverly Hills and London, 1973.

White, James W., and Munger, Frank, eds. *Social Change and Community Politics in Urban Japan*. Chapel Hill, N.C., 1976.

Willmott, P., and Young, M. *Family and Class in a London Suburb*. London, 1960.

Wirt, Frederick M. "The Political Sociology of American Suburbs: A Reinterpretation." *Journal of Politics*, 27, no. 3 (August 1965): 647–666.

Wirt, Frederick, et al., eds. *On the City's Rim: Suburban Politics and Policy*. Lexington, Mass., 1972.

Wood, Robert C. *Suburbia: Its People and Their Politics*. Boston, 1958.

Yazaki, Takeo. *The Japanese City: A Sociological Analysis*. Rutland, Vt., 1963.

INDEX

Designer: Al Burkhardt
Compositor: Viking Typographics
Printer: Braun-Brumfield
Binder: Braun-Brumfield
Text: VIP Times Roman
Display: Photo Typositor Gill Sans Extrabold
Cloth: Holliston Roxite C 56508
Paper: 50 lb. P&S Offset vellum

DATE DUE